Beyond Divorce

Beyond Divorce

Navigating Life After Separation

Morgan Reynolds

BAL
KON
media

BEYOND DIVORCE
NAVIGATING LIFE AFTER SEPARATION

Published by Balkon Media

Paperback edition ISBN: 978-1-916970-04-5
Also available in e-book format

This book is not intended as a substitute for the medical advice of physicians. The reader should regularly consult a physician in matters relating to his/her health and particularly with respect to any symptoms that may require diagnosis or medical attention.

A CIP catalogue record for this title is available from the British Library.

www.balkon.media

Contents

Introduction

Welcome to *Beyond Divorce: Navigating Life After Separation.* If you're holding this book, you might be standing at one of life's most daunting crossroads, seeking guidance, comfort, or simply a sense that you're not alone on this journey. I'm Morgan Reynolds, and like you, I've navigated the turbulent waters of divorce and emerged on the other side with a deeper understanding of myself, a renewed sense of purpose, and an unshakeable belief in the possibility of a fulfilling life post-divorce.

Divorce is more than just a legal dissolution of a marriage; it's a profound emotional upheaval that can shake the very foundations of your identity and your life. It's a time of loss, change, and, inevitably, transformation. But amidst the challenges and the pain, there is immense potential for growth, healing, and new beginnings. This book is a testament to that potential.

Beyond Divorce is not just another guide through the legalities and logistics of divorce—though these aspects are unavoidably part of the process. Instead, this book is a companion for your journey through the emotional landscape of ending a marriage, a roadmap for rebuilding your life, and a beacon of hope for what lies ahead. It's structured to guide you step-by-step through the various stages of post-divorce life, from the immediate aftermath and coping with the whirlwind of emotions to finding your feet as a single individual, navigating co-parenting, rediscovering your identity, and eventually, opening up to new relationships.

Each chapter in this book is designed to address a specific aspect of the post-divorce experience, offering insights, practical advice, and strategies to help you move forward. Whether you're struggling with the idea of being alone, adjusting to single parenthood, or wondering how you'll ever find love again, *Beyond Divorce* aims to provide answers and guidance. But more than that, this book is a space for reflection, offering exercises and questions to help you engage deeply with your own journey of healing and self-discovery.

Divorce can feel like an end, but it's also a beginning—a chance to redefine your life on your own terms. It's an opportunity to become the person you've always wanted to be, free from the constraints of a relationship that no longer serves you. My hope is that *Beyond Divorce* will not only help you navigate the practicalities of this new chapter but also inspire you to embrace the journey with courage, grace, and a sense of adventure.

Your path through divorce and beyond is uniquely yours, but you don't have to walk it alone. Let this book be your guide and companion as you move through the pain and towards a brighter, hopeful future. Together, we'll explore the vast landscape of life after divorce, finding beauty and strength in the process of rebuilding. Here's to new beginnings and the incredible journey ahead.

—Morgan Reynolds—

Chapter 1
Facing the Reality of Divorce: Understanding and Accepting Your New Reality

Divorce, as you've come to know it, is not just a word on paper. It's a shift in the very essence of your day-to-day life. It's okay to feel a range of emotions, from relief to profound sadness, sometimes all within the span of a few minutes. This chapter is about acknowledging those feelings and understanding that acceptance is a journey, one that you're embarking on starting right now.

Imagine we're sitting together, you and I, in a quiet, comfortable space. There's a sense of peace here, and it's okay to lower your guards and be truly honest about how you're feeling. I've been through this journey, and while our paths may not be the same, I understand the terrain you're navigating. It's rugged, unpredictable, and at times, it feels downright impossible. But it's also a path that leads to growth, self-discovery, and, believe it or not, new joys.

Accepting your new reality doesn't mean you have to like it, at least not right away. It means acknowledging that this is where you are at this moment in your life. It's about saying,

"This is my starting point," without judgment. It's the ground zero from which you will rebuild.

This process of acceptance is deeply personal. You might find yourself grappling with questions of identity—who are you outside of the relationship? You might be facing fears about the future or how to navigate the world as a single individual again. These are all normal, valid concerns.

Let's talk about those first few nights alone, the silence that seems louder than any conversation you ever had. It's in these moments that you might feel the weight of your new reality the most acutely. It's also here, in the quiet, that you'll begin to find your strength. You'll start to realise that within you lies a resilience that is greater than any challenge divorce throws your way.

Let me share a piece of my own story with you. After my divorce was finalised, I found myself sitting alone in what used to be our shared living room. The house felt eerily quiet—a stark contrast to the life that once filled its spaces. I remember looking around and thinking, "This is really happening." Despite the turmoil leading up to that moment, facing the reality of my divorce still felt like a punch to the gut. It was in that moment of profound solitude that I realised the journey ahead was as much about accepting this new reality as it was about navigating the practical aspects of life post-divorce.

It's important to remember, as you walk this path, that time is a healer. It might not feel like it in the throes of your current emotions, but with each passing day, the weight of your divorce will start to lift. You'll find moments of joy in the midst of sorrow, glimpses of hope in despair. These moments are sign-posts, reminders that healing is happening, even if it's imperceptible in the moment.

In the early days following my divorce, I clung to the idea

that time would heal my wounds. It seemed like a platitude, something people said when they didn't know what else to offer. But as weeks turned into months, and months into years, I began to see the truth in those words. The pain that once felt all-consuming began to fade, giving way to new experiences, new joys, and a new understanding of myself.

Activity: Crafting Your Acceptance Statement

Today, I want you to create what I call an "Acceptance Statement." This is a personal declaration that acknowledges your current reality and your commitment to move forward from this point.

Grab a piece of paper and write down what accepting your divorce means to you. It doesn't have to be profound or eloquent. It could be as simple as, "I accept that my marriage has ended, and I am open to discovering what's next for me." You can place this statement somewhere you'll see it every day —by your bedside, on your fridge, or in your wallet. Or you can destroy immediately after writing. The important thing is to craft the statement.

Let this statement be a reminder that acceptance is your first step towards healing. It's a signal to yourself that you're ready to embark on this journey, no matter how daunting it may seem at the outset.

Remember, acceptance is not a destination but a process. It's okay to have days where you feel like you're taking steps backward. What matters is that you're committed to moving through this, one step at a time. And I'm here, walking alongside you, every step of the way.

As you engage with this activity and the days ahead, remember that this chapter of your life, though challenging, is also a chapter of immense potential. You're not just facing the reality of divorce; you're stepping into a broader, richer understanding of yourself and what you're capable of.

Chapter 2
Embracing Change: Finding Strength in Transformation

Change, especially when it's not chosen but rather thrust upon us, can be disorienting and frightening. Yet, it's within this very upheaval that we find the seeds of growth and transformation. Embracing change isn't about discarding the past or ignoring the pain; it's about acknowledging that within every ending lies the potential for a new beginning.

Why Embrace Change

You might wonder why, amidst the turmoil of divorce, you should even consider embracing change. The answer lies in the inherent opportunity that change presents. It offers a rare chance to reset, to re-evaluate what truly matters to you, and to live in alignment with those values. Embracing change is not a denial of your past experiences or the love you once shared; it's an affirmation of your ability to adapt and find happiness again.

In my own journey, the realisation that change was not just inevitable but also a gateway to rediscovery was a turning point.

I learned that moving forward didn't mean forgetting the past but building upon it. My divorce, though painful, was a catalyst for examining my life's path and making conscious choices about my future.

The Process of Transformation: The process of transformation post-divorce can be likened to rebirth. It's a profound shift that encompasses every aspect of your being—from your identity and beliefs to your hopes and dreams. This transformation doesn't happen overnight. It's a gradual process that unfolds in its own time, often in unexpected ways.

Self-Reflection: The journey starts with self-reflection. This involves asking yourself hard questions about what you want from life, what brings you joy, and what values you hold dear. It's an opportunity to get to know yourself on a deeper level, perhaps for the first time in many years.

Setting New Goals: With reflection comes the opportunity to set new goals. These goals don't have to be monumental. They can be as simple as reading more books, taking up a new hobby, or spending more time in nature. The act of setting goals is a declaration of your intent to move forward and a commitment to your personal growth.

Exploring New Interests: Embracing change often leads to the exploration of new interests. This exploration is about allowing yourself to be curious, to try new things without the pressure of perfection. Whether it's taking a cooking class, joining a hiking group, or learning to paint, each new interest is a step towards rediscovering your passions and joy.

Building New Relationships: Transformation also involves the people around you. As you change, you may find that your relationships evolve as well. This is a natural part of the process. Building new relationships, based on your current interests and values, can be incredibly rewarding. These connections can offer support, laughter, and companionship on your journey.

Embracing a New Identity: Perhaps the most significant aspect of transformation is the embrace of a new identity. This new identity is not a replacement of who you were but an evolution. It's the version of you that has learned, grown, and emerged stronger from the experience of divorce.

Activity: Mapping Your Transformation

Let's put these concepts into practice with an activity designed to map your personal transformation. Create a Transformation Map by drawing two circles on a piece of paper. Label one circle "Before" and the other "After."

In the "Before" circle, write down words that described your life and identity before your divorce. In the "After" circle, envision how you'd like to see yourself and your life post-transformation. Focus on feelings, qualities, and experiences you wish to cultivate.

Between the two circles, draw arrows and label them with steps you can take to move from "Before" to "After." These could include specific activities, changes in mindset, or goals you want to achieve.

This map is a visual representation of your journey of transformation. It's a living document that can evolve as you do. Refer back to it often, and allow it to guide you as you embrace the changes ahead.

Embracing change and undergoing transformation in the aftermath of a divorce can be one of the most challenging yet rewarding experiences. It's a journey that asks for courage, patience, and a willingness to explore the unknown. Remember, within every moment of change lies infinite possibilities for growth and new beginnings. Your journey of transformation is not just about finding a new way of living; it's about discovering a deeper, more authentic way of being.

Chapter 3
Emotional Tides: Managing the Rollercoaster of Post-Divorce Emotions

Post-divorce life can often feel like being adrift in the open sea, where calm waters can suddenly turn turbulent without warning. Navigating this emotional rollercoaster requires understanding, patience, and tools to manage the highs and lows. Just as the sea eventually settles, so too will your emotions, but the journey to that peace is both challenging and transformative.

Navigating the Emotional Waters

The spectrum of emotions you may experience after a divorce is vast and varied. It's common to feel relief one moment, only to be overwhelmed by sadness, anger, or fear the next. These emotions are natural responses to the significant changes happening in your life. It's important to allow yourself to feel them fully, rather than pushing them away or judging yourself for them.

In my own journey, I remember days when I felt like I was finally moving forward, only to find myself in tears over a memory or a missed moment. It was a reminder that healing is not linear, and emotions are complex, often tied to our deepest hopes and fears.

The Importance of Emotional Acceptance

The first step in managing this emotional rollercoaster is acceptance. Acceptance does not mean resignation or giving up; it means acknowledging your emotions for what they are: natural responses to loss and change. By accepting your feelings, you give yourself permission to heal at your own pace.

One of the most powerful lessons I learned was that my emotions, however intense, did not define me. They were simply part of the process of adjusting to a new reality. This realisation can be liberating, as it shifts your perspective from being at the mercy of your emotions to observing and managing them as they come.

The Importance of Loving Yourself

In the aftermath of a divorce, it's alarmingly easy to fall into the trap of self-doubt and negative self-talk. You might find yourself questioning your worth, wondering if you are lovable, or blaming yourself for the dissolution of your marriage. These thoughts, if left unchecked, can spiral into a dangerous pattern of self-loathing. It's crucial, then, to understand the importance of loving yourself, especially during this vulnerable time.

Loving yourself isn't an act of selfishness; it's a fundamental aspect of your well-being. It's about recognising your inherent worth, independent of your marital status or any external validation. Remember, your relationship does not define you—your kindness, strengths, resilience, and compassion do.

. . .

Personal Reflection: Rediscovering Self-Love

I recall a period when I looked in the mirror and barely recognised the person staring back at me. I was so consumed by feelings of failure and self-doubt that it began to reflect in my physical appearance—I was neglecting both my health and my spirit. It was a wake-up call. I realised that if I continued down this path, I would not only be failing myself but also setting a precedent that might influence how others treat me.

I made a conscious decision to start treating myself with the same compassion and kindness that I offered to others. I began with small acts of self-care, like cooking myself a healthy meal, taking walks in nature, and setting aside time each day for reflection and meditation. Gradually, these acts of self-love helped rebuild my confidence and self-esteem. I learned to forgive myself, to celebrate my strengths, and to embrace my imperfections.

Breaking the Cycle of Negative Self-Talk

The journey to self-love begins with challenging and changing the negative narratives you might have about yourself. This involves being mindful of your internal dialogue and actively replacing critical thoughts with affirmations of your worth and achievements. It's not about denying your feelings but acknowledging them without judgment and reminding yourself that you are deserving of love and happiness.

Physical and Mental Self-Care

Loving yourself also means taking care of your physical and mental health. This goes beyond just exercise and diet; it's about treating your body with respect and kindness. It means not using food, alcohol, or isolation as ways to cope with your pain but instead choosing activities that nourish and rejuvenate your body and mind.

Mental self-care involves giving yourself permission to grieve, to seek joy, and to embrace your journey of healing. It might mean setting boundaries to protect your energy, pursuing hobbies that make you happy, or simply allowing yourself moments of rest without guilt.

The Danger of Self-Fulfilling Prophecies

When you're caught in a cycle of negative self-talk and self-doubt, there's a risk of these thoughts becoming a self-fulfilling prophecy. If you believe you're unworthy of love or happiness, you might subconsciously sabotage potential opportunities for joy and connection. Recognising this pattern is the first step toward breaking it. By actively practicing self-love and self-care, you affirm your worth and open yourself up to the positive possibilities that lie ahead.

Activity: The Emotional Weather Report

For this activity, you'll create a daily "Emotional Weather Report." Each day, take a moment to check in with yourself and write down what kind of emotional "weather" you're experiencing. Are you feeling sunny, cloudy, stormy, or calm? Next to each weather report, write down one activity you can do that day to honour or manage those emotions.

This practice encourages regular self-reflection and provides a visual record of your emotional journey. Over time, you may notice patterns or triggers for certain emotions, helping you to manage them more effectively. It's also a reminder that, just like the weather, your emotions are subject to change, and brighter days are always ahead.

In the midst of my own post-divorce journey, I found myself standing on the beach one early morning, watching the sun rise over the horizon. The sea before me was a tumult of waves, each crashing onto the shore with relentless energy. It was in this moment, with the rhythmic sound of the sea filling my ears, that I experienced a profound realisation about my emotional state.

For months, I had been riding an emotional rollercoaster, feeling at times like I was being swallowed by the depths of my sadness, anger, and confusion. Other times, I felt numb, as if floating aimlessly on the surface of my own life. Standing there, watching the dawn break, I saw my emotions reflected in the sea's waves—powerful, unpredictable, but also beautiful in their raw intensity.

I remember feeling a wave of emotion so strong it took my breath away, much like the cold ocean spray. Tears began to fall, not from sadness, but from a sudden, overwhelming sense of release. I allowed myself to truly feel the depth of my emotions, to acknowledge the pain and the loss, but also the beauty of being so deeply connected to my own heart.

This moment was a turning point for me. I realised that, just like the ocean, my emotions were a natural force, not to be feared or suppressed, but acknowledged and respected. They were a part of my journey, indicators of where I had been, and guides to where I needed to go.

From that day forward, I began to approach my emotional landscape with a new perspective. I practiced mindfulness, allowing myself to feel each emotion fully but without letting it define or control me. I found solace in writing, pouring my thoughts and feelings onto the page as a way to process and understand them. Exercise became a refuge, a way to channel my energy and clear my mind. And perhaps most importantly, I learned to seek and accept support, to share my emotional burdens with those who cared for me and to listen when they shared theirs with me.

Chapter 4
Strengthening Connections: Building and Utilising Your Support System

In the wake of a divorce, it's easy to feel isolated, as though you're navigating this tumultuous journey alone. Yet, one of the most significant steps you can take towards healing and growth is to recognise the value of connections—both in maintaining existing relationships and in building new ones. This chapter explores the importance of a support system and offers guidance on how to cultivate these essential connections.

The Importance of a Support System

A support system is more than just a network of people who offer sympathy in times of trouble. It's a community that provides emotional sustenance, practical assistance, and a sense of belonging. This network might include family, friends, colleagues, or members of support groups who share similar experiences. Each person brings a unique form of support, whether it's a listening ear, a distraction from your troubles, or sage advice based on their own experiences.

. . .

Maintaining Existing Relationships

In the aftermath of a divorce, some relationships might feel strained. It's crucial to communicate openly with loved ones about your needs, boundaries, and how they can best support you. Remember, it's okay to ask for space or to express when you're ready to talk or seek company. Equally, it's important to let them know how much their support means to you.

Building New Connections

Expanding your support network post-divorce is equally important. New connections can offer fresh perspectives and experiences, helping you to rediscover joy and interest in life. Consider joining clubs, groups, or classes that align with your interests. Support groups specifically for divorced individuals can also be invaluable, providing a space to share experiences and advice with those who truly understand what you're going through.

The Power of Reciprocity

Building and utilising your support system is not just about seeking support; it's also about giving it. The act of supporting others can be incredibly healing, reminding you of your strengths and the positive impact you can have on others' lives. This reciprocity fosters deeper connections and reinforces the value of community during challenging times.

Nurturing Your Support System

Like any relationship, your support system requires care and attention. Make an effort to reach out, check in with your network, and participate in communal activities. Celebrate successes together, offer your help when needed, and be open to receiving help in return. This mutual exchange nurtures a strong, supportive community around you.

Navigating Shared Friends and Choosing Sides

One of the more delicate aspects of a divorce can be the shifting dynamics within your circle of shared friends. It's not uncommon for friends to feel compelled to choose sides, whether due to loyalty, personal beliefs, or their own comfort. This can be painful, as it may feel like you're losing not just a spouse but also friends you once held dear.

Navigating this terrain requires a blend of honesty, openness, and sometimes, the acceptance of letting go. It's important to communicate with these friends, express your hope to maintain the friendship, and clarify that you do not expect them to choose sides. However, it's equally important to prepare yourself for the possibility that some relationships may change or even end. This isn't a reflection of your worth but rather a natural part of the transition process.

Remember, the goal isn't to 'win' friends over but to cultivate a support system that is positive, understanding, and supportive. In some cases, this may mean broadening your social circle to include new connections who align more closely with your current path and values.

After my divorce, I found the dynamics within my circle of friends shifting in ways I hadn't anticipated. Some friends whom I expected to be my strongest advocates withdrew, seemingly uncomfortable with the situation, and perhaps unsure of how to support me without taking sides. It was a painful realisation, one that left me feeling even more isolated during a time when I needed support the most.

However, it was also during this time that I discovered the true strength of other friendships. Friends who, perhaps not as close before, stepped forward with words of encouragement, offers of help, or simply their presence. It was a lesson in the unpredictable nature of relationships and the beauty of unexpected support.

I also made the conscious decision to reach out and form new connections. I joined a local hiking group, something I'd always wanted to do but never found the time for, (or made the time for) during my marriage. Through this group, I met individuals who were not only unaware of my divorce but who also shared a common interest that brought us together. These new friendships provided a fresh perspective and a sense of adventure at a time when it was most needed.

This experience taught me the importance of being open to new beginnings. While it's natural to mourn the loss of certain friendships, it's also crucial to remain open to the possibility of new connections. The end of one relationship can be the catalyst for many more, each bringing its own unique support and joy into your life.

Activity: Reflecting and Reaching Out

In light of navigating shared friends and embracing new connections, take a moment to reflect on your current social landscape:

List the Friends: Make a list of shared friends and note any changes in these relationships since the divorce. Identify which relationships you wish to maintain and which may be naturally concluding.

Outreach Plan: For those you wish to keep, consider

reaching out with a simple message or invitation to catch up. Make it clear that your intention is to maintain a friendship without putting them in the middle of your past relationship.

New Opportunities: Make another list of interests or hobbies you'd like to explore. Next to each, research and note down potential groups, clubs, or classes in your area that align with these interests. Commit to attending at least one in the next month.

The changing dynamics of shared friendships post-divorce can be challenging but also illuminating. It highlights the importance of clear communication, the acceptance of change, and the opportunity to forge new paths. As you navigate these shifts, keep your focus on building a support system that uplifts and aligns with your journey towards healing and growth. Remember, each interaction, whether with an old friend or a new acquaintance, is a step towards a richer, more supportive social tapestry in your life after divorce.

Chapter 5
Mourning the Loss: Grieving the End of Your Marriage

Grief after divorce is as real and intense as any form of loss. It's a multifaceted emotion, encompassing sadness, anger, relief, and confusion. Recognising that grief is a natural response to divorce helps validate your feelings and facilitates the healing process.

The stages of grief—denial, anger, bargaining, depression, and acceptance—may be experienced differently by everyone and not necessarily in order. You might find yourself cycling through these stages, revisiting some as you navigate your post-divorce life. It's important to allow yourself the space and grace to experience these emotions without judgment.

The Importance of Mourning

Mourning the loss of your marriage is crucial for moving forward. It's a process that allows you to come to terms with the end of one chapter in your life and gradually open yourself to the possibility of new beginnings. Mourning is not a sign of weakness; it's a step toward healing.

During this time, it's essential to seek support from friends, family, or professionals who can provide comfort and understanding. Sharing your grief can lighten the burden, offering perspectives that help you see beyond the immediate pain.

Personal Anecdote: Embracing the Waves of Grief

I remember the first night in my empty home after the divorce was finalised. The silence was deafening, a stark reminder of my new reality. I felt a wave of grief so intense that it momentarily took my breath away. It was a mixture of sorrow for what was lost and fear of the unknown future. That night, I allowed myself to truly mourn the end of my marriage, to feel every painful, messy emotion without restraint. It was a turning point for me, the beginning of my journey through grief toward acceptance.

In the weeks that followed, I found solace in writing. I poured my thoughts and feelings into journals, letters I would never send, and even poems. This act of expressing my grief helped me navigate through the darkest moments, gradually finding flickers of hope and moments of peace amidst the turmoil.

Navigating Your Grief

Allow Yourself to Feel: Give yourself permission to grieve. Suppressing your emotions only prolongs the healing process.

Seek Support: Lean on friends, family, or support groups. Speaking about your grief can help diminish its intensity.

Find an Outlet: Engage in activities that allow you to express your feelings, whether it's through writing, art, music, or physical exercise.

Practice Self-Compassion: Be gentle with yourself. Recognise that healing takes time, and there's no right or wrong way to grieve.

Activity: The Healing Box

Create a "Healing Box" as a physical space to place your grief and memories. Fill it with items that remind you of your marriage and the journey you're grieving—photos, letters, or even small mementos. Whenever you're ready, you can choose to revisit these items, allowing yourself to process your emotions. This box serves as a symbolic gesture of acknowledging your grief while also containing it, making it a part of your history but not your entire story.

Grieving the end of your marriage is a deeply personal and necessary process. It's about acknowledging the loss, experiencing the pain, and gradually finding your way toward acceptance and healing. Remember, grief is not a linear journey; it's a series of waves, each bringing you closer to the shore of healing and renewal. By embracing your grief, you're taking the first steps toward rebuilding a life filled with hope, purpose, and joy.

Celebrating the Positive Aspects of Your Marriage

In the midst of mourning the loss of your marriage, it can be easy to overlook the aspects that were positive and meaningful. However, acknowledging and celebrating what worked in the marriage—and why—is an essential step in the healing process. This recognition serves not only as a balm for your grief but also as a bridge to understanding and moving forward, both individually and in any necessary interactions with your ex-partner.

. . .

Finding Balance in Remembrance

Reflecting on the positive aspects of your marriage doesn't mean ignoring the reasons it ended. Instead, it's about finding a balanced view that honours the complexity of your relationship. There were moments of joy, achievement, and deep connection that deserve to be remembered and celebrated. These memories are a testament to the love that once was, providing valuable insights into what you value and seek in relationships.

Lessons Learned and Gratitude

Every relationship, no matter its outcome, offers lessons about love, compatibility, and oneself. Acknowledging the strengths of your marriage can help clarify these lessons, contributing to personal growth and future relationship success. Expressing gratitude for these lessons and the good times can shift your focus from what was lost to what has been gained—an enhanced understanding of love, relationships, and your own desires and boundaries.

Facilitating Healthy Communication and Closure

Remembering the positive aspects of your marriage can also facilitate healthier communication with your ex-partner, especially if you need to co-parent or manage shared responsibilities. Approaching interactions with a mindset that recognises the good alongside the bad helps foster a respectful and constructive dialogue. This balanced perspective can make moving on easier for both parties, providing a foundation for mutual respect and closure.

. . .

Activity: Gratitude and Lessons Journal

Create a journal dedicated to recognising the positive aspects of your marriage, the lessons learned, and the gratitude you hold for those experiences. Start by writing down three positive memories and what they meant to you. Reflect on what these moments taught you about love, partnership, and even yourself.

Next, list the qualities in the relationship you are thankful for. This could include shared adventures, mutual support during tough times, or growth experiences that occurred during your marriage.

Finally, consider how these reflections help clarify what you seek in future relationships or personal growth paths. Revisit and add to this journal as you continue your journey of healing, allowing it to be a reminder of the love you're capable of giving and receiving.

Reflecting on the positive aspects of your marriage and acknowledging the growth and lessons from that chapter of your life is a powerful healing tool. It allows you to honour the past, appreciate the present, and look forward to the future with a heart that's open to love and enriched by experience. Celebrating what worked in your marriage is not about clinging to the past but about building a bridge to a future where those lessons help guide you toward fulfilling relationships and a deeper understanding of yourself.

Chapter 6
The Stigma of Divorce: Dealing with Judgment and Moving Forward with Confidence

Navigating the aftermath of a divorce often means confronting not just personal upheaval but also societal perceptions and stigmas associated with ending a marriage. This chapter delves into strategies for dealing with external judgment and reclaiming your story, empowering you to move forward with confidence and resilience in the face of outdated stigmas.

In the early days post-divorce, I felt weighed down by the whispers and judgments, both real and imagined, from those around me. It was during a solo trip I mentioned in an earlier chapter that I had planned as a declaration of my independence that I found my turning point. In a new town, away from home, I realised the only judgment that truly mattered was my own. I returned with a newfound confidence, determined to live my life on my own terms. I began to share my story, not as a tale of failure but as one of resilience and self-discovery. With each person I reached, I felt the stigma lose its power over me, transforming it into a source of strength and a tool for advocacy.

. . .

Understanding the Stigma

The stigma surrounding divorce stems from cultural, religious, and societal norms that historically valued marital permanence above individual well-being. Recognising that these perceptions are rooted in the past is crucial for overcoming them.

Acknowledge External Perceptions: Be aware of the societal judgments regarding divorce but remember that these do not define your worth or the validity of your decision.

Educate Yourself and Others: Understanding the reasons behind the stigma can empower you to challenge and educate others, shifting perceptions starting within your circle.

Dealing with Judgment: Facing judgment from family, friends, or society can be one of the most challenging aspects of navigating post-divorce life.

Stay True to Your Story: Own your story with confidence. You made the best decision based on your circumstances and understanding.

Seek Supportive Communities: Surround yourself with people and communities that support and uplift you. Support groups, online forums, and therapy can provide a judgment-free space to express yourself and find encouragement.

Rebuilding Confidence: The key to overcoming stigma is to rebuild and maintain your confidence. Your self-worth should not be tied to your marital status.

Beyond dealing with societal judgments and misconceptions about divorce, a crucial aspect of moving forward is coming to terms with your new normal. Embracing your identity beyond the confines of marriage allows you to redefine yourself on your own terms, recognising that while divorce is a part of your story, it does not define you.

Embracing Your New Normal: Adjusting to life after divorce involves accepting changes in your daily routine, social circles, and even your plans for the future. This new normal, though daunting at first, is ripe with opportunities for growth and self-discovery.

You Are More Than Your Divorce: It's easy to feel like your divorce defines you, especially when it's fresh. However, it's important to remind yourself that you are a complex, multifaceted individual with unique talents, passions, and experiences that extend far beyond this chapter of your life.

Shifting the Narrative: How you talk about your divorce, both to yourself and others, can significantly impact how you view your identity post-divorce. Shifting the narrative from one of failure to one of growth and resilience can be empowering.

The stigma of divorce, while rooted in historical and societal norms, does not have the power to define your personal journey or the quality of your life post-divorce. By confronting judgment with confidence, embracing your independence, and living authentically, you can move forward empowered and unapologetic. Remember, your courage to choose happiness and well-being paves the way for a more accepting and compassionate society.

Chapter 7
Rediscovering Your Identity: Who Are You Beyond Your Marriage?

Divorce often prompts a profound questioning of one's identity. Freed from the roles you played within the marriage, you're now faced with the task of rediscovering who you are as an individual. This chapter guides you through the journey of self-discovery, encouraging exploration, self-compassion, and the embrace of new opportunities for growth and fulfilment.

For so long, your sense of self may have been intricately woven with your role as a partner. Now, standing on the precipice of this significant life change, you're confronted with a powerful and sometimes daunting question: Who are you beyond your marriage?

The Journey of Self-Discovery

Rediscovering your identity post-divorce is a journey that requires patience, curiosity, and an openness to exploration. It's an opportunity to reconnect with your interests, passions, and values—some of which may have been overshadowed by the compromises and dynamics of married life.

Exploration: Begin by exploring activities and interests that resonate with you. Whether it's picking up old hobbies or discovering new ones, allow yourself the freedom to explore without judgment.

Reflection: Spend time reflecting on your values and what brings you joy and fulfilment. This can be through journaling, meditation, or even conversations with close friends who know you well.

Experimentation: Don't be afraid to step out of your comfort zone. Always fancied learning to play the piano, or dancing, or mixed martial arts? Now's your chance. Experimentation is key to discovering new facets of your identity. Join clubs, attend workshops, or travel to new places—each experience contributes to your understanding of yourself.

Embracing Change: Embracing the changes in your identity can be both exhilarating and intimidating. It's important to remember that change does not imply losing the essence of who you are, or re-inventing yourself; rather, it's an expansion of your self-understanding and capabilities.

Self-Compassion: Be kind to yourself throughout this process. Change is challenging, and self-discovery does not happen overnight. Practice self-compassion and give yourself grace during moments of doubt or frustration.

Positive Mindset: Approach this period of change with a positive mindset. View it as an opportunity for growth and learning, rather than a loss of your former self.

The Importance of Community: Rediscovering your identity is not a journey you have to embark on alone. Surrounding yourself with a supportive community can provide encouragement, insight, and companionship.

Seek Support: Lean on friends, family, and groups that

share your interests. These connections can offer valuable perspectives and encouragement.

Share Your Journey: Don't hesitate to share your journey of self-discovery with others. You might be surprised by how much you learn about yourself in the process.

Activity: The Vision Board

A tangible way to explore and visualise your emerging identity is to create a vision board. Gather magazines, photos, quotes, and anything else that resonates with you. I find Pinterest particularly good, but an old-school scrapbook is just as effective. As you assemble your board, pay attention to themes that emerge—these are clues to your interests, aspirations, and values. Place your vision board somewhere you'll see it daily as a reminder of your journey and the future you're creating for yourself.

Moving Forward with Confidence

Rediscovering your identity after divorce is an empowering journey that can lead to a deeper understanding of yourself and a more fulfilling life. It's about piecing together the aspects of yourself that you cherish, discovering new ones, and moving forward with a sense of wholeness and confidence. Remember, the end of your marriage is not the end of your story—it's the beginning of a new chapter, one where you are the author of your own journey.

Chapter 8
New Living Arrangements: Creating a Comfortable, Safe Space for Your New Start

Transitioning to new living arrangements post-divorce represents a significant change for both you and your children, if you have any. This chapter focuses on transforming a new space into a comfortable and nurturing home environment that supports the well-being and healing of everyone involved.

Embracing Your New Space

Moving to a new living space can feel daunting, especially after the shared history and memories of a former home. However, this transition also offers a unique opportunity to redefine your environment in a way that reflects your current needs and the new chapter you're embarking on.

Personalisation: Personalise your new space with items that make you feel happy and relaxed. This could be as simple as photos, artwork, or decorative items that reflect your personality and interests. Try and add this personal touch as soon as possible to avoid the new space feeling foreign, or borrowed, or temporary. Whilst it might not be your forever home, and might be something of a compromise compared to what you have been used to, the more it looks like home, the quicker it will feel like home.

Comfort: Invest in making your new home as comfortable as possible. Focus on creating cosy areas for relaxation and family time, ensuring your space is a sanctuary for healing and growth. This isn't the time to invest in to new technology or enormous televisions—make sure you've got all the essentials, even if it means scouring charity shops, second-hand stores, online marketplaces, or community groups for furniture and decor. You can most certainly find unique and affordable items to add character to your home. If you're going to spend on anything, a simple reading nook will be worth the investment one-hundred-fold.

Creating a Home for Your Children

Ensuring your children feel safe, secure, and happy in the new living arrangements is crucial. Their comfort in the new home can significantly impact their adjustment to post-divorce life. Children adapt remarkably fast. They may be used to bigger, better furnishings and belongings, but that might not be possible from day one.

Involvement: Involve your children in setting up their rooms or shared spaces. Allowing them to make choices about decorations or layout can help them feel a sense of ownership and comfort. Where possible engage in DIY projects to personalise and enhance your space. This can be a fun and therapeutic activity for you and your children, fostering a sense of accomplishment, ownership and togetherness.

Familiarity: Incorporate familiar items from their previous home to help maintain a sense of continuity. Familiar bedding, toys, or even wall colours can make the new environment feel more like home.

Your new living arrangements offer a canvas for expressing your renewed sense of self and creating a nurturing environment for you and your family. By thoughtfully setting up your space, you can help ensure that "home" feels like home, providing a stable and comforting base from which to rebuild and move forward. Remember, the essence of home is not in the perfection of your decor but in the love, safety, and comfort that dwells within its walls.

Chapter 9
Mastering Your Finances: From Independence to Long-Term Planning

Divorce not only marks a significant change in your personal life but also necessitates a thorough reassessment and restructuring of your financial landscape. This chapter focuses on navigating the transition from financial partnership to independence, emphasising the importance of establishing a solid financial foundation for your future.

The Impact of Partnership on Financial Identity

Being part of a partnership often means shared financial responsibilities and goals. For many, this partnership plays a significant role in shaping financial habits and perspectives. When children are part of the equation, the intertwining of finances and family responsibilities becomes even more pronounced, with long-term decisions made jointly and often centred around the needs of the family unit.

The dissolution of this partnership requires not only a division of assets but a re-evaluation of your financial identity and priorities. Suddenly, responsibilities once shared are shouldered independently, and plans once made with a partner must be reconsidered from the standpoint of a single individual.

Steps Toward Financial Independence

Assessment and Budgeting: Begin with a comprehensive assessment of your financial situation—assets, debts, income, and expenses. Crafting a budget that reflects your current income and lifestyle is crucial. This budget will serve as a roadmap, helping to guide your spending and saving decisions moving forward.

Emergency Fund: If not already in place, prioritise the creation of an emergency fund. This fund acts as a financial buffer, offering security in the face of unexpected expenses or income disruptions.

Credit and Debt Management: Establishing or maintaining good credit is essential post-divorce. Take steps to manage existing debts and be cautious of incurring new debts that could strain your budget.

Savings and Investment: Re-evaluate your savings goals and investment strategies to reflect your current circumstances and future aspirations. This may involve adjusting your retirement savings plan or exploring new investment opportunities.

Long-Term Financial Planning

Retirement Planning: Regardless of your age at the time of divorce, it's important to assess the impact on your retirement plans. You may need to adjust your savings rate or investment choices to stay on track for your retirement goals.

Estate Planning: Update your will, beneficiaries, and

any other estate planning documents. This ensures that your financial affairs are in order and aligned with your current wishes.

Insurance: Review and adjust your insurance policies as needed. This includes health, life, and disability insurance, ensuring you and your dependents are adequately protected.

Navigating Financial Independence with Children

For those with children, managing finances post-divorce includes not only personal financial planning but also planning for the needs and futures of your children. This encompasses everything from day-to-day expenses to savings for their education. Coordinating with your ex-partner to ensure that financial responsibilities and goals for your children are clearly defined and mutually supported is essential.

Activity: Financial Independence Plan

Create a detailed Financial Independence Plan that outlines your short-term budget, long-term financial goals, and action steps to achieve them. This plan should include:

- A monthly budget that accounts for all income, expenses, savings, and debt repayment.
- A list of financial goals (e.g., building an emergency fund, saving for a home) with specific, measurable objectives.
- A checklist for updating your estate planning and insurance policies.

Regularly review and adjust this plan as your financial situation and goals evolve.

Embracing Your New Financial Journey

The journey to financial independence and security post-divorce is both challenging and empowering. It's an opportunity to take control of your financial future, make informed decisions that reflect your individual goals and values, and lay the groundwork for a prosperous life ahead. Remember, mastering your finances post-divorce is not just about navigating the immediate aftermath but about building a secure and fulfilling future for yourself and your loved ones.

Chapter 10
Career Adjustments: Managing Work Life During and After Divorce

Divorce can have a profound impact on all aspects of life, including your career. This chapter addresses the challenges and opportunities related to managing your professional life during and after the divorce process. It offers strategies for maintaining productivity, seeking new opportunities, and balancing work with the demands of your changing personal life.

Navigating Work During Divorce

The emotional and logistical complexities of divorce can sometimes spill over into your work life, affecting your focus, productivity, and professional relationships. In addition,

Communication at Work: The process of separation and divorce may require you to take time off from work to meet with solicitors and/or to attend court. Whilst no one wants to air their 'dirty laundry', it is often best to inform your line manager and human resources that you are going through this process. While privacy is important, a brief explanation of your situation can foster understanding and support during this period.

Setting Boundaries: Establish clear boundaries between work and personal life. This might involve limiting personal calls or emails during work hours and ensuring that work commitments do not encroach on time dedicated to dealing with divorce-related matters.

Career Development Post-Divorce

Post-divorce life may prompt you to reassess your career goals and aspirations. This period of change can be an opportunity for significant professional growth and development.

Re-evaluating Career Goals: Reflect on your career path and consider whether it aligns with your personal goals and new life circumstances. Divorce can offer a chance to pursue new directions or advancement opportunities that were not feasible before.

Professional Development: Invest in yourself by seeking professional development opportunities, such as workshops, courses, or certifications that can enhance your skills and marketability.

Networking: Expand your professional network by attending industry events, joining professional organisations , or engaging with online professional communities. Networking can open doors to new opportunities and provide support from peers who understand your career aspirations.

Balancing Work and Personal Life

Finding a balance between work responsibilities and your

personal life, especially in the context of post-divorce adjustments, is crucial for overall well-being.

Time Management: Implement effective time management strategies to maximise productivity at work and ensure you have time for self-care and family responsibilities.

Flexible Work Arrangements: If needed, explore options for flexible work arrangements with your employer, such as remote work, flexible hours, or part-time schedules, to better accommodate your new personal circumstances. This is especially pertinent when you have children.

Activity: Career Vision Board

Create a Career Vision Board that represents your professional aspirations and goals for the future. Use images, quotes, and symbols that inspire you and reflect the career path you wish to pursue or the achievements you aim to realise. Place your vision board where you can see it daily as a motivational reminder of your goals and the steps you need to take to achieve them.

While a divorce can permeate every aspect of your life, maintaining your professional life not only provides financial stability and routine but can also be a welcome source of distraction and personal fulfilment. By prioritising your job and professional development during this time, you secure a vital foundation from which to rebuild and move forward.

Chapter 11
The Adventure of Travel: Solo Travel as a Path to Self-Discovery

In the aftermath of a divorce, solo travel emerges not just as a means of escape but as a profound journey towards self-discovery, healing, and empowerment. This chapter delves into the transformative power of solo travel, offering insights on how venturing into the unknown alone can lead to a deeper understanding of oneself and a renewed sense of freedom.

Embracing the Solo Journey

Solo travel challenges you to step out of your comfort zone, pushing you to confront and overcome fears and insecurities. It's an invitation to explore not just new places but the landscapes of your own inner world. The good news is that booking a trip is straightforward, but if you would prefer to have some assistance, travel agents can offer a huge range of locations, hotels and travel options specifically designed for adult solo-travellers.

. . .

Freedom of Choice: Solo travel offers unparalleled freedom to make your own decisions, follow your intuition, and engage with your surroundings on your terms. Not to be glib, but you can eat where *you* want. Stay at the hotel or guesthouse that *you* like. Fancy a lazy morning sipping coffee and reading a book – no problem! It's your holiday, do what *you* want.

Self-Reliance: Being solely responsible for navigating new environments strengthens your independence, problem-solving skills, and confidence.

Cultural Immersion: Experiencing different cultures and ways of life can provide fresh perspectives, fostering gratitude and a sense of connection to something larger than oneself.

Natural Wonders: Immersing yourself in the beauty of the natural world can be incredibly healing, offering moments of peace and a deep sense of awe that reinvigorates the spirit.

Planning Your Solo Adventure

Embarking on a solo trip requires careful planning to ensure a safe and fulfilling experience. Consider what type of journey will serve you best at this point in your life—be it a quiet retreat, an adventurous exploration, or a cultural immersion.

Destination Selection: Choose destinations that resonate with your interests and where you feel safe and excited to explore.

Safety Precautions: Research your destination thoroughly, plan your accommodations and transport in advance, and stay informed about local customs and safety advice.

Openness to Serendipity: While planning is important, be open to the unexpected. Some of the most memorable experiences come from spontaneous decisions and unforeseen encounters.

Following my divorce, I felt an overwhelming need to reclaim my sense of self. On a whim, I booked a solo trip to a small coastal town I'd never visited. It was less than one hundred miles away from my home but the experience was transformative. Each day, I walked the beach at sunrise, reflecting on my journey and the person I was becoming. I interacted with locals, spent time walking without a plan, allowing curiosity to be my guide.

This trip was about more than just seeing a new place; it was about learning to be comfortable in my own company, trusting myself to navigate the unknown, and finding joy in my own existence. I returned home with a renewed sense of confidence and a deep belief in my ability to rebuild my life on my own terms.

Activity: Solo Travel Dream Planning

Create a plan for your dream solo trip. Start with a journal entry detailing where you'd like to go, what you want to experience, and why this trip is meaningful to you. Then, outline the steps needed to make this trip a reality, considering budget, timing, and any preparations required.

Solo travel as a path to self-discovery offers a unique and powerful way to connect with your inner self, embrace independence, and view the world through a new lens. It's an opportunity to heal, grow, and find joy in the journey of life, reminding you of your resilience and the boundless possibilities that await when you dare to explore alone.

Chapter 12
Solo Parenting Challenges: Adjusting to Life as a Single Parent

Transitioning to life as a single parent after a divorce can be one of the most significant adjustments you'll face. This chapter explores the complexities of solo parenting, offering guidance on how to navigate this new reality with grace, resilience, and a focus on the well-being of your children and yourself.

Embracing Your New Role

As a single parent, you may find yourself juggling the dual roles of caregiver and provider, often without the immediate support of a partner. Embracing this new role means recognising your strengths, acknowledging your limits, and understanding that perfection is not the goal—love, stability, and presence are.

Quality Time Over Quantity

For those not living with their children full-time, it's vital to focus on the quality of the time spent together rather than the quantity. Every moment with your child is an opportunity to strengthen your bond, create lasting memories, and affirm your love and commitment.

Plan Engaging Activities: Use your time together to engage in activities that foster connection, whether it's a simple picnic in the park, a board game night, or working on a project together. These moments can be deeply meaningful for both you and your child.

Stay Present: When you're with your child, be fully present. Put away distractions and focus on being in the moment, showing them that they have your undivided attention.

Co-Parenting - Aligning on Rules and Behaviours: Successful co-parenting after a divorce requires communication and cooperation with your ex-partner, especially when it comes to parenting decisions. Agreeing on rules, behaviours, and parenting strategies is crucial for providing your children with a sense of stability and consistency. See more below.

Establish Common Ground: Work with your ex-partner to establish common rules and expectations for your children. This might involve regular discussions and compromises but ensures that your children receive a consistent message from both parents.

Focus on the Children's Best Interests: Keep conversations with your ex-partner focused on the well-being and best interests of your children. Avoid letting personal grievances influence these discussions.

Navigating the Emotional Landscape: Children may struggle with their emotions following their parents' divorce, and as a solo parent, you play a crucial role in helping them navigate these feelings.

Open Communication: Encourage your children to express their feelings and thoughts about the divorce. Listen without judgment and reassure them of your unconditional love and support.

Seek Support When Needed: Don't hesitate to seek external support if you or your children are struggling. Family therapists or counsellors can provide valuable guidance during this transition.

Co-parenting is Collaborative

In the initial months following our divorce, I noticed a trend that concerned me. My children would return from weekends with their father full of stories about going to the cinema, amusement parks, and late-night snacks. While I was glad they were having fun, I realised they weren't keeping up with their homework and were staying up late, creating a disconnect between our households.

I decided it was crucial to address this with my ex-husband for the sake of our children's well-being and consistency. I approached the conversation with the aim of collaboration, not criticism. I suggested we both could blend fun activities with learning opportunities and shared responsibilities. For instance, cooking could become a fun activity that also served as a lesson in responsibility and self-care. I also asked for consistency with bedtimes – whilst there should be some flexibility at weekends, they still need a routine and not left exhausted for school on Monday mornings.

To my relief, he was open to the idea. We agreed to more closely align our weekend plans with weekday routines, ensuring that our children enjoyed their time at both homes without neglecting their responsibilities. This adjustment helped our children adapt more easily to the changes in our family dynamic, reinforcing that both parents were equally invested in all aspects of their lives, from their education to their emotional well-being.

Balancing fun and responsibilities in co-parenting requires effort, communication, and a commitment to consistency from both parents. By sharing the joys and duties of parenting, co-parents can support their children's growth into well-rounded individuals, ensuring they feel loved and guided no matter which parent they are with. This balanced approach lays a strong foundation for children to thrive in the new family dynamic.

Activity: Planning Your Special Traditions

Create a list of activities or traditions you'd like to start with your child, focusing on things that reflect your shared interests and values. It could be anything from a monthly hiking trip, weekly cooking nights, or daily bedtime stories over a video call. Schedule these activities, making them a non-negotiable part of your routine. This not only strengthens your bond but also creates a series of positive, predictable moments for your child in the midst of change.

Adjusting to life as a single parent post-divorce presents a unique set of challenges and opportunities. By focusing on quality time, aligning on co-parenting strategies with your ex-partner, and navigating the emotional complexities with compassion and openness, you can build a nurturing and stable environment for your children. Remember, the essence of parenting lies not in the perfection of the circumstances but in the love and intention behind your actions.

In the whirlwind that followed my divorce, the reality of becoming a single parent didn't truly hit me until the first night it was just me and my child at home. That evening, as I tackled the bedtime routine solo, I was struck by the enormity of my new role. Gone were the days of shared responsibilities; it was now up to me to provide the care, discipline, and emotional support my child needed, all on my own.

I remember one particularly challenging evening. My child, struggling with their own emotions about the divorce, was acting out in ways they hadn't before. Exhausted and overwhelmed, I felt a moment of despair. How was I going to do this on my own?

It was in this moment of vulnerability that I realised the strength of the bond between my child and me. Instead of focusing on discipline, I chose connection. We sat down, just the two of us, and talked openly about our feelings, fears, and the new shape our family was taking. This heart-to-heart didn't solve all our problems overnight, but it marked the beginning of a new understanding and approach to our relationship.

I learned the importance of being present, truly present, during the time we had together. We started small traditions, our own little rituals, that brought joy and a sense of stability to both of our lives. These moments were our building blocks toward healing and adapting to our new family dynamic.

Chapter 13
The Kids' Perspective: Helping Children Navigate the Divorce

Divorce isn't just a transition for the adults involved; it's a significant upheaval in the lives of the children, too. This chapter delves into understanding divorce from your children's perspective, offering strategies to support them through the process, ensuring their emotional well-being, and fostering a positive environment for their growth and adjustment.

Understanding Their Feelings

Children may experience a range of emotions in response to their parents' divorce, from confusion and sadness to anger and guilt. They may worry about the future, feel torn between parents, or even believe they are somehow to blame for the divorce. Recognising and validating these feelings is the first step in helping them navigate this challenging time.

Open Communication: Create a safe space for your children to express their feelings. Encourage honest discussions, and reassure them that all their emotions are valid and understandable. Remember that they might not be on the same timeline as you, and they may not feel ready or able to vocalise how they are feeling immediately.

Consistency and Reassurance: Children thrive on routine and predictability. Maintaining consistency in daily routines and reassurances of both parents' love and commitment can provide a sense of security amidst the changes. Maintaining their school attendance as well as any clubs, groups or sports clubs they may be members of is imperative.

Supporting Their Adjustment: The adjustment period following a divorce can be difficult for children as they come to terms with their new family dynamic. Supporting them through this time involves patience, understanding, and proactive steps to address their needs.

Unified Parenting Approach: Whenever possible, collaborate with your ex-partner on parenting decisions and approaches. Presenting a united front can help mitigate confusion and provide a stable environment for your children.

Professional Support: Consider seeking support from child psychologists or family therapists who specialise in divorce. They can offer valuable guidance and strategies to support your children's emotional health.

Fostering a Positive Environment: Creating a positive, nurturing environment post-divorce is crucial for your children's well-being and resilience. This includes not only the physical environment but the emotional and relational environments they inhabit.

A Truce: Demonstrate respect and cooperative behaviour with your ex-partner in front of your children. This helps them feel more secure and models healthy relationship dynamics. Keep talk of the divorce procedure, your feelings about your ex-partner and any shouting matches private.

Encourage New Relationships: Be supportive of

your children developing positive relationships with new significant others or step-siblings, ensuring they know these new connections do not replace the love and importance of their biological parents.

Activity: Creating a Family Transition Plan

Together with your children, create a Family Transition Plan that addresses both logistical arrangements (like living arrangements and visitation schedules) and emotional support strategies (like regular check-ins or family activities). This plan should be flexible and open to adjustments as everyone settles into the new family structure.

Include Your Children in the Planning: Involve your children in discussions about the transition plan, ensuring they feel heard and have a say in decisions that affect them.

Regular Re-evaluations: Set times to revisit and assess how the plan is working, allowing for adjustments based on everyone's evolving needs and feedback.

Age-Appropriate Conversations

Understanding how to approach conversations about divorce with your children requires sensitivity to their age and developmental stage. Tailoring your discussions to be age-appropriate ensures that your children receive the information and reassurance they need in a way they can understand and process.

- For Young Children (ages 3-7): Focus on simple, clear explanations and reassurances of safety and love. Young children benefit from knowing who will take care of them and what their daily routines will look like.
- For Middle Childhood (ages 8-12): Children in this age group can understand more complex emotions and situations. Be honest but optimistic, focusing on the practical changes they can expect and reassuring them that both parents will continue to love and support them.
- For Teenagers (ages 13-18): Teenagers are capable of understanding nuanced explanations and may have more direct questions about the reasons behind the divorce. It's important to communicate openly, respect their feelings, and involve them in discussions about future arrangements, emphasising that the divorce is not their responsibility.

Navigating the Path Forward

Helping your children navigate the divorce means being there for them through the uncertainty, offering love and support, and ensuring they have the resources they need to adjust healthily. Remember, every child is different, and the way they process and cope with the divorce will be unique. By staying attuned to their needs, maintaining open lines of communication, and providing a stable and loving environment, you can help them emerge from this experience stronger and more resilient.

Chapter 14
Navigating Family Dynamics: Handling Family Gatherings and Traditions Post-Divorce

The aftermath of a divorce often brings significant changes to family dynamics, especially when it comes to family gatherings and long-standing traditions. This chapter focuses on navigating these changes with grace, maintaining relationships within the extended family, and creating new traditions that honour your new life chapter.

Acknowledging Changes in Family Dynamics

Divorce can alter the landscape of family relationships, affecting not just the immediate family but extended relatives as well. Recognising and accepting these changes is the first step in navigating post-divorce family gatherings and traditions.

Open Communication: Communicate openly with family members about your divorce and any changes it may bring to family interactions. Honesty helps set realistic expectations for both you and your relatives.

Setting Boundaries: Establish clear boundaries with family members regarding discussions about your ex-spouse, the divorce, and any topics you're not comfortable addressing during gatherings.

Maintaining Relationships with Extended Family

It's important to maintain positive relationships with extended family members, even if the dynamics may shift. This is especially true if you have children.

Direct Relationships: Continue to nurture relationships with your in-laws and other extended family if you and they desire. Determine the most comfortable way to maintain these connections, whether it's through direct communication, social media, or family events.

Children's Relationships: Facilitate your children's relationships with extended family members from both sides. These connections can provide a sense of continuity and stability for your children during times of change.

Respect for New Boundaries: Respect the new boundaries and relationships within the extended family. This includes acknowledging new significant others when they become part of the family dynamic.

Navigating family dynamics post-divorce requires patience, open communication, and the willingness to adapt. By maintaining positive relationships with extended family, creating new traditions, and handling family gatherings with grace, you can foster a sense of continuity and support for yourself and your children. Remember, it's possible to honour the past while embracing the changes and opportunities that lie ahead in your newly redefined family structure.

Chapter 15
The Dating Scene: When and How to Step Back into Dating

After a divorce, the thought of trusting someone new with your heart can seem daunting. This chapter explores how to navigate the waters of trust and vulnerability as you begin to open yourself up to new relationships post-divorce. It's about moving past the pain and fear to find connection and intimacy with potential partners, without letting past experiences overshadow the possibility of future happiness.

Rebuilding Trust

Trust is the foundation of any meaningful relationship, but after a divorce, your trust in romantic partners may be shaken. Rebuilding trust starts with self-reflection and understanding what trust means to you now.

Self-Trust: The first step in rebuilding trust is to trust yourself—your judgment, instincts, and decisions. This comes from self-reflection and learning from past experiences.

Slow and Steady: Trust doesn't happen overnight. Allow it to build gradually as you get to know someone new. Pay attention to actions over words, and look for consistency and reliability.

Embracing Vulnerability

Vulnerability is crucial for emotional intimacy, yet it can feel risky after experiencing the hurt of a divorce. Being vulnerable means opening yourself up to the possibility of hurt, but it also opens you up to deeper connections.

Identify Fears: Understand the fears holding you back from being vulnerable. Is it the fear of being hurt again, of being judged, or of not being accepted for who you are?

Small Steps: Start with small acts of vulnerability and build from there. Sharing personal stories, expressing your feelings, and being honest about your needs are ways to gradually open up.

Avoiding the "Divorce Bore" Trap

In new relationships, it's important to be mindful of not dwelling excessively on your past and particularly the details of your divorce. While it's okay to share parts of your past, focusing too much on your ex, or the divorce, can be off-putting and signal that you may not be ready to move on. If you do find yourself talking excessively about your ex or your divorce, it might be a sign you're not quite ready to date. That's okay. Healing is a personal journey, and everyone moves at their own pace.

Focus on the Present: Make a conscious effort to focus

conversations on your interests, aspirations, and getting to know the other person.

Mutual Sharing: Aim for a balance in sharing personal histories. It's about building a new connection, not rehashing the past.

Navigating the Dating World

The dating world may have changed significantly since you were last single, especially with the rise of online dating and social media. Navigating these new dynamics requires patience and an open mind.

Online Dating: If you choose to explore online dating, take the time to research and select a dating site or app that aligns with your dating goals. Be honest in your profile about your status and what you're looking for.

Meeting New People: Beyond online platforms, consider joining clubs, groups, or activities that interest you. These can be great ways to meet new people who share your interests, in a more organic setting.

Setting Boundaries and Communication

As you begin to date again, setting clear boundaries and maintaining open communication are key to forming healthy connections.

Boundaries: Be clear about your boundaries and respect those of others. This includes physical boundaries, emotional boundaries, and boundaries regarding your time and energy.

. . .

Telling your Children

If you have children, deciding when and how to introduce them to someone you're dating is a significant consideration. It's generally advisable to wait until a relationship becomes serious and you feel confident about its stability and future. Give your children time to adjust to the idea of you dating. Have open conversations about their feelings and reassure them of your love and commitment to them.

Re-entering the dating world post-divorce is a journey of exploration, self-discovery, and, ultimately, opening yourself up to the possibility of love again. By taking the time to ensure you're ready, setting clear intentions and boundaries, and navigating the dating scene with honesty and openness, you can create the foundation for meaningful and fulfilling connections. Remember, there's no rush or right way to start dating again—the best path is the one that feels right for you, at your own pace.

Activity: Trust and Vulnerability Reflection

Write a letter to yourself that explores your fears and hopes about trust and vulnerability in future relationships. What does trust mean to you now? What are you afraid of, and what are you hopeful for? Reflect on the steps you can take to slowly build trust in others and how you can start to open up in safe and measured ways.

Chapter 16
Avoiding Negative Patterns: Recognising and Avoiding Old Relationship Pitfalls

Moving forward after a divorce provides a unique opportunity to reflect on past relationships and the dynamics that contributed to their dissolution. This chapter focuses on the crucial process of recognising and avoiding the repetition of negative patterns in future relationships. By identifying these patterns and understanding their roots, you can pave the way for healthier, more fulfilling connections.

Identifying Negative Patterns

The first step in breaking free from negative relationship patterns is to identify them. These patterns might include poor communication, unmet emotional needs, or recurring conflicts over similar issues.

In the journey to avoid repeating old relationship pitfalls, an often overlooked but invaluable source of insight can come from reflecting on the criticisms or feedback provided by your ex-partner. While the end of a marriage can be fraught with emotional turmoil and conflict, there may be kernels of truth in the observations shared by your ex that can serve as catalysts for personal growth.

Listening to Criticisms with an Open Mind

It's natural to defensively reject criticisms, especially those delivered during heated moments or as part of the divorce process. However, approaching these criticisms with an open mind can provide valuable insights into Behaviours or patterns you may be unaware of.

Reflection: Set aside time to reflect on the criticisms or feedback you received from your ex-partner. Try to distil any emotional charge from the feedback and identify if there are consistent themes or Behaviours mentioned.

Objective Analysis: It can be challenging to assess criticisms objectively. Writing them down and examining them when you're feeling calm can help you analyse them more rationally.

Seeking Second Opinions

Sometimes, it's hard to discern the validity of the feedback on your own. Seeking the perspectives of trusted friends or family members can provide clarity and confirmation.

Ask for Examples: If the feedback resonates, ask for specific examples of when they've observed the behaviour in question. This can help you understand the impact of your actions and how they're perceived by others.

Self-Improvement Plans: Based on the feedback and your reflections, develop a plan for addressing the identified issues. This might involve reading books on communication, attending workshops, or seeking therapy.

. . .

Personal Growth Through Criticism

While it may not be comfortable, viewing criticisms through the lens of personal growth can transform potentially painful feedback into a roadmap for positive change. This approach not only benefits your future relationships but also contributes to your overall emotional and psychological well-being.

In my marriage, I struggled to communicate my needs clearly, often opting to keep the peace instead of addressing issues that were important to me. After my divorce, I realised this pattern of avoidance contributed significantly to my unhappiness. Determined to change, I began working with a therapist to understand why I felt uncomfortable expressing my needs and how I could do so more effectively.

With practice and support, I learned to recognise when I was suppressing my feelings and developed strategies for open, honest communication. This journey wasn't easy, and there were moments of discomfort and fear, but the outcome was transformative. In my current relationship, I prioritise clear communication, and it has made all the difference in establishing a healthy, supportive partnership.

The end of a relationship often brings with it hard truths about ourselves that, if approached with openness and a willingness to grow, can lead to significant personal development. By listening to and reflecting on the criticisms of our ex-partners, seeking objective second opinions, and committing to change, we can work to ensure that our future relationships are healthier and more fulfilling.

Chapter 17
Forgiveness and Letting Go: The Journey Towards Forgiving Your Ex and Yourself

Forgiveness, especially after the emotional turmoil of a divorce, is a profound and often challenging journey. It involves releasing resentment and anger towards your ex-spouse and, equally important, forgiving yourself for any perceived shortcomings or mistakes. This chapter explores the path to forgiveness and how it can lead to healing and personal growth.

Understanding Forgiveness

Forgiveness doesn't mean condoning hurtful actions or denying your pain. Instead, it's about letting go of the hold that anger and resentment have on your heart. It's a process that frees you to live more fully in the present and look towards the future with hope.

Forgiveness Is For You: Recognise that forgiveness is something you do for yourself. It's a gift that releases you from the burden of negative emotions that can hinder your healing and happiness.

It Takes Time: Forgiveness is a process, not a one-time

act. It may involve layers of emotion and require time to work through fully.

The Steps to Forgiveness

The journey towards forgiveness often involves several stages, including acknowledgment of hurt, empathy, and the decision to forgive.

Acknowledgment: Acknowledge the pain and allow yourself to feel the emotions associated with it. This acknowledgment is crucial for healing.

Empathy: Trying to understand the perspective of your ex-spouse can sometimes aid in the forgiveness process. This doesn't excuse their actions but can provide a context that makes forgiveness feel more accessible.

Decision to Forgive: Forgiveness is a choice. It's a decision that you may need to make repeatedly as you navigate the ups and downs of post-divorce emotions.

Learning from the Experience: View your marriage and divorce as opportunities for growth. Reflect on what you've learned and how you can use these lessons to improve your future relationships and personal happiness.

After my divorce, I found myself trapped in a cycle of anger and bitterness. Every time I thought about my ex-spouse, a tidal wave of negative emotions would overwhelm me. It was exhausting. It was all-consuming and it was tearing me apart. It wasn't until I recognised that this resentment was hindering my ability to move forward that I truly began to consider forgiveness.

The turning point came one evening during a quiet

moment of reflection. I realised that holding onto my anger was only causing me more pain. I decided then that I needed to forgive—not for my ex-spouse, but for myself. I started by writing a letter to my ex that I never intended to send. In it, I poured out all my feelings, acknowledged the pain, and ultimately expressed my decision to forgive.

This act of writing was cathartic. It didn't erase the past or the hurt, but it allowed me to start letting go of the anger that had been weighing me down. The most challenging part was forgiving myself for not being able to make the marriage work. With time, I learned to extend the same compassion to myself that I was learning to extend to my ex. This self-forgiveness was crucial in reclaiming my happiness and moving forward with my life.

Forgiveness is a powerful step in the journey of healing from divorce. By forgiving your ex and yourself, you open the door to a life defined not by past hurts but by peace, growth, and new possibilities. Remember, forgiveness is a personal journey that unfolds in its own time. Be patient and gentle with yourself as you navigate this path towards freedom and healing.

Afterword

As we reach the conclusion of this journey through the challenges, emotions, and growth that follow a divorce, it's important to recognise that this ending is, in truth, a beginning. A new chapter awaits, one not written by the past but inspired by it, driven by the strength you've garnered and the lessons you've learned. This afterword is a celebration of the resilience of the human spirit and an affirmation of the endless possibilities that life offers, even after the most significant changes.

The Journey of Self-Discovery

Divorce, while often marked by loss, serves as a catalyst for profound self-discovery. You've navigated through the depths of grief, climbed the heights of personal growth, and emerged with a clearer understanding of who you are and what you desire from life. This journey is a testament to your resilience, a reminder that within you lies the strength to overcome adversity and the courage to face the unknown.

The Gift of Second Chances

Life is an anthology of chapters, each with its own narrative arc. The end of a marriage is not the conclusion of your story but a transition, an opportunity to write new chapters that reflect your growth, aspirations, and newfound wisdom. Embrace this gift of a second chance with open arms and an open heart, ready to explore new paths and pursue dreams that were once deferred.

Embracing Life's Possibilities

Beyond divorce lies a landscape brimming with possibilities. Whether it's finding love again, pursuing passions with renewed vigour, or discovering joy in the smallest moments, life post-divorce is ripe with opportunities for fulfilment and happiness. Allow yourself to dream, to hope, and to embrace the myriad possibilities that await. Remember, your potential is limitless, and your future is bright.

Building New Connections

The relationships you form post-divorce—friendships, romantic connections, or communal ties—are enriched by your experiences. These relationships are built on a foundation of authenticity, mutual respect, and shared growth. Cherish these connections, for they are the threads that weave the tapestry of your new life, adding depth, colour, and warmth.

A Celebration of You

As you stand at the threshold of this new beginning, take a moment to celebrate yourself. Celebrate your journey, your resilience, and the person you've become. You've navigated the storm and found your way to the shore, stronger, wiser, and more vibrant. The world is yours to explore, filled with endless opportunities for joy, love, and fulfilment.

Final Reflection

The end of a marriage marks not just the close of a chapter but the start of something new and beautiful. As you move forward, carry with you the lessons learned, the strength gained, and the hope that illuminates your path. Embrace this new beginning with the knowledge that you are capable of crafting a life filled with happiness, love, and meaning. Beyond divorce lies not just a new chapter but a whole new book waiting to be written by you.

Here's to new beginnings, to the endless possibilities that lie ahead, and to you—resilient, hopeful, and ready to embrace all that life has to offer.

The road post-divorce is often winding, marked by moments of doubt, loneliness, and reflection. Yet, it is also a path lit by the opportunity for profound personal growth, the chance to redefine your identity, and the freedom to pursue your dreams unencumbered. It's a journey of learning to stand on your own, finding strength in your resilience, and discovering that you are capable of navigating life's challenges with grace and courage.

As someone who has walked this path, I want to share with you a personal message of encouragement and solidarity. When I embarked on my own post-divorce journey, I felt a mixture of fear and liberation. The future seemed uncertain, and the prospect of rebuilding my life from the ground up was daunting. Yet, it was in this space of uncertainty that I discovered my strength, my capacity for resilience, and my ability to shape my destiny.

I learned to embrace solitude as a gift, an opportunity to reconnect with myself and explore my passions without compromise. I discovered the joy of setting new goals, the thrill of new adventures, and the warmth of forging new connections. Most importantly, I realised that my happiness and fulfilment were in my hands, and the end of my marriage was not the end of my story.

Through the ups and downs, I found a wellspring of hope and a renewed sense of purpose. I came to see that life beyond divorce is not just about moving on but moving forward, carrying the lessons and insights gained into a future brimming with possibilities.

To you, the reader, standing at the threshold of your new beginning, know that you are not alone. The path ahead is yours to shape, filled with endless opportunities for joy, growth, and adventure. Embrace the journey with an open heart, a curious mind, and the knowledge that the best is yet to come.

Let this book be a companion and a guide as you navigate the complexities of life post-divorce. May it offer comfort, inspiration, and practical advice to support you in embracing life's possibilities beyond divorce.

Remember, every ending is a new beginning. Here's to your journey towards a vibrant, fulfilling future—one step, one breath, one moment at a time.

With warmth and solidarity,

Morgan

About the Author

Morgan Reynolds is a fervent believer in the transformative power of positive thinking. Having navigated the tumultuous journey from a mindset ensnared by negativity and self-doubt to one flourishing with positivity and resilience, she has become a beacon of hope for those embarking on a similar path. Her mission is clear: to guide others as they traverse the challenging yet rewarding journey to reframe their mindsets and embrace a life of optimism and growth.

Drawing from a wellspring of personal experiences, including overcoming alcohol dependency and the trials of rebuilding her life post-divorce, Morgan's commitment to helping individuals unlock the full potential of their minds is unwavering. She understands first-hand the profound impact a positive mindset can have on overcoming life's obstacles and achieving lasting fulfilment.

As a lifelong learner and advocate for holistic well-being, Morgan continuously explores innovative approaches to mindset change. She integrates principles of mindfulness, self-care, and personal growth not only into her own life but also into the lives of those she touches through her writing and coaching. Her dedication to personal development is matched only by her sincere desire to inspire and uplift others.

Morgan offers more than just empathetic guidance and practical strategies; she provides a roadmap to a more positive mindset that inspires hope, boosts confidence, and celebrates the transformative power of embracing positivity. Her work shines a light on the path toward a fulfilling life characterised by resilience, self-belief, and an unwavering optimism.

Note from the author

Hi,

Thanks so much for reading *Beyond Divorce:Navigating Life After Separation.*

I hope you found it helpful and you were able to incorporate some of the advice, tips and techniques into your life.

If you think others would benefit from reading this book, whilst on their own journey , I would be incredibly grateful if you'd be so kind as to leave a review.

Reviews really help authors for a number of reasons, not least, providing feedback on what readers like, and improving visibility of the book on online retail sites.

Thanks in advance and once again I wish you well on your life journey.

Morgan Reynolds

Printed in Dunstable, United Kingdom

68310779R00047

Contents

Preface

On 8 May 1918, in one of the tragedies of war, 20-year-old Ted Ambler was patrolling No-Man's-Land in northern France when he was shot by a nervous young sentry; both were from the same Company, 2nd Battalion, Scots Guards. Today, all his family is dead and his story almost forgotten. This made me decide to research War Memorials, to share more information about those who are commemorated.

Deddington War Memorial was my starting point; but then the story evolved as I looked more carefully and talked to people. WWI military records show the names of people who claimed Deddington, Clifton or Hempton as their birthplace or their residence. This revealed others who could be included on the Memorial. Then I was lent a Roll of Honour printed in the latter stages of WWI which is a comprehensive listing of all those serving at that time. This revealed a far broader picture of the Parish's contribution and clearly showed the very significant proportion of the community who were engaged in military duties not just on the Western Front but all round the world.

When Rob Forsyth uploaded all this War Memorial information onto Deddington OnLine, the village website, it stimulated considerable interest locally, nationally and internationally, and encouraged him to join me in this project to research WWII and the post-war period and also to undertake the onerous, but rewarding, task of bringing all of the material into publishable form.

Michael Allbrook

It has been my very great privilege to meet personally a large number of those who served or, sadly, their widows and families. I would like to say a very big thank you to everyone for their patience with my notebook and innumerable questions and, of course, for the many cups of tea. Several of my visits have been to those in their 80s, or even 90s and so I also must record how impressed I have been by their near total recall of the WWII years.

The average age of WWII servicemen was their early twenties - many were still teenagers - and most had not travelled much beyond their own county town when they suddenly found themselves variously flying over Germany, on the sands of North Africa, in the icy wastes of the arctic on convoy duty, wading ashore on D-day or in the monsoon heat of the Burmese jungle looking for crashed aircraft. Each and every one of them could write their own book; one has to read between the lines to understand just what the reality of serving really was for them.

My meetings also triggered a host of recollections of Deddington in the 1930s and 40s. We have restricted ourselves for reasons of space to military matters but are left with an overwhelming sense of how strong the ties were between families and friends during long periods in which they had little or no knowledge of where their loved ones were or what they were doing. We can only echo Prince Charles' own words as quoted on the title page.

Rob Forsyth

Deddington’s military past

Deddington had a castle but, as there is no record of military activity, we move swiftly to 1643 and the Battle of Deddington and, to be honest, there is little known about that particular Civil War skirmish. The following year, King Charles I won the Battle of Cropredy Bridge and he, and his army, slipped away from the battlefield in the ensuing darkness. King Charles is reputed to have stayed that night in Castle House, Deddington.

But let us concentrate on the people of the Parish.

Our first is a soldier who has been the subject of a book entitled *Matthew Bishop of Deddington in Oxfordshire* by Brian Carter. ‘Matthew Bishop was born in Deddington ... Being of a “rambling disposition”, he joined the Navy in 1702 during the War of Spanish Succession, seeing action in Spain and Gibraltar and later proved to be a wily press gang operator in Ireland.

He married in 1706 but decided that his Queen commanded his duty despite the risk of consequential neglect of his wife and he joined the Army, subsequently fighting at Oudenard (1708) and Malplaquet (1709). His army career ended in 1711 with an expedition to New England and Canada.’

Our second soldier is William Parish who enlisted as Matthew Vincent in 2nd Battalion, Coldstream Guards in Lt Colonel D MacKinnon's Company and fought at Waterloo. He was awarded the Waterloo Medal.

The Waterloo Medal

The Parish Burial Register has an entry on 5 November 1875 that William Parish of Clifton was buried age 87 years 11 months.

Deddington had its representative in the Crimean War too. In 1899 *Jackson's Oxford Journal* reports that Sergeant Major John Brotherton Wilkie was buried in Deddington. He had served in the Crimea and been awarded 'several medals and clasps.' This included the Crimean Medal with clasp for Sebastopol whist serving with Major M Clifford's Company, 1st Battalion, Royal Artillery.

Also in 1899, *Jackson's Oxford Journal* makes a passing reference to four Deddington men who had served with General Kitchener in the Second Sudan War. It is implied that they had fought in two major British victories, the Battle of Atbara and the Battle of Omdurman in 1898. We have not found the names of these four men.

At this time Britain was gearing up for the Boer War, now called the Second Anglo-Boer War and, as usual, there were parades and committees supporting our men.

But the only named people we have found are George Bott and those to whom he refers in his letters:

Jackson's Oxford Journal 14 July 1900: A Deddington Man's Letter

The following letter is from a Private in the 1st Oxfordshire Light Infantry (O L I) sent to his parents at Deddington.

Kroonstad, June 13

Dear Mother,

I have not fired a shot yet but I have not lost the chance. We have been making trenches and powder mines. We are expecting an attack on Kroonstad tonight.

We are in the trenches day and night, but I got a day off, and I am going to do some washing. We have a big river close by, but the worst is they throw dead horses and bullocks into it. Kroonstad is a pretty place, but there are no Boers in it. They left everything behind them. We fetched a few in this morning.

We don't live so bad. We got some bread this morning, the first time for a week. But we lie out of the veldt with nothing a blanket to cover us, and we are covered with frost every morning. It isn't as if we get up and have a good breakfast. We get a biscuit and about a pint of coffee. But for all that I am happy enough. I think myself that we should get home some time before next March. I think they will keep us twelve months: I hope they will, I am just getting used to it. I think our next shift will be Pretoria. I am longing to go there. We get rum twice a week - two drams. I have had no beer yet.

I was sorry to hear about Mr. Whetton's death. I should like a night or two on the old sofa, it doesn't make your bones ache like the veldt. Remember me to Edmund, Harry and Will. Tell them I think of them very often. Tell Jo Ell I am alright and also tell Mr and Mrs Checkley and Mrs Miller. We have got to stand to arms.

Your loving son

George Bott

Jackson's Oxford Journal 21 July 1900: A Deddington Man's Letter

Riet Spruit, Sunday, June 17

Dear Mother,

We had to shift from Kroonstad in a hurry to Ventersburg. The Boers had blown up the railway each side of Zand River and cut the wires. There are about 900 Boers, and we were 400 militia. When they found we were coming they bolted, so we had to chase them. But they had horses, so we left them for the night. Some men were wanted to volunteer for plate laying, so I went with five others and an Officer. We took an engine and truck and soon did the job. The niggers [*sic*] did the work. We went down to where the fighting was, a distance of about five miles. The Officer told us to shoot at first sight, so you can bet I had a shot. We came back to Riet Spruit, and had to entrench ourselves. They afterwards went back to Kroonstad leaving two companies behind, so I had to work night and day. I have not had my shoes off for a week; we had no tents and only one blanket. We got the cotton khaki and it is so thin most of us are in rags, and we are as chatty as pigs living! Well, dogs live better at home. We get two dog biscuits and army rations. People at home think we get everything we want, but let me tell you we don't. I have only one pipe of tobacco left. I had to lose all I had – the only comfort I had: but it is no use grousing. They say there are 2,000 Boers around us, but they will find us a hard nut to crack. We have two guns, 25 mounted men, and 250 of us. We have a good position. I wish they would let us go for them and get it over.

Wednesday – some tents came today and we are in hopes of getting some better grub; we can do with it. I am about as fat as a match, and I've got whiskers three inches long, so you can tell what a mug I look. Knees out and sleeves all in rags, and it's too cold to wash. Never mind, roll on, old England. Jack Vincent has gone back to Kroonstad but Will Williams is with me, and we get on alright together. We often have a talk over the old "show." I've had no beer yet. We have plenty of money but it's no use, for we can buy nothing with it. We are about 950 miles from Cape Town, and I think we should go to Pretoria. I hope so anyway. Don't forget to send some writing paper. Remember me to all I know.

Best love to Harry, Will and Edmund.

Your loving son

George Bott

Jackson's Oxford Journal 15 September 1900: A Deddington Man's Letter

Bloemfontein, August 22

Dear Mother,

A few lines to let you know I am getting stronger. I am still in a convalescent home. We get everything we want here, but I expect we shall be going to Norvals Pont about 135 miles away, though I hope they won't shift us yet. There are about 1,200 here of all sorts. I found a mate from Steeple Aston, one of Mr. John Weston's sons. We don't know when we shall be coming home, though it won't be just yet: but we are only playing "fox and hounds": there is no fighting much now. I hope to let you have some good news next time I wrote [*sic*]. We can buy butter, eggs, fish, biscuits etc., but they are still very dear. We can go into town when we like. After tea last night we went for a bit of a walk, but I had to turn back; I'm so weak in the legs. I am going to write a few lines to Ernest and I am sending Harry a little book. (this is the soldier's New Testament, specially printed for the forces in South Africa. Nice ornamental and appropriate covers, and profusely illustrated by Messrs H A Harper and J Clack) [1]. I hope Harry has grown a deal stronger and that Will is a good boy. Tell Edmund I still have his pipes for him. I very often think about you all. I lie awake many hours some nights. I am sending some newspapers to Deddington. I shall have a lot to tell you some day. Remember me to Mr and Mrs Checkley, Mrs Miller, Mr and Mrs Belcher. Tell them that I am a teetotaller, but it's not my fault. I am going to try to do without or not have so much. Think of me when you are eating green peas, kidney beans, new spuds, etc.

I am having my photo taken, but it wont be much to look at. I expect J. Miller will be married by the time I get back. We have some nice looking girls here, but they are all black. I get one to do my washing.

I remain your loving son

Georg T. Bott

At the time these letters were written, George Bott was a 28-year-old bachelor. His mother had been widowed twice and lived in the Market Place. George returned to England, married Isabella Boyles, moved to London and they had at least two children, Charles and Eva.

Editors' note:

Nationally the first memorials for non-commissioned servicemen are those of the fallen of the Second Anglo-Boer War but these are few and far between and no such memorial exists in Deddington.

[1] This comment may possibly have been inserted by the editor of *Jackson's Oxford Journal* as it has a different 'ring' to Bott's own words.

Graves and memorials

The names in this chapter of those who served

There are over 600 people named in this book, many of whom came from a relatively small number of families during WWI and WWII: for example, there are 17 different Callows and the same number of Sykes, while other families, such as Garrett, Cowley, Davis, Hawkins and Smith all have multiple (but slightly fewer) entries. So it is all too easy to make incorrect assumptions as to which names and initials relate to which person. The lists at the start of each chapter therefore contain only the surnames of those who served contained in that particular chapter.

Adey
Austin
Bannard
Bliss
Bolton
Bull
Callow
Carvill
Castle
Checkley
Chislett
Churchill
Coulton
Curryer
Davis
Deane
Deeley
Dore
Dumbleton
Dunn
Ell
Fletcher
Freeman
French
Gardiner
Gardner
Garrett
Gilkes
Godfrey
Gomm
Grace
Greenaway
Griffin
Hall
Hancox
Hawkins
Hicks
Hiorns
Hitchman
Hutt
Jordon
Lewis
Manchip
Mundy
Pinfold
Pyman
Smith
Sorrell
Spencer
Stanley
Stevens
Sykes
Taylor
Tustain
Twissell
Waddup
Weaver
Wheeler
White
Wilkins
Woolgrove
Yerbury

The War Memorial

Deddington War Memorial 2011

Age shall not weary them
Nor the years condemn
At the going down of the sun
And in the morning
We will remember them.

Laurence Binyon

When the War Memorial was erected in 1922, it was sufficient for the inscription to be simply a name and an initial. Everybody knew them. Now more information is necessary to tell us about these men of Deddington. You will see that the names include men who had emigrated to Australia, Canada and New Zealand and still they volunteered to support the land of their birth.

Men of Deddington died in Belgium, Canada, England, France, Germany, Greece, India, Iraq, Israel, Italy, Malaysia, Sicily, Syria and Turkey where their graves and official memorials may be found. It was government policy that all those who died overseas would be buried where they died, irrespective of their rank.

If you wish to visit any of the graves look at the Commonwealth War Graves Commission website (www.cwgc.org/) and it will give you precise details about how to reach the cemetery and the location of the grave.

Extracts from *Deddington Deanery Magazine* (1919-22) relating to the War Memorial

Deddington Parish War Memorial is not on the village green but is located in the lower churchyard.[1] The minutes of *Deddington Deanery Magazine* record the lengthy process of erecting the Memorial.

May 1919 At a public meeting on 31 March it was decided to have a monument in the church or in the church porch.

June 1919 At a specially convened meeting on 20 May, it was decided that the Memorial should be in the churchyard.

August 1919 The Memorial would be designed by Mr Smithin. It would be twelve feet 6 inches high, executed in Portland Stone and cost about £230.

January 1920 An apology for the delay.

March 1921 A brass plaque commemorating those who died was erected through the instrumentality of Miss Ellen Bessie Hands. [This plaque hangs inside the church to the right of the East door and is reproduced on the facing page. The names are the same as those later inscribed on the War Memorial.]

Sunday 6 August 1922

The War Memorial was unveiled by Major General Sir Robert Fanshawe KCB DSO.[2]

Dedicated by the Vicar of Deddington, Reverend Thomas Boniface and the Assistant Clergy and Reverend T Buckingham (Wesleyan) and Reverend J Carter representing the Congregationalists.

Wreaths were placed by relatives and friends of the Fallen, also by The Queen's Own Oxfordshire Hussars and Ex-Servicemen of the Parish of Deddington.

A muffled peal was rung at the conclusion of the service.

The Memorial was executed by Messrs. Smithin and Cambray

[1] The War Memorial is actually in the New Churchyard which is an extension to the east of the original one.

[2] Major General Sir Robert Fanshawe (1863-1946) had commanded 48th (South Midland) Division on the Western Front and in Italy from 1915 until June 1918.

Brass plaque donated by Miss E B Hands in 1921

Names on the War Memorial from WWI

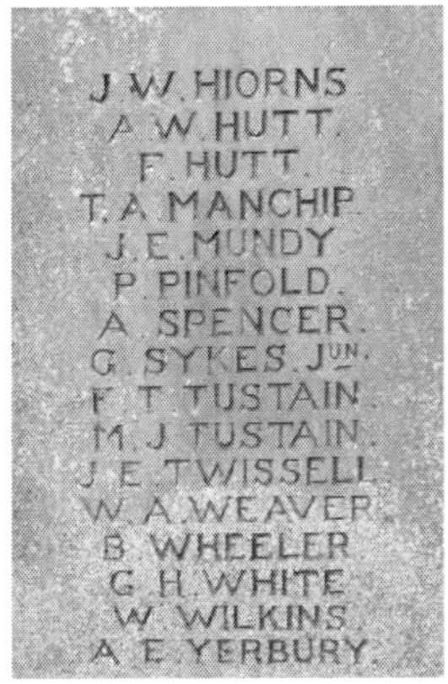

More details of these men are contained on pages 23 - 30

Names on the War Memorial from World War II and later

More details of these men are contained on pages 55 - 58 (1939-45) and page 95 (1950)

Memorials in the Church

Wooden crosses from WWI to the right of the north door of the church

(l to r) **F Tustain, O A J H Dore, R Bull and A E Hancox**

The wooden crosses or gravemarkers are preserved from their original WWI graves some of which were in France. O A J H Dore also has a CWGC headstone in the churchyard.

Above these crosses is a stone memorial to Ronald Page Bull who died in WWI and was reinterred in Highland British Cemetery, near Le Cateau, France, in 1920. He was the only son of Richard Page Bull, veterinary surgeon for this largely agricultural village.

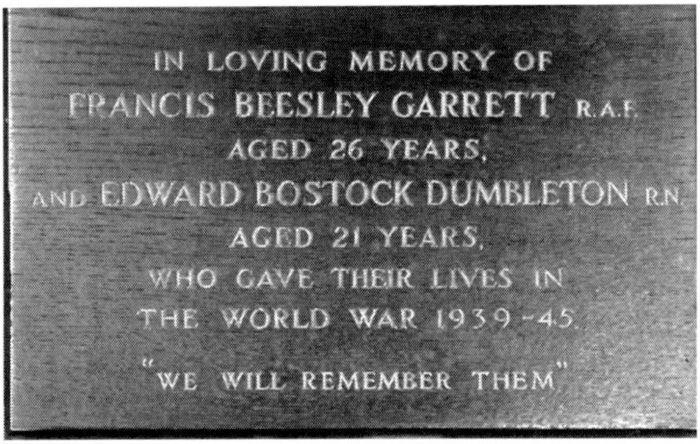

The wooden plaque immediately below the Royal British Legion Standard is in memory of Francis Garrett and Edward Dumbleton, two friends from Clifton who died in WWII. The plaque originally hung in the Church of St James in Clifton but was moved to the Church in Deddington when St James was closed in 1976.

Wooden crosses from WWI to the left of the north door

The names on the crosses are:

B Wheeler*,

A Ell*,

A Castle*,

W D Hancox,

W L French*

* These men also have CWGC headstones in the churchyard

A wooden plaque on the north wall of the baptistry - WWI

carved by David Hancox, their father

Inscription

IN LOVING MEMORY OF
OF
WALTER DAVID HANCOX.
N° 140053.R.E.
KILLED IN ACTION IN FRANCE.
JULY 1ST 1916.
AGED 30 YEARS.
WILLIAM RUFUS HANCOX.
N° 1907 OXFORD & BUCKS.LT INFTY.
KILLED IN ACTION IN FRANCE.
AUGUST 14TH 1916.
AGED 20 YEARS.
ALBERT EDWARD HANCOX.
N° 139675.R.E.
DIED IN BELGIUM OF WOUNDS RECEIVED IN ACTION.
JULY 24TH 1917.
AGED 19 YEARS.

GREATER LOVE HATH NO MAN THAN THIS,
THAT A MAN LAY DOWN HIS LIFE FOR HIS FRIENDS.

South aisle - a slate plaque commemorating Lt Churchill - WWII

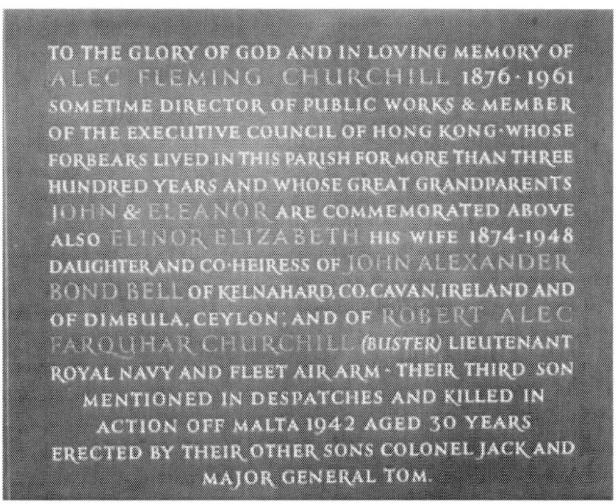

Lt Robert (Buster) Churchill's name is not on the War Memorial – possibly because his family were not resident in Deddington at the time. However, the plaque indicates the family's very strong attachment to the parish.

Graves in the Churchyard

Commonwealth War Grave Commision headstones - WWI

The CWGC erected headstones at the graves of those who died as a consequence of war. Those in Deddington are in the New Churchyard in which the War Memorial is also located. The New Churchyard is an extension to the east of the original one.

The New Churchyard

Private W L French

Private O A J H Dore

Private R W Wheeler

Private A C Ell

Private A J Castle

Gravestones from WWII

Private W C Coulton

He was in the 1st Battalion Oxfordshire and Buckinghamshire Light Infantry. His name is not on the War Memorial. A family could choose its own headstone.

Private J R F Gilkes

He was in the 1st Battalion Oxfordshire and Buckinghamshire Light Infantry. He is buried in Brouay War Cemetery, France and named on the War Memorial.

War Memorial and Grave in the Churchyard of All Saints, Croughton

Private F Hawkins was in the Royal Army Service Corps. His parents lived in Croughton and his widow, Emily Teresa Hawkins, lived in Market Place, Deddington

The Croughton War Memorial stands in the north east corner of the churchyard

There are 4 Hawkins named on the Croughton Memorial. Fred and 2 of his brothers are on this face

His CWGC gravestone stands at the far west end of the churchyard. The inscription is hard to read because of lichen and weathering.

M/323118 PRIVATE
F. HAWKINS
ROYAL ARMY SERVICE CORPS
18TH JANUARY 1918 AGED 29

The Menin Gate, Ypres

Percival B BANNARD
George W H CASTLE
Arthur J CHISLETT
Norman CHISLETT
Alec C TAYLOR
William WILKINS

and more than 54,800 other soldiers

The Thiepval Memorial

Harold FREEMAN
Archie A GOMM
W Rufus HANCOX
George W JORDON
Isaac SMITH
Mathew J TUSTAIN

and more than 94,930 other soldiers

The Tyne Cot Memorial

Clarence B GILKES
Ernest J HAWKINS
Hubert C SYKES

and more than 73,350 other soldiers

Where they rest or are commemorated

England	
St Peter and St Paul, Deddington	Alfred J CASTLE
	Robert A F CHURCHILL
	William C COULTON
	O Arthur J H DORE
	Alfred ELL
	William L FRENCH
	Bernard WHEELER
All Saints Church, Croughton	Fred HAWKINS
Falmouth Cemetery, Cornwall	Walter A GARDNER
Lee on Solent Memorial	Robert A F CHURCHILL
Norwich Cemetery	Ernest C HITCHMAN
Preston Cemetery, Tynemouth	Edward B DUMBLETON
Runnymede Memorial	Francis B GARRETT
St Peter's Church, Wolvercote	William T STANLEY
Belgium	
The Menin Gate, Ypres	Percival B BANNARD
	George W H CASTLE
	Arthur J CHISLETT
	Norman CHISLETT
	Alec C TAYLOR
	William WILKINS
Ploegsteert Memorial	Harry G GRIFFIN
Talana Farm Cemetery	Frederick R HUTT
The Tyne Cot Memorial	Clarence B GILKES
	Ernest J HAWKINS
	Hubert C SYKES
Canada	
Calgary Union Cemetery	James E TWISSELL
France	
The Arras Memorial	Benjamin HAWKINS
	Thomas A MANCHIP
	William H V TUSTAIN
	Frank WADDUP
	George H WHITE
Bienvillers Military Cemetery	Walter D HANCOX
Boulogne Eastern Cemetery	Charles G FLETCHER
Brouay War Cemetery, Normandy	John R F GILKES

Brewery Orchard Cemetery, Bois-Grenier	William A WEAVER
Cabaret Rouge British Cemetery, Souchez	Albert ADEY
Calais Southern Cemetery	Lawrence L PYMAN
Corbie Communal Cemetery	Fred C WOOLGROVE
Daours Communal Cemetery Extension	John H CHECKLEY
Doingt Communal Cemetery Extension	Ernest W CURRYER
Doullens Cemetery Extension No.2	Louis H GARDINER
Étaples Military Cemetery	James GODFREY
	Alfred E YERBURY
La Ferté-sous-Jouarre Memorial	Charles CALLOW
Givenchy-en-Gohelle Canadian Cemetery	Joseph AUSTIN
Godewaersvelde British Cemetery	Albert E HANCOX
Guards' Cemetery, Combles	Percy PINFOLD
Guards' Cemetery, Lesboeufs	Frederick T TUSTAIN
Highland Cemetery, Le Cateau	R Page BULL
Iwuy Communal Cemetery	Joseph W HIORNS
Longuenesse (St Omer) Cemetery	Wallace J CARVILL
Lonsdale Cemetery, Authuile	Edwin SYKES
The Messines Ridge (NZ) Memorial	Henry G S CHURCHILL
Montescourt Lizerolles Cemetery	Archie W HUTT
Namps-au-Val British Cemetery	Albert STEVENS
Orchard Dump Cemetery, Arleux-en-Gohelle	John E MUNDY
The Pozières Memorial	William J DUNN
The Soissons Memorial	Stanley H DEELEY
The Thiepval Memorial	Harold FREEMAN
	Archie A GOMM
	W Rufus HANCOX
	George W JORDON
	Isaac SMITH
	Mathew J TUSTAIN
Thistle Dump Cemetery, Longueval	Norman W SYKES
Le Touret Memorial	Albert F SPENCER
	George SYKES

Germany

Berlin 1939-1945 War Cemetery	William R GREENAWAY

Greece

Mikra British Cemetery, Kalamaria	George I DAVIS

India

Kirkee 1914-1918 Memorial,	Edwin BLISS

Iraq	
North Gate War Cemetery, Baghdad	Frederick DEANE
The Basra Memorial,	John F HAWKINS
	James HICKS
Kut War Cemetery	Harry GRACE
Italy	
Catania War Cemetery, Sicily	Ernest S G HALL
Cassino War Cemetery	John H LEWIS
Malaysia	
Batu Gajah, God's Little Acre	
Roll of Honour and grave	Richard L HALL
Singapore	
The Singapore Memorial	Henry SORRELL
Syria	
Damascus Commonwealth Cemetery	Ernest A SYKES
Turkey	
The Helles Memorial	William F BOLTON

The First World War
(1914-18)

The names in this chapter of those who served

Adams
Adey
Allen
Austin
Bannard
Beesley
Bennet
Berridge
Berry
Bletsoe
Bliss
Boffin
Bolton
Bowler
Breen
Brooks
Brookes
Browning
Bull
Callow
Cambray
Carvill
Castle
Checkley
Cherry
Chislett
Churchill
Clark
Clarke
Clutterbuck
Collect
Compton
Course
Cowley
Curryer
Darlington
Davis
Deane
Deeley
Dodwell
Dore
Drinkwater
Dunn
Durran
Ell
Field
Finch
Fincher
Fletcher
Fox
Freeman
French
Gardiner
Gardner
Garrett
Gibbs
Gilkes
Godfrey
Gomm
Grace
Green
Gregory
Griffin
Hall
Hancox
Hands
Harmsworth
Harper
Harris
Hawkins
Hicks
Hickson
Higham
Hiorns
Hirons
Hitchman
Hodges
Holiday
Hopcraft
Hore
Hunt
Hutt
Jennings
Jones
Jordon
Kelley
Large
Lewis
Long
Luker
Malcher
Malings
Manchip
Mayo
Meadon
Miller
Mitchell
Mobley
Morton
Mundy
Nichols
Page
Paginton
Payne
Pearson
Pinfold
Quarterman
Rees
Regan
Roberts
Sanders
Shirley
Smith
Spencer
Spenser
Stanley
Stevens
Stimpson
Stockford
Stone
Sturch
Sykes
Taylor
Thornewill
Tomkinson
Tustain
Twissell
Valentine
Vincent
Waddup
Wallin
Warren
Watts
Weaver
Wheeler
Whetton
White
Whitton
Wilkins
Williams
Woolgrove
Yerbury

See the note on page 6 for a further explanation about names

The men named on the War Memorial

'SACRED TO THE HONOURED MEMORY OF THESE MEN
WHO FELL IN THE GREAT WAR 1914-1918'
(Inscription on the War Memorial)

Albert ADEY
Lance Corporal, 2nd Battalion, The Oxfordshire and Buckinghamshire Light Infantry, 5 Brigade, 2nd Division.
He was killed in action near Arras, Somme on 1 May 1918 age 38.
He is buried in grave VIII Q3, Cabaret Rouge British Cemetery, Souchez.
His parents were Josiah and Sarah A Adey and he was the husband of Mary C Adey, Beaumaris, Upland Road, Sutton.

Joseph AUSTIN
Private, 50th Battalion, Alberta Regiment, Canadian Infantry, 24th Canadian Division, 1st Corps.
He died near Hill 145 on the second day of the Battle for Vimy Ridge on 10 April 1917 age 25.
He is buried in grave B19, Givenchy-en-Gohelle Canadian Cemetery, Souchez.
He had emigrated to Canada in 1913 and lived in Clover Bar, Alta.
His parents, Arthur and Eliza Austin of Hempton, had both died and he was survived by his sister, Ellen (Nellie) Churchill of Westcote Barton, Middle Barton.

Edwin BLISS
Private, 1st Garrison Battalion, The South Staffordshire Regiment formerly with the Royal Warwickshire Regiment.
He died on 23 November 1918 age 25 presumably from illness.
He is remembered on face 6 of the Kirkee 1914-1918 Memorial, Poona, India.
His parents were George and Caroline Bliss of Philcote Street.

William Frederick BOLTON
Private, 2nd Battalion, The Royal Fusiliers (City of London Regiment), 86 Brigade, 29th Division.
He was killed in action during the Gallipoli campaign on 4 December 1915 age 29.
He is remembered on panel 37-41 of the Helles Memorial, Gallipoli, Turkey.
His parents were Frederick T and Catherine E Bolton of Deddington.

Ronald Page BULL
Second Lieutenant, 4th Battalion, The Northamptonshire Regiment and previously a Private in The Oxfordshire and Buckinghamshire Light Infantry.
He was killed in action in the final advance in Picardy on 30 October 1918 age 19.
He is buried in grave XII A9, Highland Cemetery, Le Cateau.
His parents were Richard Page Bull MRCVS and Annie Bull of New Street.

Charles CALLOW
Pioneer, 2nd Signal Company, Royal Engineers, formerly with The Oxfordshire and Buckinghamshire Light Infantry.
He was killed in action on 16 September 1914 age 28.
He is remembered on La Ferte-sous-Jouarre Memorial.
His parents were Thomas and Ruth Callow, Market Place.

Wallace James CARVILL
Private, 139th Field Ambulance, Royal Army Medical Corps.
He died from measles on 3 March 1917 age 36.
He is buried in grave IV B 34, Longuenesse (St Omer) Souvenir Cemetery.
His parents were Charles and Jane E Carvill of Deddington.

Alfred John CASTLE
Private, The Oxfordshire and Buckinghamshire Light Infantry, who was transferred to The Labour Corps.
He died on 12 November 1918 in hospital in Bristol age 33.
He is buried in the churchyard of St Peter and St Paul.
His parents were Alfred M and Mary J Castle of Clifton.

George William Henry CASTLE
Rifleman, 4th Battalion, The King's Royal Rifle Corps, 80 Brigade, 27th Division.
He died of wounds received during the Battle of Frezenberg Ridge on 25 May 1915 age 32.
He is remembered on panel 51 and 53 of The Menin Gate, Ypres.
His parents were Albert J and Lydia Castle.

John Hawtin CHECKLEY
Private, 1st/4th Battalion, The Oxfordshire and Buckinghamshire Light Infantry, 145 Brigade, 48th Division.
He died on 20 July 1916 of wounds received during the Battle of the Somme age 21.
He is buried in grave I B 24, Daours Communal Cemetery Extension.
His parents were William and Louisa Checkley, Market Place.

Two brothers
The sons of Emily and the late James Chislett of Deddington.

Arthur Joseph CHISLETT
Private, 27th Battalion, Canadian Infantry (Manitoba Regiment), 6 Infantry Brigade, 2nd Canadian Division.
He died on 6 November 1917 at the Battle of Passchendaele age 27.
He is remembered on panel 24-26-28-30 of The Menin Gate, Ypres.
He had emigrated to Canada in August 1912 on *SS Tunisian*.

Norman CHISLETT
Rifleman, 18th (Arts and Crafts) Battalion, The King's Royal Rifle Corps, 122 Brigade, 41st Division.
He was killed in action at Pilckem Ridge, near Ypres on 31 July 1917 age 31.
He is remembered on panel 51 and 53 of The Menin Gate, Ypres.

Henry George Stratford CHURCHILL
Private, 2nd Battalion, Auckland Regiment, 1st New Zealand Infantry Brigade, NZEF.
He was killed in action at the Battle for Messines Ridge near Ypres on 7 June 1917.
He is remembered on the Messines Ridge (NZ) Memorial in Mesen.
He had emigrated to Wellington, New Zealand, on 1 October 1908 on the *MV Ruapehu.*
His parents were Richard C and Thurza Churchill, Market Place.

George Isaac DAVIS
Gunner, 98 Anti-Aircraft Section, Royal Garrison Artillery.
He died on 24 December 1918 age 26.
He is buried in grave 1143, Mikra British Cemetery, Kalamaria, Greece.
His parents were Harry and Charlotte Davis of Deddington and he was the husband of Nora B Davis of 42 Duns Tew.

Stanley Hubert DEELEY
Private, 3rd Battalion, The Worcestershire Regiment, 74 Brigade, 25th Division.
He was killed in action at the Battle of the Aisne on 27 May 1918 age 19.
He is remembered on the Soissons Memorial.
His parents were Edwin and Eliza Deeley of Castle Street.

O Arthur John H DORE
Private, 53rd (Graduated) Battalion, The Royal Warwickshire Regiment.
He died of pneumonia on 6 October 1918 age 18 in Ludgershall, Suffolk, where his regiment was stationed.
He is buried in the churchyard of St Peter and St Paul, Deddington.
His parents were Arthur George and Rosina Dore of Victoria Terrace.

William James DUNN
Private, 1st/1st Battalion, Queen's Own Oxfordshire Hussars, 4 Cavalry Brigade, 4th Cavalry Division.
He was killed in action on 1 April 1918 at Rifle Wood age 27 when The Oxfordshire Yeomanry (The Queen's Own Oxfordshire Hussars) suffered its worst casualties.
He is remembered on panel 6 of the Pozières Memorial, near Albert.
He lived in Deddington and his parents were Thomas and Jenett Dunn.

Alfred Christian ELL
Private, 12th Battalion, The Duke of Cornwall's Light Infantry.
He died from his wounds in hospital in Chichester on 3 March 1917 age 37.
He is buried in the churchyard of St Peter and St Paul.
His parents were George A and Frances Ell of New Wiggington but Alfred was born in Deddington.

Harold FREEMAN
Private, 9th Battalion, The Royal Fusiliers (City of London Regiment), 36 Brigade, 12th Division.
He was killed in action at the Battle for Transloy Ridge on 7 October 1916 age 19.
He is remembered on pier and face 8C, 9A and 16A of The Thiepval Memorial.
He was the son of Joseph and Jane E Freeman, Market Place.

William Loder FRENCH
Private. He served with The Oxfordshire Yeomany (The Queen's Own Oxfordshire Hussars) before emigrating to Australia in 1913 where he served with the 11th Battalion, Australian Infantry, AIF.
He died on 10 February 1916 age 25 in Deddington where he had been convalescing from the illnesses contracted in Gallipoli.
He is buried in the churchyard of St Peter and St Paul.
He was buried with full military honours by the Australian Army on 14 February.
His parents were William J and Emily French, Council Street, now Hopcraft Lane.

Louis Henry GARDINER
Private, 2nd/4th Battalion, The Oxfordshire and Buckinghamshire Light Infantry, 148 Brigade, 61st Division.
He died on 2 December 1918 age 22.
He is buried in grave IE1, Doullens Communal Cemetery Extension No 2.
He was the husband of Ellen K Gardiner of Laurel Cottage, Barford St. Michael.

Walter Albert GARDNER
Private, 1st/1st Battalion, The Oxfordshire and Buckinghamshire Light Infantry, 145 Brigade, 48th Division.
He died on 5 January 1916 age 24 in Cornwall before embarking for France.
He is buried in grave KH62, Falmouth Cemetery, Cornwall.
He was born in Deddington. His parents were Frank and Elizabeth Gardner of Cardiff.

James GODFREY
Lance Corporal, 5th Battalion, The Oxfordshire and Buckinghamshire Light Infantry, 42 Brigade, 14th Division.
He died on 29 September 1915 from the wounds received in the attack on Bellewaarde age 27.
He is buried in grave IV H 16, Étaples Military Cemetery.
His parents were Samuel and Martha Godfrey and he was the husband of Rose Godfrey, Bishops Itchington, Leamington Spa. He lived in Clifton when he enlisted.

Archie Andrew GOMM
Private, 6th Battalion, The Oxfordshire and Buckinghamshire Light Infantry, 60 Brigade, 20th Division.
He was killed in action between Combles and Bapaume on 27 February 1917 age 25.
He is remembered on pier and face 10A and 10D of The Thiepval Memorial.
His parents were Harriet and the late Andrew Gomm.

Harry GRACE
Private, 1st Battalion, The Oxfordshire and Buckinghamshire Light Infantry, 17 Brigade, 6th (Poona) Division.
He died of fever on 12 February 1916 age 27.
He is buried in grave H4, Kut War Cemetery, Iraq.
His parents were Deborah and the late William Grace, Earl's Lane, and he was the husband of Lillian R Grace.

Harry Gerard GRIFFIN
Private, 2nd Battalion, The Worcestershire Regiment, 100 Brigade, 33rd Division.
He was killed in action at the Battle of Messines on 11 April 1918 age 21.
He is remembered on panel 5 of the Ploegsteert Memorial, Belgium.
His parents were the late Henry Griffin and his widow Elizabeth Grimn, formerly Griffin, Hillbre, 25 Bowling Green Road, Stourbridge.

Three brothers
The sons of David and Ellen Hancox of Grove Lodge.

Albert Edward HANCOX
Sapper, 101 Field Company, Royal Engineers.
He died of his wounds on 24 July 1917 in hospital near Ypres age 19.
He is buried in grave 1 A 4, Godewaersvelde British Cemetery, France.

Walter David HANCOX
Sapper, 154 Field Company, Royal Engineers.
He was killed in action on 1 July 1916 age 30 on the first day of the Battle of the Somme. Over 60,000 men were killed or wounded on that day.
He is buried in grave VIII B13, Bienvillers Military Cemetery.

William Rufus HANCOX
Corporal, 1st/4th Battalion, The Oxfordshire and Buckinghamshire Light Infantry, 145 Brigade, 48th Division.
He was killed in action near Pozières Ridge on 14 August 1916 age 20.
He is remembered on pier and face 10A and 10D of The Thiepval Memorial.

Fred HAWKINS
Private, 700 MT Company, Royal Army Service Corps formerly with The Worcestershire Regiment.
He died on 18 January 1918 after an accident age 29.
He is buried in the churchyard of All Saints Church, Croughton.
His parents were George and Annie Hawkins of Croughton and he was the husband of Emily T Hawkins, Market Place.

Two brothers
The sons of Josiah J and Caroline J Hawkins of Clifton.

Benjamin HAWKINS
Private, 6th (Royal Wiltshire Yeomanry) Battalion, The Duke of Edinburgh's (Wiltshire Regiment), 58 Brigade, 19th Division.
He was killed in action on 23 March 1918 at the Battle of St Quentin age 19.
He is remembered on bay 7 of the Arras Memorial.

John Frederick HAWKINS
Lance Corporal, 1st Battalion, The Oxfordshire and Buckinghamshire Light Infantry, 17 Brigade, 6th (Poona) Division.
He was killed in action on 22 November 1915 age 25.
He is remembered on panel 26 and 63 of the Basra Memorial, Iraq.

Joseph William HIORNS
Lance Corporal, $1^{st}/4^{th}$ Battalion, Duke of Wellington's (West Riding Regiment), 147 Brigade, 49th Division.
He was killed in action on 11 October 1918 during the Pursuit to the Selle age 30.
He is buried in grave B44, Iwuy Communal Cemetery, France.
His parents were William and Emma Hiorns of Castle Street.

Two brothers
The sons of John W and Mary F Hutt of Deddington.

Archie William HUTT
Sergeant Major, 5th Battalion, The Oxfordshire and Buckinghamshire Light Infantry, 42 Brigade, 14th Division and formerly a Sergeant with The Oxfordshire Yeomanry (The Queen's Own Oxfordshire Hussars) who had been in France since 1914.
He was killed in action at the Battle of St Quentin on 21 March 1918 age 32.
He is buried in grave 141, Montescourt Lizerolles Communal Cemetery.
He was the husband of Margaret Hutt of Deddington.

Frederick Rowland HUTT
Private, 5th Battalion, The Oxfordshire and Buckinghamshire Light Infantry, 42 Brigade, 14th Division.
He was killed in action near the Ypres Salient on 8 February 1916 age 25.
He is buried in grave III C5, Talana Farm Cemetery, Belgium.

Thomas Alexander MANCHIP
Private, 20th Battalion (The 3rd Public Schools), The Royal Fusiliers (City of London Regiment), 19 Brigade, 33rd Division.
He was killed in action at the second Battle of the Scarpe on 25 April 1917 age 35.
He is remembered on bay 3 of the Arras Memorial.
His parents were Elizabeth J and the late Thomas A Manchip of Deddington and he was the husband of Grace L Manchip, 89 Hayes Road, Bromley, Kent.

John Ernest MUNDY
Private, 2nd Battalion, The Oxfordshire and Buckinghamshire Light Infantry, 5 Brigade, 2nd Division.
He was killed in action in the Somme on 3 June 1917 age 22.
He is buried in grave III K24, Orchard Dump Cemetery, Arleux-en-Gohelle.
He was a native of Hinton-in-the-Hedges.
His parents were Albert T J and Caroline Mundy of the Paper Mills, Adderbury.

Percy PINFOLD
Private, 2nd Battalion, Prince of Wales' Own (West Yorkshire Regiment), 23 Brigade, 8th Division.
He was killed in action on the Somme on 1 January 1917 age 24.
He is buried in grave Priez Farm Mem 5, Guards Cemetery, Combles, France.
His parents were Joseph and Elizabeth Pinfold of Clifton.

Albert Edward SPENCER
Private, 2nd Battalion, The Oxfordshire and Buckinghamshire Light Infantry, 5 Brigade, 2nd Division.
He was killed in action on 16 May 1915 age 32.
He is remembered on panel 26 of the Le Touret Memorial.
He was born in Banbury and lived in Hempton. His parents were William and Adelaide Spencer of Hook Norton and he was the husband of Sarah R E Spencer, Queen Street, Hook Norton.

George SYKES
Private, A Company, 2nd Battalion, The Oxfordshire and Buckinghamshire Light Infantry, 5 Brigade, 2nd Division.
He was killed in action on 16 May 1915 during the Battle of Festubert age 22.
He is remembered on panel 26 of Le Touret Memorial.
His parents were George D and Louisa Sykes of The Green.

Two brothers
The sons of William and Eliza Tustain of Victoria Terrace.

> **Frederick T TUSTAIN**
> Private, 3 Company, 1st Battalion, Coldstream Guards, 2 Guards Brigade, Guards Division.
> He was killed in action near Lesboeufs on 29 September 1916 age 30.
> He is buried in Guards Cemetery, Lesboeufs.
> He was the husband of Agnes Tustain, 267 Alama Street, Rockhampton, Queensland, Australia where he had emigrated on the *SS Kaikoura* in 1911.
>
> **Matthew James TUSTAIN**
> Lance Corporal, C Company, 1st/4th Battalion, The Oxfordshire and Buckinghamshire Light Infantry, 145 Brigade, 48th Division.
> He was killed in action at Pozières Ridge on 23 July 1916 age 23.
> He is remembered on pier and face 10A and 10D of The Thiepval Memorial.

James Ethelbert TWISSELL
Private, 82nd Battalion, Abegweit Light Infantry Regiment, Canadian Infantry.
He died on 1 June 1916 age 32 in Holy Cross Hospital Calgary.
He is buried in grave L 95 B 7 S P, Calgary Union Cemetery.
He had emigrated on 20 April 1912 on the *SS Tunisian* bound for Saint John.
He was married to Edith M Twissell of Cabin Lake, Alberta.
His parents were Emily and the late Frank Twissell of New Street.

William Alfred WEAVER
Private, 7th Battalion, The East Surrey Regiment, 37 Brigade, 12th Division.
He was killed in action near Armentières on 17 January 1918 age 33.
He lived in King's Sutton.
He is buried in grave IV F24, Brewery Orchard Cemetery, Bois-Grenier.
His parents were George and Mary A Weaver of Deddington.

Bernard WHEELER
Private, Training School, Canadian Army Medical Corps.
He died on 18 November 1916 age 29. He is buried in the churchyard of St Peter and St Paul.
His parents were James and Sarah Wheeler of Deddington and he was the husband of Janet Wheeler of Winnipeg where he had emigrated on 28 February 1907 sailing on the SS *Southwark* to Halifax, Nova Scotia, Canada.

George Henry WHITE
Private, 5th Battalion, The Oxfordshire and Buckinghamshire Light Infantry, 42 Brigade, 14th Division.
He was killed in action at the third Battle of the Scarpe on 3 May 1917 age 30.
He is remembered on bay 6 and 7 of the Arras Memorial.
He was born in Over Norton and lived in Hempton. His parents were Job and Eva A White of Hempton and he was married to Emma E White, The Bank, Hempton.

William WILKINS
Private, 2nd Battalion, The Oxfordshire and Buckinghamshire Light Infantry, 5 Brigade, 2nd Division.
He was killed in action during the First Battle for Ypres on 21 October 1914 age 31.
He is remembered on panel 37 and 39 of The Menin Gate, Ypres.
His parents were George and Lavinia Berry (previously Wilkins) of Earl's Lane.

Alfred Edwin YERBURY
Private, 2nd Battalion, The South Wales Borderers, 87 Brigade, 29th Division formerly with The Oxfordshire and Buckinghamshire Light Infantry.
He died of wounds received at the Battle of the Scarpe on 27 April 1917 age 19.
He is buried in grave XIX L10A, Étaples Military Cemetery.
His parents were Alfred and Cicely Yerbury of Castle Street.

The men whose names are not on the War Memorial

The War Memorial currently includes names of men who are not from Deddington and it includes men who were dear to the people who were living in the Parish after the wars. This list is of men who have an officially recorded link to the Parish of Deddington, either by birth or residence, and whose names do not appear on the War Memorial.

Percival Bryan BANNARD
Corporal, 1st/4th Battalion, The Oxfordshire and Buckinghamshire Light Infantry, 145 Brigade, 48th Division.
He was killed in action on 7 August 1917 age 21 during the Battle of Passchendaele.
He is remembered on panel 37 and 39 of The Menin Gate, Ypres.
He was born in Deddington and was the son of Frederick P and Florence N A Bannard, 4 Grosvenor Road, Banbury.

Ernest Walter CURRYER
Gunner, Royal Horse Artillery and Royal Field Artillery, 44 Brigade.
He died of wounds received during the fighting on the Somme on 30 September 1918 age 29.
He is buried in grave III B 14, Doingt Communal Cemetery Extension near Peronne.
He was born in Hempton and was the son of Frederick and the late Mary Curryer, Kempton Green, Princes Risborough.

Frederick DEANE
Private, 1st Battalion, The Oxfordshire and Buckinghamshire Light Infantry, 17 Brigade, 6th (Poona) Division.
He died on 30 June 1916 probably from illness age 24.
He is buried in Islahie Mem 201, North Gate War Cemetery, Baghdad.
He was born in Deddington but moved to Compton, Berkshire. He was the son of James T and Agnes A Deane.

Charles George FLETCHER
Private, 2nd Battalion, The Oxfordshire and Buckinghamshire Light Infantry, 5 Brigade, 2nd Division.
He was wounded near Ypres and died on 26 October 1914 age 33.
He is buried in grave III A 12, Boulogne Eastern Cemetery.
He was born in Deddington, the son of John and Elizabeth Fletcher.

Clarence Bert GILKES
Private, 5th Battalion, The Oxfordshire and Buckinghamshire Light Infantry, 42 Brigade, 14th Division.
He was killed in action between Gheluvelt and Polygon Wood in the Battle of Passchendaele on 16 October 1917 age 20.
He is remembered on panel 96-98 of The Tyne Cot Memorial.
He was the son of George and Susan Gilkes of New Street.
His name is recorded by the Vicar in the Deanery magazine (p.40)

Ernest James HAWKINS
Private, 202 Company, Machine Gun Corps (Infantry), formerly with The Royal Army Service Corps.
He was killed during the Battle for Passchendaele on 9 October 1917 age 22.
He is remembered on panel 154 to 159 and 163A of The Tyne Cot Memorial.
He was born in Deddington, the son of Stephen H and Martha Hawkins.

James HICKS
Private, 5th Battalion, The Duke of Edinburgh's (Wiltshire Regiment), 40 Brigade, 13th Division, formerly with The Oxfordshire and Buckinghamshire Light Infantry.
He was killed during the second assault on Sanniyat on 9 April 1916 age 31.
He is remembered on panel 30 and 64 of the Basra Memorial, Iraq.
He was born in Deddington, the son of James and Sarah Hicks, Rock Farm, Baginton, Coventry.

Ernest Charles HITCHMAN
Private, 51st (Graduated) Battalion, The Royal Warwickshire Regiment, 205 Brigade, 68th Division.
He died on 23 October 1918 age 18 whilst he was stationed in East Anglia.
He is buried in grave 54 197, Norwich Cemetery.
He lived in Deddington and he was the son of Mrs Fanny G Symonds, 31 St Mary's Road, Cowley St John, Oxford.

George William JORDON
Lance Corporal, 5th Battalion, The Oxfordshire and Buckinghamshire Light Infantry, 42 Brigade, 14th Division.
He was killed in action at Delville Wood on 24 August 1916 age 19.
He is remembered on pier and face 10A and 10D of The Thiepval Memorial.
He was born in Deddington, the son of John and Annie Jordon.

Isaac SMITH
Private, 6th Battalion, The Oxfordshire and Buckinghamshire Light Infantry, 60 Brigade, 20th Division, formerly with The Oxfordshire Yeomanry (The Queen's Own Oxfordshire Hussars).
He was killed in action during the Battle of Transloy Ridge on 7 October 1916, age 26.
He is remembered on pier and face 10A and 10D of The Thiepval Memorial.
He was born in Deddington, the son of the late George and Ellen Smith.
His Army records show that he had no known living relatives.

William Thomas STANLEY
Private, Royal Army Ordnance Corps.
He died of double pneumonia in Halifax on 14 January 1918 age 33.
He is buried in St Peter's Churchyard, Wolvercote.
He was the son of Thomas J and Eliza A Stanley and the husband of Alice M Edwards (formerly Stanley) of Wytham, Oxford.
His Army records state that he was born in Deddington but there is no other evidence of this and it is probable that he was born in Ledwell.

Albert STEVENS
Corporal, 5th Battalion, The Oxfordshire and Buckinghamshire Light Infantry, 42 Brigade, 14th Division.
He was killed in action during the retreat after the Battle of St Quentin on 31 March 1918 age 25.
He is buried in grave 1 D 22, Namps-au-Val British Cemetery.
He was the brother of Ellen Prew, Adlestrop, Kingham and lived in Deddington.

Edwin SYKES
Sergeant, 11th (Lonsdale) Battalion, The Border Regiment, 97 Brigade, 32nd Division.
He was killed in action during the attack on Albert on 1 July 1916, the first day of the Battle of the Somme age 36.
He is buried in grave 1 G 20, Lonsdale Cemetery, Authuile.
He was the son of John and Elizabeth Sykes of Deddington.

Hubert Charles SYKES
Rifleman, 2nd/9th County of London Battalion, The London Regiment (Queen Victoria's Rifles), 175 Brigade, 58th Division.
He was killed in action in the Battle of Passchendaele on 3 October 1917 age 37.
He is remembered on panel 151 of The Tyne Cot Memorial.
He was the son of Joshua and Mary A Sykes of New Street and the husband of Harriet C Bennetton (formerly Sykes), 99 Evelyn Street, Deptford.
His name is recorded by the Vicar in the Deanery magazine (p.42.)

Norman William SYKES
Rifleman, 1st Battalion, Rifle Brigade (The Prince Consort's Own), 11 Brigade, 4th Division.
He was killed in action near Albert on 1 July 1916 age 20.
He is buried in grave B5, Thistle Dump Cemetery, High Wood, Longueval.
He was born in Deddington, the son of Henry and Martha J Sykes, of North Aston.

Alec Charles TAYLOR
Private, 2nd Battalion, The Oxfordshire and Buckinghamshire Light Infantry, 5 Brigade, 2nd Division.
He was killed in action in the first Battle of Ypres on 26 November 1914.
He is remembered on panel 37 and 39 of The Menin Gate, Ypres.
He was born in Deddington and the husband of Ethel M H Geen (formerly Taylor), 7 Clarke Street, Ebey, Cardiff.

William Henry Valentine TUSTAIN
Private, 7th Battalion, The Leicestershire Regiment, 110 Brigade, 37th Division.
He was killed in action during the Battle of Arleux on 28 April 1917 age 33.
He is remembered on bay 5 of the Arras Memorial.
He was born in Hempton. His parents were Sarah and the late George Tustain.

Frank WADDUP
Private, 5th Battalion, The Oxfordshire and Buckinghamshire Light Infantry, 42 Brigade, 14th Division.
He was killed in action during the third Battle of the Scarpe on 3 May 1917 age 20.
He is remembered on bays 6 and 7 of the Arras Memorial.
He was the son of Thomas H and the late Harriet Waddup of Deddington.

Fred Cecil WOOLGROVE
Corporal, 7th Battalion, The Queen's (Royal West Surrey Regiment), 55 Brigade, 12th Division.
He died of his wounds on 9 December 1915 age 24. He had probably been wounded at Hulluch in late October.
He is buried in plot I row B grave 6, Corbie Communal Cemetery.
He was born in Deddington, the son of Joseph and Annie Woolgrove of North Aston.

The men who served and returned

The names on the two lists that follow have been taken from *Deddington Deanery Magazine*, extracts of which are on page 39 and from a contemporary Roll of Honour reproduced on page 44. The combination of these two sources provides a comprehensive, but probably incomplete, record of those who served, a list that is too often not available.

These men are known to have been wounded and/or discharged.

William Allen discharged
Alec Austin Hempton
Cpl John Beesley discharged
Frederick G Berry
Geoffrey Bowler foot amputated
E Browning discharged
Allan Callow discharged
Frank H Callow
A Cambray
A Castle discharged
E Cherry discharged
F Clarke
G Clarke
P Dunn
Christopher J Ell leg amputated
H Freeman
M French invalided from the Front
William J Gardner discharged
G Gilkes
R Gilkes
Rev H Tyrell Green
A Hands discharged
L Hands
William J Harper Royal Berkshire Reg't 1916 Medical discharge
John A Higham
E A Hicks invalided from the Front
H Hicks
G Hodges discharged
Cpl Thomas P Holiday discharged
Capt. D Hopcraft
A Hunt
Henry J Malcher
P Mayo discharged
H Miller
W Mitchell
B Paginton disabled
S Payne discharged
L Rees
O Regan
E Shirley
J Smith
G Smith discharged

These men are known to have served but no additional details are held.

These men are known to have served but there is no record of their wartime service or whether they should be included in any of the other categories. Unfortunately there is no longer any comprehensive archive which enables us to add to this information. The surviving records of soldiers in WWI are very poor having largely been destroyed in a bombing raid in WWII.

G Adams
C Austin
Richard G Beesley
G Bennet, Clifton
M Bennett
J Berridge
William G Berry
B Bletsoe
D Bliss
S Boffin, Clifton
E Bolton
J Bolton, Clifton
R F Bolton, Clifton
W Brooks (or Brookes?)
James H Callow
P Callow
Robert Callow
R Callow, Clifton
R Cambray
P Carvill
J Castle
W Checkley
P Churchill
W Churchill
H Clark, Clifton
R Clarke
E Clutterbuck, Hempton
F Clutterbuck, Hempton
H Collect
John Compton
W Course
F Cowley
Jacob Cowley
John Cowley
Fred W Davis (RHA)
B Dodwell
W Dodwell
F Durran
E Field
F Finch
W Fincher, Clifton
S Fox, Clifton
H Gardiner
Charles E Gibbs
Walter E Gibbs
C Gilkes
F Gregory
H Griffin
S Hall
E Hancox
Arthur Harper, Clifton
H Harper
A Harris, Clifton
F Hawkins
E Hickson, Clifton
B Hiorns
John Hiorns
S Hiorns
William Holiday
F Hopcraft
S Hopcraft
E Hore
W Jennings
C Jones
Lieut D Jones
C Large
John H Lewis
T Luker
Frederick C Mayo
G Meadon, Clifton
E Mobley
L W Morton
L Nicholls, Hempton
F Page
W Page
J Quarterman, Clifton
T Quarterman, Clifton
W Sanders
Alfred A Smith
W G Smith
W O Smith
W Smith
E Stimpson
E Stockford
Stone
B Sykes
F Sykes
George Sykes
G I Sykes
Hubert Sykes
Joseph Sykes
John Sykes
R Sykes
Ro. Sykes
S Sykes

The details of these men have been provided from other sources

These names are not recorded in either the Vicar's notes or the Roll of Honour (p.44) but have Deddington connections by birth or residence. They have been sourced either from a recently discovered 1953 membership list of the then named British Legion (see next page) or from information provided by their families.

Leonard George A BOFFIN (1900–73) Sergeant.
The Oxfordshire Yeomanry (The Queen's Own Oxfordshire Hussars) – he enlisted underage and was discharged in 1915 – subsequently he joined The Royal Welch Fusiliers and later served with The Hong Kong Police from 1926 to 1932.

Frank Colman BOWLER (1898-1989) 2nd Lieutenant Royal Flying Corps.
His story and that of his two brothers can be read on page 114.

Leslie William Harold BOWLER MC (1893-1981) Captain.
He joined the 16th (Public Schools) Battalion Middlesex Regiment as a Territorial soldier age 21. He was commissioned in June 1915 into 22nd County of London Regiment (The Queen's), 142nd Brigade, 47th Division. His story and that of his two brothers can be read on page 114.

James H BREEN Flight Lieutenant.
Royal Flying Corps.

Bartholomew (Bart) CALLOW (1881-1964).
Royal Army Service Corps. Driver. He was a well-known Deddington character whose considerable skills as a singer and musician have been researched and recorded in an article by Professor Michael Pickering of Loughborough University.

Lewis DARLINGTON (1891-1991) Guardsman.
The Grenadier Guards.

John Maurice FRENCH (1893-1985).
The Oxfordshire Yeomanry (The Queen's Own Oxfordshire Hussars).

Francis (Frank) **Beesley GARRETT** (1891-1955).
The Oxfordshire Yeomanry (The Queen's Own Oxfordshire Hussars) (see p.134).

Henry Thomas HARPER (1898-1966) Private.
Princess Charlotte of Wales (Royal Berkshire Regiment). Son of William Jesse Harper who also served.

Frank Seymour HIRONS (1885-1969).
5th Battalion, The Royal Fusiliers (City of London Regiment).

Arthur John (Jack) MALCHER (1898-1997) Private.
The Gloucestershire Regiment. More about the Malcher men who served can be read on page 161.

Henry James MALCHER (1878-D) Private.
The East Yorkshire Regiment, part of the British Expeditionary Force (BEF). He was discharged wounded and awarded the Silver War Badge on 13 July 1915. This badge absolved the wearer of any possible charge of 'shirking' military service (p.161).

James Henry Hone MALINGS (1885-1929) Private.
He served from 1914 to 1920 in The Royal Engineers and then The Northumberland Fusiliers.

John Frederick MALINGS (1872-1933).
He enlisted into the 20th Hussars in 1900 saying he was 19 whereas he was actually 29! He served abroad in South Africa (1901-02), Egypt (1903-04) then emigrated to Canada in 1907 where he enlisted in the Canadian Expeditionary Force in 1915 by, once again, subtracting years from his age (43) saying he was only 37 and born in 1878!

Ernest Cecil PEARSON (1890-1956) Corporal.
The Essex Regiment. He received a bullet wound to his ankle in France in 1916.

Reginald Geoffrey ROBERTS (1890-1946) Major.
4th/7th Battalion, Dragoon Guards, then 10th Battalion, (Prince of Wales' Own Royal) Hussars.

William Frederick (Fred) SANDERS (1876-1932).
The Oxfordshire and Buckinghamshire Light Infantry and Princess Charlotte of Wales (Royal Berkshire Regiment).

Bernard WALLIN (1892-1960) Sergeant.
1st/4th Battalion, The Oxfordshire and Buckinghamshire Light Infantry.

The Royal British Legion

The British Legion was formed as a national organisation on 15 May 1921, bringing together four organisations of ex-Service men that had established themselves after WWI. Its main purpose was to care for those who had suffered as a result of service in the Armed Forces in the Great War, whether through their own service or through that of a relative. It was awarded the appellation 'Royal' in 1971.

The Deddington Branch was formed in 1925. The building it occupies on High Street was formerly an axle-tree factory belonging to the local firm of Mason & Hard. It subsequently passed into the hands of William Cox of South Newington. In 1920 the trustees of "The Red Triangle Club" and "The Deddington Institute" raised funds by means of a public collection and purchased the property from William Cox to be their club premises for the sum of £350.

In 1925, at a General Meeting of the two organisations, the Trustees handed over the Club premises to the newly formed Deddington Branch of the British Legion to use in perpetuity; although it was also stated in the deed that ..."the trustees shall in the event of the said Deddington Branch of the British Legion ceasing to exist hold the said heraditaments and premises in trust for the Parish Council of Deddington ..".

The Officers of the Deddington Branch in 2011 were:

President: **Major D Hood MC**
Chairman: **Mr A Humphries MBE**
Standard Bearer: **Mr DA Keats**

Extracts from *Deddington Deanery Magazine* (1914-19) relating to the men who served

These records are the work of the Reverend Thomas Boniface, Vicar of Deddington. At the time of writing them he had been Vicar since 1878 and if you read the original magazine, which is held in the Oxford Record Centre, you will detect the increasing level of despair in the records.

December 1914

Chas. Callow Killed in Action
Wm Wilkins Killed in Action
John Beesley Wounded
Wm Tustain Wounded

January 1915
Corporal J Beesley Convalescent
A Spencer Convalescent
M French Invalided from Front
E A Hicks Invalided from Front
George Castle Killed

February 1915
We were delighted recently to welcome from the Front (on leave)
R Beesley **W Holiday** **J M French**
S R Hall **W Page** **J C Warren**

June 1915
The Curate, **the Rev Tyrell Green** has joined the Royal Army Medical Corps

July 1915
G Sykes jnr Killed
Sergeant Major Warren Wounded
Corporal T Holiday Wounded
L/Cpl. D Hopcraft Wounded
Private H Miller Wounded
Private H Checkley Wounded

Killed previously and not recorded were:
W Wilkins **C Callow** **G Castle**
[In fact, the names of all these men had been recorded already]

Wounded previously but not recorded.
J Beesley **W Tustain** **W Brooks**
J H Warren **A Callow**

August 1915

A Spenser of Hempton Wounded

Clarence Gilkes Wounded

[Private Clarence Bert Gilkes, 5th Battalion, The Oxfordshire and Buckinghamshire Light Infantry died on 16 October 1917. He has no known grave but his name is recorded on panel 96-98 of The Tyne Cot Memorial yet he is not on the Deddington Memorial. For more details see page 31.]

October 1915

Private Spenser of Hempton. Killed

Lieut. Geoffrey Bowler Wounded in the Dardanelles Campaign

November 1915

William Allen Wounded and in Manchester

Albert Tustain Wounded and in Netley

Walter Gibbs Dangerously ill

Loder French Welcome home

February 1916

J F Hawkins of Field Barn. Killed

W F Bolton of Clifton. Killed

Walter Albert Gardner Died in Cornwall on home service

March 1916

Loder French Died age 24. Elder son of Mr and Mrs W J French

April 1916

Lieut. G Bowler Wounded and his foot was amputated whilst serving in the Dardanelles. He has been promoted to Captain

Sgt Major Warren DCM Now commissioned and has transferred from the Queens Own Oxfordshire Hussars

Sergeant H Grace DCM Died of fever in the Persian Gulf

F Hutt Killed in action 8 February 1916

August 1916

Walter D Hancox Royal Engineers, killed 1 July. A ringer at the Church and Captain of the Football and Cricket Clubs

Private J E Twissell Serving with 32 Battalion Canadian Infantry, he died in Calgary Holy Cross Hospital. A former chorister he was buried on 5 June

Lieut. Warren Wounded for the second time

Private G Clarke Wounded

H Checkley Wounded

J W Cowley Prisoner of War in Turkey

October 1916

Corporal W Rufus Hancox Killed age 20 serving in The Oxfordshire and Buckinghamshire Light Infantry
He was a bell ringer at the Church, a Scout and a Territorial

November 1916	
Private J H Checkley	Killed in action in July. Previously wounded
L/Cpl M J Tustain	Killed in action in July
F Tustain	His brother. Coldstream Guards. Killed
December 1916	
Bernard Wheeler	Died in Shorncliffe Military Hospital on 18 November and was buried on 23rd. He was the son of James Wheeler and he had become a Canadian Resident
February 1917	
Percy Pinfold	of Clifton. Killed in action 1 January 1917

[The Vicar comments that this is the 20th Death and that there were 209 Deddington men in the armed forces]

March 1917	
A Ell	Wounded a second time and in hospital in Chichester
April 1917	
Wallace Carvill	Died on 3 March in hospital in France, he had been suffering from measles
Alfred Ell	Died on 3 March, in Chichester Hospital
June 1917	
Joseph Austin	of Hempton. Killed
Alfred Yerbury junior	Killed
Alex Manchip	Killed
July 1917	
John Ernest Mundy	Killed on Sunday 3 June
Private H White	of Hempton is missing
October 1917	
D Hopcraft	Promoted and commissioned
J Watts	Promoted and commissioned
N Chislett	Killed in July
A Hancox	Wounded
R, W and T Wheeler	All three wounded
E Shirley	Wounded
W Mitchell	Wounded
F Callow	Wounded
P Dunn	Wounded

The marriage of **Private R E Weaver** to Miss G M Miller

November 1917	
Sapper E Hancox	Killed in action 24 July, a bell ringer
Harold Freeman	Killed in action

January 1918

E and B Paginton	Both badly wounded and disabled
J Higham	Badly wounded
Alec Austin	Badly wounded
A Hunt	Badly wounded
A Cambray	Badly wounded
R Gilkes	Badly wounded
M French	Indisposed
H Churchill	From New Zealand. Killed

February 1918

Private F Drinkwater	Awarded Military Medal for rescuing two comrades
Lieut D Jones	Has returned
Private F Hawkins	Died 18 January after an accident

March 1918

Private A Weaver	Killed. He was a resident and Chorister who had moved to Sutton. A nephew of the Wright family in Clifton
M French	on sick list
E and B Paginton	on sick list
W White	Missing
Lieut. L Bowler	Mentioned in Despatches

May 1918

A Hutt	Killed
W Dunn	Killed
Rev. Tyrell Green	Wounded
Lieut. Watts	Wounded
H Hicks	Wounded
Captain L Bowler	Awarded Military Cross
J Higham	RFC won a Belgian Award

June 1918

F Valentine	At first believed killed but this was corrected in July which states he is a Prisoner of War
A Adey	of Clifton. Killed

The total number of deaths has reached 34

Hubert Sykes has fallen; he is the son of Joshua
[Hubert Charles Sykes, Rifleman, London Regiment (Queen Victoria's Rifles) died on 3 October 1917 age 37. His name is not on the War Memorial. For more details see page 33.]

August 1918

C J Ell	Wounded and his leg amputated
F Berry	Wounded
H Griffin	Killed
H Deeley	Missing

September 1918	
B Hawkins	of Field Barn Missing
F Berry	Wounded
D Hopcraft	Promoted Captain
CQMS H J Harmsworth	in the London Gazette for Gallantry
November 1918	
Captain L Bowler	Awarded bar to his Military Cross
B Cambray	From Canada. Awarded Military Medal
B Hawkins	Believed to be a Prisoner of War
O Dore	Who has recently enlisted died of pneumonia on 5 October
December 1918	
Joseph Hiorns	Killed 11 October 1918
R Page Bull	Killed 30 October 1918
Leonard A Long	Is a Prisoner of War
January 1919	
Harry Gardner	Killed 2 December 1918 in France. He was a Scout and a bell ringer
February 1919	
George Davis	Died in Salonica
Edwin Bliss	Died in India
Bernard Hawkins	Has died. He was not a prisoner as was earlier reported. Some others have returned home
Leonard Long	He was a prisoner in Germany
James Cowley	He was a prisoner in Mesopotamia
QMS H J Harmsworth	From Italy, awarded the Meritorious Service Medal

A Roll of Honour

This is a copy of a Roll of Honour provided by courtesy of Albert Harper whose family members are included on it. It is undated but probably was compiled sometime prior to the spring of 1917. It is not a complete record but nonetheless it has been a very valuable source document.

ROLL OF HONOUR (*revised*).

REFERENCE—*a*. Killed in Action. *b*. Wounded. *c*. Discharged.

DEDDINGTON.

Adams, G.
Allen, W.*bc*
Austin, C.
Beesley, J.*bc*
Beesley, R.
Bennett, M.
Berridge, J.
Berry, F.
Berry, W.
Bletsoe, B.
Bliss, D.
Bolton, E.
Bowler, G.*b*
Bowler, L.
Brookes, W.
Browning, E.*c*
Callow, Al.*bc*
Callow, A.
Callow, C.*a*
Callow, F.
Callow, J.
Callow, P.
Callow, R.
Cambray, A.
Cambray, B.
Carvill, P.
Carvill, W.
Castle, A.*c*
Castle, G.*a*
Castle, J.
Checkley, H.*b* (dead)
Checkley, W.
Cherry, E.*c*
Chislett, A.
Chislett, N.
Churchill, H.
Churchill, P.
Churchill, W.
Clarke, F.*b*
Clarke, G.*b*
Clarke, R.
Collect, H.
Compton, John
Course, W.
Cowley, F.
Cowley, Jacob
Cowley, John
Cowley, Jas.
Davis, F.
Davis, G.
Dodwell, B.
Dodwell, W.
Dunn, W.
Durran, F.
Ell, A.
Ell, C.
Field, E.
Finch, F.
Freeman, H.*b*
French, L. (dead)
French, M.
Gardiner, H.
Gardner, A. (dead)
Gardner, H.
Gardner, W.*c*
Gibbs, C.
Gibbs, W.
Gilkes, C.*b*
Gilkes, G.
Gilkes, R.*b*
Gregory, F.
Griffin, H.
Grace, H. (D.C.M.) dead.
Green, H. T.
Hall, S.
Hancox, A.
Hancox, E.
Hancox, R.*a*
Hancox, W.*a*
Hands, A.*c*
Hands, L.*b*
Harmsworth, J.
Harper, W.*c*
Harper, H.
Hawkins, F.*a*
Hicks, E.
Hicks, H.
Higham, J.
Hiorns, B.
Hiorns, John
Hiorns, Jos.
Hiorns, S.
Hodges, G.*c*
Holiday, T.*bc*
Holiday, W.
Hopcraft, D.*b*
Hopcraft, F.
Hopcraft, S.
Hore, H.
Hutt, A.
Hutt, F.*a*
Hunt, A.
Jennings, W.
Jones, G.
Kelley, F.
Large, C.
Lewis, [illegible].
Luker, T.
Malcher, H.*b*
Manchip, H.
Mayo, F.
Mayo, P.*bc*
Miller, H.*b*
Mitchell, W.*b*
Mobley, E.
Morton, L. W.
Mundy, J. F.
Page, F.
Page, W.
Paginton, E.
Payne, S.*c*
Rees, L.*b*
Regan, D.*b*
Sanders, F.
Sanders, W.
Shirley, E.
Smith, A.
Smith, G.*c*
Smith, J.*b*
Smith, W. G.
Smith, W. O.
Smith, W.
Stimpson, E.
Stockford, E.
Stone
Sturch, H.*c*
Sykes, B.
Sykes, F.
Sykes, G.*a*
Sykes, G. D.
Sykes, Jos.
Sykes, John
Sykes, R.*a*
Sykes, Ro.
Sykes, S.
Sykes, T.*c*
Sykes, W.
Taylor, E.
Taylor, V.*b*
Taylor, P.
Thornewill, A.
Thornewill, L.
Tomkinson, H.
Tustain, A.*bc*
Tustain, F.*a*
Tustain, M.*a*
Tustain, S.
Tustain, T.
Tustain, W.*bc*
Twissell, B.
Twissell, E. (dead)
Vincent, R.
Warren, J.*b*
Watts, J.
Weaver, H.
Wheeler, B. (dead)
Wheeler, Jas.*c*
Wheeler, Jas.
Wheeler, R.
Wheeler, W. E.
Whetton, H.
Whitton, D.
Wilkins, W.*a*
Wilkins, W.
Williams, A.
Williams, B.
Williams, F.
Williams, J.
Yerbury, A., sen.
Yerbury, A.

CLIFTON.

Adey, A.
Bennett, G.
Boffin, S.
Bolton, J.
Bolton, R. E.
Bolton, W. F.*a*
Callow, B.
Castle, A.
Clark, H.
Fincher, W.
Fox, S.
Garrett, F.
Godfrey, J.*a*
Gomm, A.
Harper, A.
Harris, A.
Hickson, E.
Meadon, G.
Pinfold, P.
Quarterman, J.
Quarterman, T.
Warren, J. (D.C.M.)

HEMPTON.

Austin, A.
Clutterbuck, E.
Clutterbuck, F.
Nichols, L.
Spencer, A. (dead)
White, H.
White, J.

Total ... 209

Photographs and illustrations

A group of Deddington soldiers

The Oxfordshire and Buckinghamshire Light Infantry, Banbury TA Company

Photograph courtesy of Clive Sanders

(Rear row l to r) **Rufus Hancox, John Beesley, Tom Holiday, <u>John Lewis</u>**

(Front row l to r) **Anon - a Hancox?, Douglas Hopcraft, <u>Stanley Hall</u>, Wilf Mitchell**

The photograph was probably taken at a pre-war summer camp.

The men whose names are <u>underlined</u> were not from Deddington at the time but Richard Stanley Hall became publican of the King's Arms in due course. His son, Robin, died while on National Service in 1950 (p.95)

The Oxfordshire and Buckinghamshire Light Infantry, Banbury TA unit, 1914 - just before they were sent to France

(courtesy of Clive Sanders)

(Back row l to r) Mr R E Lewis, **W Wilkins, J H Lewis***, **Wilfrid Mitchell***

(2nd row l to r) **Mr (W) Allen♦, Mr (W J) Harper♦**, H Gardner, **C. Ell,** Mr Mold, **Phil Bannard**, Sep Mold, Mr Harris and Harold Slaymaker

(3rd row seated on chairs l to r) **Matt Tustain*, Rufus Hancox*, H E Hopcraft, J H Harmsworth**#, **Bob Giles (probably Gilkes), T P Holliday♦,** G Coleman, A Singleton

(4th row seated on the ground l to r) H White*, Mr Meadows, Mr Alexander*, S F Hands, **H Checkley, J H Callow*, J Holton**

The names are handwritten on the back of the photograph but two names are missing from the second row so we cannot be certain as to who was who in it.

Key to names:

The names in **bold** are known to have been from Deddington

* known to have died.

♦known to have been wounded.

awarded the Meritorious Service Medal

A troop of Deddington soldiers some time during 1914 – cover photograph

Courtesy of Clive Sanders, his grandfather Frederick is in the back row third from left

Bartholomew Callow

William Loder French

John Maurice French

Henry Thomas Harper

Percy Pinfold *(seated)*

John Smith *(r)*

William Smith

6th Battalion, Oxfordshire and Buckinghamshire Light Infantry
Private Archie Gomm's Company

Private Archie Andrew Gomm

Archie's family still have his medals and award certificates which we reproduce here as being typical of those awarded to many thousands of other soldiers.

Families of the fallen received this plaque known as the 'Dead man's penny'

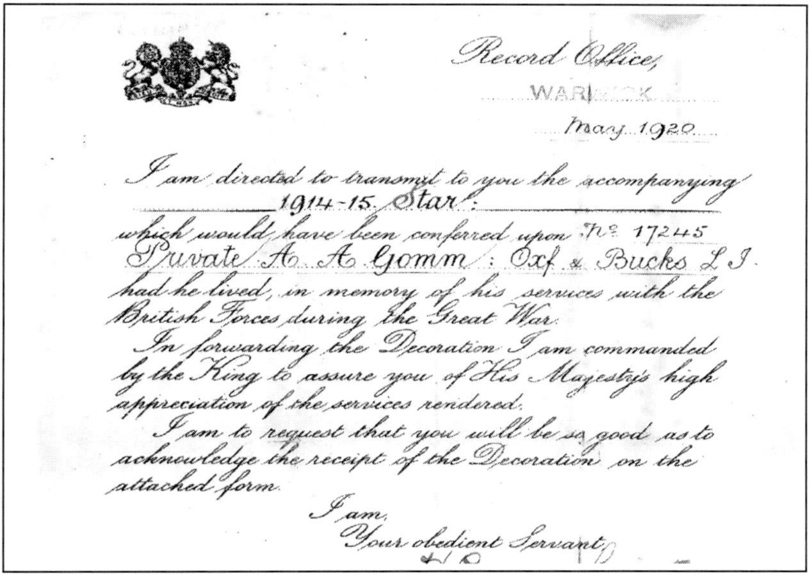

Record Office,
WARWICK
May 1920.

I am directed to transmit to you the accompanying 1914-15 Star:
which would have been conferred upon No. 17245 Private A. A. Gomm: Oxf & Bucks L.I.
had he lived, in memory of his services with the British Forces during the Great War.

In forwarding the Decoration I am commanded by the King to assure you of His Majesty's high appreciation of the services rendered.

I am to request that you will be so good as to acknowledge the receipt of the Decoration on the attached form.

I am,
Your obedient Servant,

1914-1915 Star Medal Award

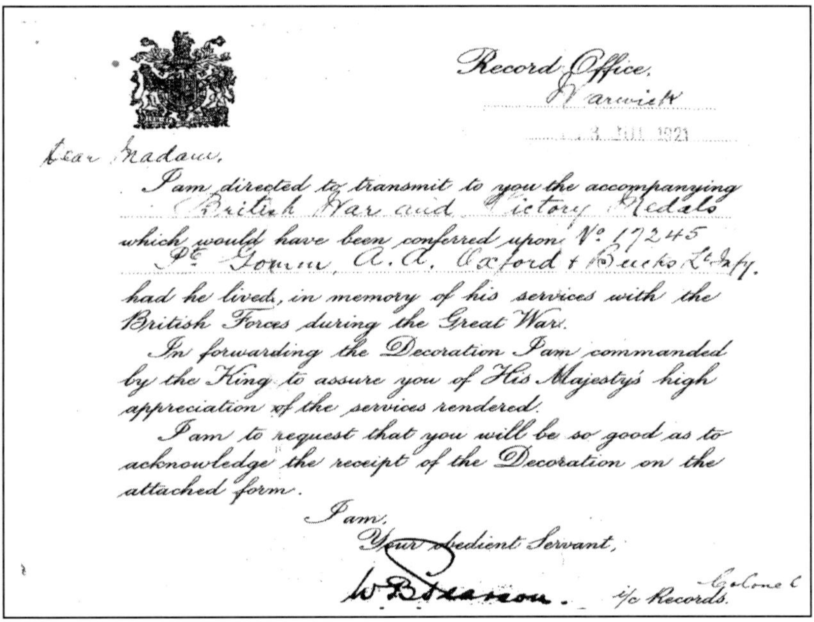

Record Office,
Warwick
3. JUL. 1921

Dear Madam,

I am directed to transmit to you the accompanying British War and Victory Medals
which would have been conferred upon No. 17245 Pte. Gomm, A.A. Oxford & Bucks Lt. Infy.
had he lived, in memory of his services with the British Forces during the Great War.

In forwarding the Decoration I am commanded by the King to assure you of His Majesty's high appreciation of the services rendered.

I am to request that you will be so good as to acknowledge the receipt of the Decoration on the attached form.

I am,
Your obedient Servant,
[illegible] Colonel i/c Records.

British War and Victory Medal Award

The Second World War
(1939-45)

Key to entries

If known by other than the first forename or (familiar) name then the used name is underlined.

*denotes has brother(s) or sister(s) who also served

D denotes deceased, but the year is unknown

The names in this chapter of those who served

Ashton	Dellar	Hunt	Sewell
Beddar	Dodd	Ivings	Sheppard
Bell	Drake	Johnson	Shirley
Berry	Drinkwater	Kerridge	Smith
Berthon	Dumbleton	Kevelos	Sones
Bignold	Ellis	Kinge	Sorrell
Bliss	Evans	Legerton	Spenceley
Bolton	Faber	Lewis	Spiers
Bowerman	Fortescue	Lloyd	Stevens
Bowler	Franklin	Love	Stewart
Boyd	Franklyn	Loveday	Stockford
Brain	French	Lowther	Sykes
Brooks	Fuller	Malcher	Tarling
Buckle	Garrett	Marmion	Tibbetts
Burton	Gilkes	Mathias	Trevor
Busby	Gill	Minnear	Tucker
Butlin	Godfrey	Minty	Turney
Callow	Green	Morris	Turrell
Canning	Greenaway	Mosedale	Tustain
Caporn	Grigg	Moseley	Tyrell
Castle	Hale	Newell	Underwood
Chaplin	Hall	O'Rourke	Unsworth
Churchill	Harper	Pacey	Vincent
Clark	Hawes	Paginton	Wales
Clarke	Hawkins	Pearson	Wallin
Cooper	Haynes	Pigott	Walsh
Cosgrove	Hayward	Plumbe	Ware
Cotteral	Heywood	Pratt	Webb
Coulton	Higham	Prew	Weedon
Cowley	Hiorns	Pyman	West
Cox	Hobart	Roberts	Wheeler
Dance	Hodges	Robbins	Wilkinson
Davidson	Holiday	Rule	Willet
Davis	Homans	Ryan	Woolgrove
Dawes	Hopcraft	Sanders	Woolley
Deeley	Humphries	Savill	

See the note on page 6 for a further explanation about names

The men named on the War Memorial

'LIVE THOU FOR ENGLAND.WE FOR ENGLAND DIED'
(Inscription on the War Memorial)

Edward Bostock DUMBLETON
Stoker 1st Class, *HMS Manchester*, Royal Navy.
He died on 24 March 1941 age 21 whilst his ship was being refitted after its role in the Norwegian Campaign.
He lived in Clifton and he is buried in section K, grave 14.442, Preston Cemetery, Tynemouth.
Elizabeth Pinfold, who was the mother of Percival Pinfold (killed in action in 1917), was listed as Edward Dumbleton's next of kin and so she received the Letter of Condolence from King George VI which is reproduced on page 91.

Francis Beesley GARRETT
Flight Sergeant and Rear Gunner, 467 Squadron (RAAF), Royal Air Force Volunteer Reserve based at RAF Bottesford.
He died on 18 August 1943 age 26 on a raid on Peenemunde in Lancaster Bomber LM342PO.
He is remembered on panel 136 of the Runnymede Memorial.
His parents were Francis B and Florence R Garrett, Home Farm, Clifton.

Additional information:
The aeroplane was lost on its first Key Operation with a total of just 42 hours flying time. LM342 was one of the two 467 Squadron Lancasters that were lost on this operation. They took off at 21.45 hours on 17 August 1943 from RAF Bottesford and the aeroplane crashed in the Baltic while approaching the target. All the crew were killed. They were:

Squadron Leader A S Raphael DFC was 'A' Flight Commander
Flight Lieutenant M H Parry was the Squadron Bombing Leader and was flying as second air bomber
Sergeant V Smith
Pilot Officer R G Carter DFC RCAF
Sergeant F Grey
Flight Sergeant D Fielden
Sergeant A C Brand
Flight Sergeant F B Garrett

John Richard Frederick GILKES
Private, 1st Battalion, The Oxfordshire and Buckinghamshire Light Infantry.
He died on 16 July 1944 shortly after the D-Day invasion of Normandy and during the Battle for Caen age 19.
He is buried in grave III E18, Brouay War Cemetery, Normandy.
He was the son of Richard and Lilian R Gilkes of Deddington.

William Reginald GREENAWAY
Sergeant (Flight Engineer), 432 (RCAF) Squadron, Royal Air Force Volunteer Reserve based at RAF Swale in Yorkshire.
He died on 27 January 1944 age 22 on a bombing raid on Berlin.
He is buried in grave 7 L 11, Berlin 1939-1945 War Cemetery.
He was the son of Reginald and Ethel M Greenaway of Deddington.

Additional information:
Lancaster no. LL638 of 432 Squadron was lost on its first operation. They had taken off at 17.51 hours on 27 January 1944 and the aeroplane crashed at Schmockwitz, a town 22 km SE from the centre of Berlin.
The crew were:

Pilot Officer D J Paterson RCAF
Sergeant W R Greenaway
Sergeant F W Heinen RCAF
Flight Sergeant C A Sherwood RCAF
Pilot Officer A S Gates RCAF
Flight Officer F/O A D G Bell RCAF
Flight Sergeant R P Wilson

Ernest Sydney G HALL
Sapper, 576 Corps Field Park Company, Royal Engineers.
He died on 13 August 1943 age 27.
The Allied Army invaded Sicily on 9 July and the island was captured on 17 August 1943, four days after he was killed.
He is buried in grave IV C27, Catania War Cemetery, Sicily.
He was the husband of Lilian M Hall of Deddington.

John H LEWIS
Private, 2nd Battalion, The Bedfordshire and Hertfordshire Regiment, 10 Infantry Brigade, 4th Infantry Division.
He died on 1 April 1944 age 25.
He is buried in grave XII J 9 XII, Cassino War Cemetery, Italy.
He was the son of Edwin and Charlotte Lewis of Deddington.

Lawrence Lee PYMAN
Pilot Officer, 65 Squadron, Royal Air Force Volunteer Reserve, previously with the Cambridge University Air Squadron.
He died on 16 August 1940 age 23.
He was a Battle of Britain fighter pilot who, on 14 August 1940, had force-landed his aircraft at RAF Manston. His aircraft was peppered with bullet holes. He was shot down and killed on 16 August 1940 in his Spitfire I (K9915) over the Channel near Deal at 17.30 hours.
He is buried in plot Q, grave 18, Calais Southern Cemetery.
He was the son of the late Ronald L Pyman (who was killed in France in 1917) and C Freyda Roberts (formerly Pyman) of Deddington House (now Deddington Manor). Freyda Roberts ran the Hospital in the Old Vicarage in Church Street.

Henry SORRELL
Driver, 18th Divisional Signals, Royal Corps of Signals.
He died on 12 September 1944 age 33.
He was captured in Thailand and was being transported in an unmarked Japanese Hell Ship, the *MV Rakuyo Maru*, when it was torpedoed by the *USS Sealion* and sank; 1,159 Allied Prisoners of War died. The Japanese transported PoWs in unmarked ships. The prisoners were usually being moved to be used as slave labour and the warships had no means of identifying which vessels were actually PoW transporters.
He is remembered on column 46 of the Singapore Memorial.
He was the son of the late H Sorrell and of Eva Sorrell who moved to Deddington after the war to join her daughters who had been evacuated to Deddington. He was the husband of Ethel M Sorrell of Islington.

Additional information:
The story of the terrible treatment that Allied PoWs received at the hands of the Japanese is recounted in *The Forgotten Highlander* by Alistair Urquhart published in paperback by Abacus (ISBN 978-0349-12257-1). It includes a full account of the sinking of *MV Rakuyo Maru* and other Hell Ships on the same day.

Ernest Arthur SYKES
Corporal, Royal Army Service Corps. He died on 24 June 1941 age 33.
He was probably involved in the capture of Damascus involving the Free French, the Indian Army, the Australians and the British from the Vichy French Army.
He is buried in grave N 23, Damascus Commonwealth Cemetery.
He was the son of George H and Clara E Sykes and the husband of Georgina F Sykes of Deddington.

A Plaque in the Church

Robert Alec Farquhar (Buster) CHURCHILL. Mentioned in Despatches.
Lieutenant, *HMS Victorious*, Royal Navy.
He died on 12 August 1942 age 31 protecting a convoy to Malta.
He is remembered on bay 3, panel 1 of the Lee-on-Solent Memorial and a stone plaque on the wall of Deddington Parish Church.
He was the son of Alec F and Elinor Churchill and the husband of Olive H D Churchill (née Townroe) of Cuckfield, Sussex.

Additional information:
Robert Churchill was serving in 884 Squadron embarked on the aircraft carrier *HMS Victorious*. At the time of his death he was protecting a convoy known as Operation Pedestal which was the last opportunity to deliver essential supplies to the besieged island of Malta. The operation succeeded but, as the diary for Operation Pedestal on 12 August 1942 shows, the cost was very high:

20 Junker 88s attack convoy.
Submarine attacks.
100 German and Italian planes attack. *MV Deucalion* sunk by aerial torpedo, dud hits aircraft carrier *HMS Victorious*.
Italian submarine forced to surface by depth charges.
30 Junker 87s attack carrier *HMS Indomitable* which is hit three times.
Destroyer *HMS Foresight* damaged by aerial torpedo and had to be sunk.
Cruisers *HMS Cairo* and *HMS Nigeria* torpedoed by Italian submarines, *HMS Cairo* abandoned, *HMS Nigeria* returns to Gibraltar.
The oil tanker *Ohio* (carrying vital oil supplies) torpedoed and bombed several times, eventually reached Malta supported and towed by destroyers and minesweepers.
20 Junker 88s attack. Gunners on *MV Almeria Lykes* shoot down two planes.
MV Empire Hope bombed, high octane gas on fire, abandoned and sunk by escort.
MV Clan Ferguson hit and explodes. Italian submarine rescues 53 survivors.
MV Brisbane Star hit by torpedo,
Cruiser *HMS Kenya* damaged by torpedo from Italian submarine.

A Grave in the Churchyard

William Charles COULTON
Private, 1st Battalion, The Oxfordshire and Buckinghamshire Light Infantry.
He died on 8 September 1941 age 27 on a training exercise.
He is buried in the churchyard of St Peter and St Paul, Deddington.
He was the son of Charles and Kate Coulton and the husband of Ivy M Busby, formerly Coulton, of Deddington.

The men and women who served and returned

Royal Navy (RN)

Sidney (Sid) William George BERRY* (1920-2006) Leading Cook.
The ships he served in were in action in the Lofoten Raid, Arctic Convoys and the hunt for the *Bismarck*. After his ship, *HMS Mashona*, was sunk he joined the submarine service for a quieter life! His story can be read on page 112.

Charles Pierre BERTHON CBE (1893-1965) Rear Admiral, Engineering Branch.
He joined the Navy as a 13-year-old cadet in 1906 and had served in the Home Fleet during WWI. In WWII he served in Malta (shore post 1940), *HMS Orion* and *Woolwich* (Med Fleet 1941). He was Mentioned in Despatches. For the rest of the war and until he retired he was responsible for the maintenance of Fleet Air Arm aircraft. He purchased Leadenporch House from General Stobart in 1948 and lived there until his death in 1965.

Frank Reginald BIGNOLD* (1923-98).

Anthony (Tony) BOLTON (1920-2010) Lieutenant Commander, Supply Officer.
He served in the RN throughout the war. He was landed at Arromanches two months after D-Day as part of a naval supply team that had the enormous administrative task of working round the clock to keep supplies moving inland from the 'Mulberry Harbours' to support the advancing troops. He was later part of the naval forces that liberated Norway in May 1945. His wife, Avis, was a Wren. He was released from war service in 1946 but remained in the Navy until 1955 and subsequently joined the RAF - see page 102 for his post-war career.

Robert (Bob) CALLOW* (1923-D).

Norman Arthur DAVIS (1917-2006) Petty Officer.
He served from 1942 in Landing Craft. He was cousin to Harold, Frederick and Ewart Davis (RAF). His father, George Davis, died in WWI and his name is on the War Memorial (p.25).

George Thomas GODFREY (1913-78) Stoker Petty Officer.
He served from August 1932 to January 1946.

Joseph (Joe) HIORNS (1920-97) Leading Stoker.
He served with Sid Berry in *HMS Mashona* but left before she was sunk. However, he later shared Sid's experience of abandoning ship because his next one (name unknown) was torpedoed and sunk by a submarine. He was the brother in law of CQMS Bill Minnear.

James (Jim) LEWIS* (1921-D).
No details of his service are known. He emigrated to New Zealand after the war. His brother John H (known as 'Gudgeon') Lewis was killed in action at Monte Cassino and his name is on the War Memorial (p.56).

William (Bill) John MALCHER* (1925-70) Telegraphist (S).
He was one of three brothers who served. Read their story on page 161.

Kenneth (Ken) TARLING*

Percy TUSTAIN* (1910-50) Chief Stoker.
He joined in 1929 and served on *HMS Suffolk*, *Repulse* and *Nelson* and a number of other ships in the Pacific Fleet. He was known to be good at boxing. He left the service in late 1946 and went to work at Morris Motors in Cowley where he suffered a fatal acccident.

Frank WEEDON Lieutenant.
Royal Naval Volunteer Reserve. He served from August 1942 to December 1945.

Women's Royal Naval Service (WRNS)

Avis BOLTON (1926-2008) née Bell, Wren.
She was the wife of Tony Bolton, Lt Cdr RN. They met and married while serving.

Stephanie HIGHAM (b 1920) née Pigott, Third Officer (Special Duties).
She was a linguist trained to read German signals for decryption by Bletchley Park. Read her story on page 149.

Edna SEWELL (b 1925) née Evans, Wren.
She joined the Navy aged 18 years old, fresh from school. Read what this was like in her story on page 177.

Royal Marines (RM)

William (Bill) COWLEY (b 1925) Corporal.
46 Commando. His Commando was part of the D-Day invasion force. Some time later he was badly wounded in the head while advancing through Europe. Read his story on page 124.

Brian Morris DAWES Marine.
30th Battalion, Royal Marines. He served from August 1942 to May 1946.

Army

Kenneth (Ken) Albert BERRY* (b 1923) Sergeant.
Driver and Transport Manager, 246 Field Company, 3rd Division Royal Engineers. He joined in May 1942 and landed on the beach in France on D-Day+6 with some replacement vehicles for those lost on D-Day. He recalls that one replacement was needed because a D-Day driver had reversed his vehicle back into the sea - and wrote it off - trying to avoid driving over piles of dead bodies on the beach. He then drove his Company Commander through Europe to Germany, being shot in the neck by a sniper en-route, but only required two weeks to recover and so arrived in Bremen on 26 April 1945 still with his Company Commander. He went with 246 Company to Palestine (now Israel) and Egypt for a while before being de-mobbed in December 1946.

William (Bill) Herbert BIGNOLD * (1919-91).
He served in the South East Asia Command (SEAC) area.

Arthur William BLISS (1913-2004) Sergeant.
The Oxfordshire and Buckinghamshire Light Infantry. He served in Ireland, Italy and Germany.

William (Bill) BOYD (1915-94) Sergeant.
He was awarded the Belgian *Croix de Guerre* for valour.

David James BRAIN (1911-88).
The Royal Artillery. He served with the 8th Army (Desert Rats) in North Africa and Italy.

Leslie George BURTON (1929-2005) Private.
Royal Electrical and Mechanical Engineers. Served in the Far East.

Frederick (Fred) BUTLIN (b 1927) Private.
General Service Corps. He joined in 1945 but was invalided out just under a year later after contracting pneumonia and pleurisy.

Denis George CALLOW* (b 1921) Private.
He served first in the Royal Artillery and with them sailed in convoy for Alexandria in Egypt the long way round via Durban and through the Suez Canal to arrive in time for the Battle of El Alamein. He then joined the 9th Battalion, The Royal Fusiliers, with whom he fought up through Italy to Pola in Yugoslavia where he recalls meeting up with Joe Tarling (p.64). After six months garrison duty they moved to Trieste where he was moved yet again to The Queen's Regiment and eventually was demobbed in late 1946 or early 1947.

Ernest Edward (Jockey) CALLOW* (1912-87) Sergeant.
Royal Electrical and Mechanical Engineers. He travelled to South Africa in the same convoy as his brother Denis but his ship carried on to Singapore where he was made a PoW when it was captured by the Japanese. He was subsequently part of the forced labour that built the infamous Burma railway.

Kenneth (Nimmer) CALLOW* (D).
The Royal Army Service Corps. He was the cousin of Denis and Ernest and brother of Robert (Navy).

Arthur Edward (Nobby) CLARKE* (1910-82) Lance Corporal.
The Royal Engineers. He served in France, Belgium and Holland.

Henry Joffre (Joffer) CLARKE* (1915-81).
The Oxfordshire and Buckinghamshire Light Infantry. He was named after a famous WWI French General admired by his father. He was wounded in the back by shrapnel while in Normandy.

Leonard (Len) John CLARKE* (1912-73).
The Oxfordshire and Buckinghamshire Light Infantry and The Hampshire Regiment. He was wounded in the leg in North Africa, recovered, but then was wounded again in the same leg at Salerno. This time he was invalided out. He married Jean Woolley who was a Land Girl stationed in Deddington (p.77).

Frederick (Fred) John DAVIDSON* (D) Corporal.
The Oxfordshire and Buckinghamshire Light Infantry. He served in Greece and Italy.

Peter Leonard DAVIDSON* (D) Sergeant Major.
The Royal Electrical and Mechanical Engineers. He served in India.

Norman Frederick DELLAR (1922-88) Sergeant.
2nd Battalion, Parachute Regiment.
He served from August 1940 to February 1950.

Peter FRANKLYN (1923-98) Lance Corporal.
The Royal Armoured Corps 10th, 7th and 3rd Royal Tank Regiments.
He met his wife, Pauline, when she was a teenage evacuee to Deddington. Peter survived the battle to liberate Europe and they married in 1947. Read their story on page 131.

Thomas (Tom) William GARRETT* (1920-2000).
The Oxfordshire and Buckinghamshire Light Infantry. Six men and women from the Garrett family served in the World Wars. Read their story on page 134.

Maurice A GILKES (1926-D) Corporal.
The Queen's Royal Regiment. He served from September 1944 to January 1948.

Albert Edward (Ted) HARPER (1920-76) Private.
The Royal Warwickshire Regiment. He was captured during the Dunkirk evacuation and became a PoW. Read his story on page 139.

Ronald Ernest HARPER (1912-76) Corporal.
The Royal Artillery.

William Henry HAWKINS Private.
The Royal Army Service Corps, Driver. He served from June 1939 to January 1946.

Percy Cleghorn HOBART KBE CB DSO MC (1885-1957) Major General.
He had previously served with the Corps of Royal Engineers throughout WWI. In 1923 he transferred to The Royal Tank Corps. His unconventional ideas on tank warfare and inability to get on with his superiors led to his dismissal in 1939 from his role of training the 7th Armoured Brigade (later to become well-known as the 'Desert Rats'). He was called back by Winston Churchill in 1941 and was given command of the brand-new 11th Armoured Division ('Black Bulls') but was again denied the chance to deploy into action due to age and ill-health. Instead he was assigned the task of using his unconventional ideas to develop specialised armoured vehicles - known as 'Hobo's Funnies' - for D-Day. These were widely credited as the key to getting Allied Forces successfully ashore and inland from the beaches of Normandy.

He was lessee and then owner of Leadenporch House from 1940 to 1948. His sister, Elizabeth, had married Field Marshall Montgomery before the war but died tragically young.

The present occupant of Leadenporch House, Jo Eames, has written a novel *Not only the good boys*, Peach Publishing, 2011, in which the General features as a major character. It covers the period between March 1943 and June 1944 when 'Hobo's Funnies' were being developed - and ultimately sent into battle.

John HODGES MC (b 1922) Captain.
The Royal Armoured Corps. He fought with distinction through North Africa and Italy where he was decorated. Read his story on page 153.

Arthur HUMPHRIES (D).
The Royal Tank Regiment.

William HUNT (D) Sergeant.
Royal Engineers. He served throughout Europe after D-Day and also in Palestine where he met up with his cousin Ken Berry.

William (Bill) IVINGS (1921-99) Corporal.
The Royal Army Service Corps, Transport Division. He was a member of the Deddington Home Guard as a despatch rider before joining the RASC in 1940. He drove 3-ton Bedford trucks and, when they came into service, DUKW amphibious vehicles. He served in Egypt and Germany and was present for the liberation of Belsen Concentration Camp.

Edward (Ted) B W JOHNSON MC (b 1922) Captain.
The Royal Irish Fusiliers. He was decorated for his actions in the Battle for Leros. Read his story - including Christmas in a PoW camp - on page 157.

Leslie (Les) LEGERTON (1916-2005) Private.
7th Battalion, Worcestershire Regiment. He survived the Burma campaign without a spare pair of glasses! Read his story on page 155.

George LOWTHER (D)
Royal Army Service Corps. He served with the 8th Army driving tank transporters.

Arthur Denis MALCHER* (b 1926) Private.
Royal Army Ordnance Corps. The story of the three Malcher brothers can be read on page 161.

Morton Griffith MATHIAS (1899-2004).
He served in The Royal Artillery initially and then transferred to a searchlight battery in The Royal Engineers.

William (Bill) Henry MINNEAR (1912-97) Company Quarter Master Sergeant.
The Somerset Light Infantry and The Duke of Cornwall's Light Infantry. Like Ted Johnson, he was taken prisoner after the Battle of Leros and spent two years as a PoW in Germany. Read his story on page 157.

Cecil Henry PEARSON* (1922-71) Sergeant.
He joined the RAF aged 16 as an apprentice instrument maker in 1939 signing on to serve 12 years from the age of 18. He was with the support units that followed the 8th Army through its North African and Italian campaigns. In 1947 he returned to the UK, was posted to Ceylon (now Sri Lanka) in 1948 and came back to UK again in 1950. He left the service in 1952 and worked initially for Alcan Laboratories in Banbury but then emigrated to Australia where he worked for Ansett Airlines. He died at the early age of 49.

Ernest Cecil PEARSON (1890-1956) Corporal.
He was the father of Cecil (above) and Edmund who joined the RAF(p.66). He had served in The Essex Regiment in WWI in France where he received a bullet wound to his right ankle. He was called up for service again in 1939 as a clerk but was invalided out in 1942.

Thomas (Tom) Charles PRATT* (1916-D) Private.
The Somerset Light Infantry.

Reginald Geoffrey ROBERTS (1890-1946) Major.
Pioneer Corps. His family lived in Deddington House. His wife, Freyda, nursed evacuee children (p.80) and their daughter, Primrose, was an ROC plotter in the Oxford Post located in the Bodleian Library (p.75).

Kenneth (Ken) SMITH (1916-2009) Trooper.
4th Royal Tank Regiment. He enlisted in 1937 and served with the BEF in France and was evacuated via Dunkirk. He then served with the 8th Army ('Desert Rats'), at El Alamein, Tobruk and Monte Cassino.

Francis (Frank) John TARLING* (1921-2003) Private.
He joined The Oxfordshire and Buckinghamshire Light Infantry's Territorial Battalion in April 1939 and transferred to The Bedfordshire and Hertfordshire Regiment in December 1943. He was wounded in Italy during the battle for Monte Cassino and was reported missing; however it subsequently transpired that he had been captured while keeping another wounded man company. He was interned as a PoW in Stalag VII/A in Germany. He married Doris Sorrell, who had been an evacuee to Deddington, in July 1945. Her brother Henry's (Harry) name is on the War Memorial (p.56)

Joseph (Joe) TARLING* (D).
London Irish Rifles.

Francis (Frank) TUSTAIN* (1915-88) Sergeant.
He was conscripted in 1940 into the 43rd Battalion, The Oxford and Buckinghamshire Light Infantry where he became a Despatch motorbike rider in the anti-tank section. He landed with his company - which included his brother Billy - on Sword Beach on D-Day+6 in 1944. He lost a leg fighting in Normandy and was invalided home. After extensive time in hospital he was discharged in 1946.

Leonard (Len) TUSTAIN* (b 1920) Private.
He was conscripted into the 52nd Battalion of the The Oxfordshire and Buckinghamshire Light Infantry in 1940. He had a bad motorbike accident in 1941 and spent time in hospital and then recuperated with The Suffolk Regiment. His nurse was Jo Kelly whom he married six months before he went to France. At the end of 1941 he joined the 43rd Battalion to serve as a Bren Gun Carrier Driver in the same 'Specialist' company as his brother Frank. They both landed on Sword Beach on D-Day+6. He was wounded 10 days later near Caen with severe phosphorus burns to arm and face. After two weeks hospitalisation in France he was sent back to the UK for treatment at the Canadian Burns Hospital in Basingstoke. This included the pioneering use of maggots to clean the area, and extensive skin grafts. He was discharged in 1946.

George UNSWORTH (D).

Anthony (Tony) VINCENT (D).
The Oxfordshire and Buckinghamshire Light Infantry.

The Auxiliary Territorial Service (ATS)

Ivy BUSBY (b 1920) née Smith.
She was previously married to Private William (Bill) Coulton who died in 1941 and whose grave is in the churchyard (pages 15 and 58). She moved to London where she joined the Royal Electrical and Mechanical Engineers in June 1942 and served until 1945 maintaining heavy artillery. She later re-married and returned to live in Deddington.

Mary TIBBETTS* (1917-D) and **Margaret TIBBETTS*** (1918-D)
They were the daughters of Horace (1887-1957) and Sarah (née Deeley) Tibbetts. Horace was the village blacksmith at the Archway on New Street; his forge subsequently became Len Plumbe's Archway garage.

Royal Air Force (RAF)

Frank Colman BOWLER* (1898-1989) Squadron Leader (acting Wing Commander).
He joined The Royal Flying Corps towards the end of WWI which then became the RAF. He was one of the four Bowler men who served in three wars with distinction. Their story is on page 114.

Thomas <u>Geoffrey</u> BOWLER* CB CBE (1895-1974) Air Vice Marshal.
He initially served as a soldier at Gallipoli in WWI, then transferred to the Royal Flying Corps. He served with distinction in WWII (p.117).

Ronald (Ron) CANNING (1924-2006) Leading Aircraftman.
He was a Wireless Operator serving at Chicksands which was an outstation of the code-breaking centre at Bletchley Park; here he met Daphne his future wife. Read their story on page 121.

Walter CAPORN (b 1922) Sergeant.
He qualified as an Engine Fitter at RAF Halton in 1939. He served in India and Burma from 1941 until war end. Post-war he spent time on various air stations including in Iraq. He left the service in 1954.

Richard Stanley CHAPLIN (b 1921) Corporal.
He was a Wireless Operator who served from April 1939 to November 1945. He subsequently moved to Australia.

Brian COSGROVE MBE (1926-2010) Sergeant.
He had a craving to fly from an early age. His first flight was aged eight in a Dragon at an Alan Cobham Circus. He enlisted in late 1943 but there were no vacancies for pilots. He therefore trained as a Meteorological Air Observer. After a spell in Yorkshire he transferred to the Far East where he was taught (quite unofficially) to fly Dakotas in which he spent a lot of time. He was demobbed in 1947 and went to work for Spillers. He joined the RAF Volunteer (Training Branch) in 1948 (p.102).

Ewart Ashley (Maxi) DAVIS* (1921-2002) Leading Aircraftman.
He served at RAF Filey, Yorkshire, as a mechanic on Mosquito aircraft.

Frederick (Fred) William DAVIS* (1916-70) Leading Aircraftman.
He served in Belgium, Germany and Malaya.

Harold (Harry) Francis DAVIS* (1913-94) Leading Aircraftman.
He served from 1940-46 at the RAF Flying School in White Waltham, Berkshire, RAF Halton in Buckinghamshire and in Havant, Hampshire.

William (Bill) Maurice DRAKE (b 1925) Squadron Leader.
He joined the RAF in 1944 as a Navigator. He flew in Mosquitos in India and Burma preparing for the relief of Singapore. Post-war he saw service in Malaya and the Suez campaign. In the Cold War, when the RAF had responsibility for the nuclear deterrent, he flew in Canberra aircraft equipped to carry the nuclear bomb. Following several years in Intelligence at MOD, he left the service in 1977. As soon as he left the service he joined the Campaign for Nuclear Disarmament (CND) and marched with them.

Frank Leslie DRINKWATER (1920-99) Leading Aircraftman.
He joined the RAF in May 1940 and served in the Middle East, India and the Western Desert with 203 Squadron Transport section. He was demobbed in 1946.

Frederick (Fred) James ELLIS (b 1923) Warrant Officer.
He joined in 1942 and qualified as a Wireless Operator. He served in India flying Liberators over Burma. He was de-mobbed in 1945 but rejoined in 1947 flying in Lincoln bombers then transferred to Coastal Command in 1951 flying in Lancasters, Shackletons and Neptunes on Cold War tracking operations against Russian submarines. After a time in Transport Command (Beverleys) he left the service in 1965 and became the well-known landlord of the Unicorn Inn on Market Place until 1987.

Kenneth (Ken) GARRETT* (1924-91) Corporal.
Served in the RAF Volunteer Reserve from 1942 to 1946 mainly in the Middle East. Read the Garrett family story on page 134.

Walter George HAYWARD (1922-2000) Leading Aircraftman.
He did his training as ground crew in Blackpool then was based at Kemble, Pershore and Bibury.

Denys Guy L HEYWOOD (1926-2010) Group Captain.
He joined at the end of WWII and later flew Vulcan Bombers carrying the nuclear deterrent during the Cold War – and over 50 other types of aircraft. Read his story on page 143.

Bruce Campbell HUNT (b 1920) Flight Lieutenant.
He served from December 1941 to January 1947.

James Carlyle MARMION OBE (b 1924) Group Captain.
He joined the RAF in 1942 and after extensive training in UK, USA and Canada graduated as a Navigator/Bomb Aimer in June 1944. His first operational flying was in Catalina flying boats based in Madras, India, in 1945. He converted to the B24 Liberator and joined 321 Squadron (Royal Netherlands Naval Air Service) in Ceylon. His service in the post-war years is on page 103.

Thomas Edward MOSELEY Corporal.
He served from April 1940 to October 1945.

Edmund Ernest PEARSON* (b 1924) Leading Aircraftman.
His involvement with the war began when he was only 15 as a member of the Home Guard at Adderbury where he then lived. At 16 he went to work for the Northern

Aluminium Company (now Alcan) at their plant for re-cycling crashed aircraft and scrap aluminium from manufacturers located on the southern of the present two trading estates to the south of Adderbury. The northern estate was Adderbury Station on the branch line from King's Sutton to Chipping Norton and Kingham.

He joined up aged 18 and trained as a Ground Wireless Operator to be posted in due course to Freetown, Sierra Leone, from where the RAF flew anti-submarine patrols to protect the convoys heading to and from South Africa. In early 1945 he was posted back to the UK and, in accordance with the policy of giving a posting as close to home as possible, he was sent to Chipping Warden where he was a wireless operator in the control tower. When hostilities ceased in Europe he had several UK postings before de-mob in 1947. As a civilian again, Edmund returned to working for his old company in Banbury.

Leonard (Len) Charles PLUMBE (b 1921) Leading Aircraftman.
He trained as a skilled Engine Fitter and was sent out to the Far East. His jungle experiences can be read in his story on page 165.

Harold Henry PRATT* (b 1922) Leading Aircraftman.
11 Squadron RAF Regiment. He joined in July 1942, trained as a Ground Gunner and then served in Burma, India, Singapore and Japan. He was demobbed in 1946.

Tom SMITH Leading Aircraftman.
He joined the RAF when he was 18, trained as driver and landed at Arromanches on D-Day.

Ray SONES (1926-2011) Leading Aircraftman.
Pre-war he was a member of the Air Training Corps (ATC). He volunteered for regular service in 1943 aged 17½ and trained as a Radar Fitter serving in Blackpool, Egypt and Malta. He was demobbed in 1948.

George SPENCELEY (b 1921) Warrant Officer Pilot.
He was shot down and spent three years as a PoW. While undergoing a forced march by the Germans, their column was attacked by Allied aircraft in error. Read his story on page 179.

William (Bill) Foster SPIERS (1922-2001) Leading Aircraftman.
He joined at the age of 18 in 1941 and, after training and qualifying with No 2 Mechanical Transport Squadron, he joined 13 Operational Training Unit based in Bicester which was one of the two principal bomber training units in Britain. After D-Day he joined the forward support units through Holland and Germany until the end of the war where he remained with the British Air Forces of Occupation Communication Wing until returning home in September 1946.

Robert (Bob) STEVENS (1921-2004) Leading Aircraftman.
He found to his surprise that he was colour blind. This meant that he could not serve as aircrew so he trained as a Radio Mechanic. He served from 1939 through to war's end. Following the Allied invasion of Europe, he was based in Belgium. He was the husband of José Stevens whose story can be read on page 184.

Bernard SYKES (1921-92) Flight Sergeant.

Women's Auxiliary Air Force (WAAF)

Daphne Maud CANNING (b 1925) née Tucker. Aircraftwoman 1st Class.
She was a Radio Operator at Chicksands. She kept in touch with her boyfriend (and future husband) in India - almost certainly illegally! - by using a spare radio channel to chat at night. Read her story on page 121.

Pamela (Pam) DANCE* (b 1924) née Lewis. Leading Aircraftwoman.
In civilian life she was a professional cook so was employed as such when she joined up in October 1942. She saw the WAAF as a better alternative to working in an ammunition factory or in the Land Army. She served mainly in Bomber Command. Part of her service time was spent at RAF Edgehill. She was demobbed in 1945 after what she looks back on as 'three good years.' In 1945 she married a naval man from Kent, Victor Jones (deceased), who had been in the Fleet Air Arm and had survived the sinking of *HMS Ark Royal*. She is the sister of Sergeant Arthur Lewis.

Edith Elsie GARRETT (b 1925) née Minty. Leading Aircraftwoman.
She was one of the six Garrett family members who served in the world wars (p.134).

Margaret (Margery) HAWES (b 1922) née Faber. Sergeant.
Her own account: 'I joined the WAAF in January 1941 and, after a week or so of training and marching round the mirrored ball room of the Majestic Hotel in Harrogate, was posted to Corsham (Wilts) to work as a plotter in one of the underground Filter rooms of Fighter Command. After a couple of years there I was sent to Inverness. This was an excellent posting as we had our bicycles and would explore the countryside, sometimes taking them on the train to the west coast and cycling back along Loch Ness. We sent our families eggs by train and they arrived intact. These were more welcome to my widowed mother than the large boxes of kippers sent by my generous brother. In 1944 I volunteered to go to Belgium and was sent to Malines near Brussels. We tracked the V2 rockets fired from Peenemunde. We saw one nasty incident when two women were chased by a crowd who shaved their heads. They had been friendly with German soldiers. On VE Day [1] we danced in the streets with the crowds, everyone so happy and smiling. I was demobbed in 1946.'

Peggy PACEY (b 1918) Section Officer.
She spent most of the war on a motorbike. Read her story on page 163.

Emily Mary WEBB (1918-92) née Garrett*. Corporal.
She was another of the six members of the Garrett family who served in two world wars (p.134).

[1] Victory over Europe Day - 8 May 1945

The Home Guard

Affiliated to The Oxfordshire and Buckinghamshire Light Infantry

On parade in the Market Place

Lewis gun detachment - outside the Primary School

(back row l to r) **'Wilkie' Wilkinson** (no relation to Fred) , **Albert Tyrell**
(front row l to r) **Herbie Smith, Sergeant Leslie Bowler, Fred Wilkinson**

This photograph and the one on the next page are courtesy of Joe Cowley who has a copy of an album presented to Major Morris (Commanding Officer) at the end of the war. A copy of the full album can be seen in the Deddington OnLine Gallery.

The Company, outside the Primary School

(Back Row l to r) **Bert Wheeler, Brian 'Harry' Cox, Jeff Woolgrove, Cliff Homans, Joe Cowley**

(Centre row l to r) **Ernie Green, Herbie Smith, Cooper, Bernard or John Bowerman, Fred Wilkinson, Jack Hiorns, Len Vincent, Hawkins, Jim Stockford, Fred Ware, Bill Harper**

(Front row l to r) **Harry Harper, 'Wilkie' Wilkinson,[1] Albert Tyrrel, Major Arthur Morris, Sergeant Leslie Bowler,[2] Boyce Paginton, B Vincent, ? Kinge**

Others who served in the Home Guard include:

Jack Beddar
Jack Brooks
George Busby
Bill Castle
Bill Harper
Ian Haynes
Dr Hodges
Bill Ivings
Denis Malcher
(?) Mosedale
Bill Prew
Bill Shirley
'Coakey' Smith
Percy Smith
George Trevor
Albert Turrell
Sidney Wales
Jeanne Wales née Rule[3]
George Willet

[1] 'Wilkie' Wilkinson had been the batman (servant) of Major Roberts of Deddington Manor during WWI and had remained with him post war.

[2] This was his Home Guard rank. He was actually Captain Bowler MC whose distinguished service in WWI can be read on page 115.

[3] Trained to be a comptometer (code machine) operator.

A pillbox at Somerton guarding the south side of the canal bridge

There are now very few examples of WWII architecture in the area. Air raid shelters and Observer Corps posts have been demolished and all that remains, beyond a few signs of old airfields (see p.92), are a pair of concrete pillboxes either side of the road from North Aston to Somerton. They guard the bridge over the canal in the foreground, the railway line and its bridge hidden behind the canal side cottages. The north side one is very similar. The embrasures would have given a good arc of fire for a machine gun along the approach road. No doubt there were also mobile road blocks (large tree trunks on wheels) as there were on each of the four roads into Deddington.

A commemorative plaque in the church bell tower recording the appreciation of the Parish.

The Royal Observer Corps

Insignia of the Corps

The crew of the Deddington Observation Post (OP) 1943/44

Photograph courtesy Clive Sanders

(Back row l to r) **Jack Malcher, Charlie Fuller, Arthur Humphries, Arthur Newell, Gill, Walter Sanders, Frank Garrett, Fred Deeley, George Clark, Percy Franklin**

(Front row l to r) **Bill Berry, George Cotteral, Bill Holiday, George Deeley (Ldg Observer and 2 i/c), Observer Officer (later Observer Lieutenant) K W J Grigg, Chief Observer Douglas Hopcraft, Smith, Ernie Dodd, Bob Churchill.**

Deddington had its own OP in the middle of the old allotments which were then up the Hempton Road in the area that is now a housing estate known as Gaveston Gardens - see map on the next page.

The original post was a very comfortable fully furnished dug-out in which Brian Fuller remembers taking tea to his father when he was on watch. The building in the photograph above - the 'tower' as it was called - replaced the dug-out and lasted into the 1950s.

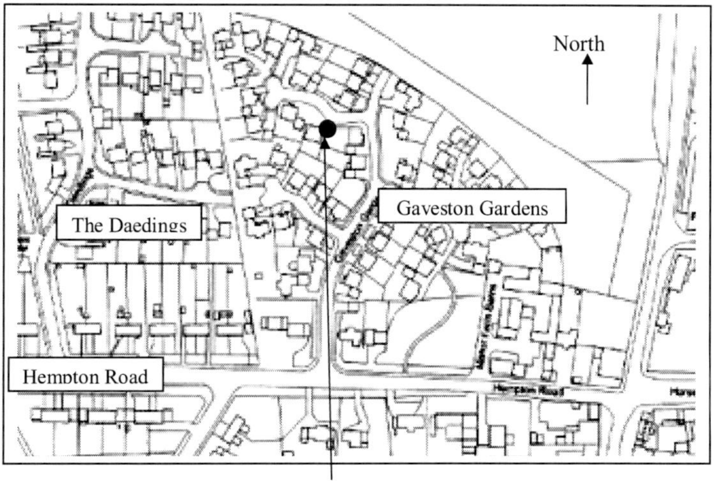

Approximate location of the OP

Map courtesy of Deddington Map Group

Unusually, the new post was a two-storey brick building whereas most ROC posts were wooden huts. It had an external iron staircase to an upstairs viewing room. Tar felted panels could be rolled back for access and clear viewing. Furniture consisted of old upholstered bus seats which were convenient for sitting and leaning back to scan the sky with binoculars - and also for courting couples!

Training of the Corps in aircraft recognition was by means of some 200 3" x 2" cards containing black and white silhouettes on one side and identity on the other - an early form of 'flash card' familiar to schoolchildren today. The full set of cards belonging to Percy Franklin (back row in photograph on previous page) is still in his family.

Jack Malcher (back row in photo on previous page) recalls seeing the top secret jet aircaft, the Gloster Meteor, conducting some of its test flights from Enstone and Barford airfields in late 1942. The Deddington crew were mystified by the very high speed and lack of propeller noise from this unknown aircraft. Derrick Robbins also recalls seeing and, more particularly, hearing it: 'I came back to Deddington on a school break late 1943 and took a bike ride one afternoon. I was just north of Adderbury on the Banbury road when a twin engine plane flew east to west pretty low. Unusually it made a swishing sort of sound which was completely unlike the usual beat of a propellor driven plane. I did not know it at the time but it was the experimental Meteor jet.'

Derrick Robbins' recollections:

Derrick was evacuated to Deddington at the start of the war. His crystal-clear and extensive recollections about life in the parish then can be found on page 168. These are his recollections about the Observer Corps: 'What was the Royal Observer Corps? I hear you cry. I would hazard a guess that there is hardly anyone alive in Deddington who could really answer that question. Started way back in

1925, the ROC, then just Observer Corps, was formed to report on enemy aircraft movements in time of war. When the Second World War actually broke out, the plan was immediately put into operation and observation posts were put in all over Great Britain. These were manned by two men in shifts 24 hours a day, seven days a week, all unpaid volunteers. Mostly over 50 years of age and too old for active service (although there was one volunteer aged 15), they wore Royal Air Force blue battledress, a black beret with a silver badge and carried a military gas mask. Their task was to report on the height, direction and speed of any aircraft entering their air space. If the aircraft were German, then this information would be transferred to a fighter pilot allowing him to proceed directly to his foe and save time searching for it. Also a downed pilot could be picked up in a short space of time. What about radar detection, you might ask. In the 1940s radar was still in its infancy and could not pick up low-flying aircraft; nor could it detect height or speed, or if it was friend or foe.

There is no record of how many enemy aircraft they counted, but they would have reported on planes going to and from the devastating attack on Coventry, and on the two unexploded bombs which fell into a field near the village. Some volunteers with above average spotting ability were transferred to an elite section known as Seaborne Ops and were put aboard ships lying off the French coast two days after D-Day to help the gunners avoid friendly fire on the numerous allied aircraft in the air at the time.'

Information provided by Tony Maatz, Chairman of the ROC Museum:

'Deddington Observation Post opened at map reference P464319 (see previous page) in December 1938 as 4/Z4, ie Z4 Post in No.4 Group Oxford. In March 1939 it became 12/Q2 but was re-allocated to Oxford Group (re-designated No.3 Group) in November 1953 as 3/K2.'

Aircraft Observation Posts were manned in shifts from a Post strength of up to 25 Observers including a Head Observer and two Leading Observer Post Instructors. Posts were linked by telephone in threes and fours, called Clusters. There was an Officer in charge of each Cluster. There were no Officers in a Post Crew. It is therefore likely that the Officer in your photograph was the one in charge of the Cluster. He was known as a Group Officer. Wartime records are rare because instructions were issued in 1945 to send them for salvage so that they could be pulped to help the shortage.'

...and from Neville Cullingford (Curator):

'Observer Officer (later Lieutenant) KWJ Grigg, wearing a cap, in the centre of the photo (p.72) was not part of the Crew of the Post but was the Group Officer for a number of adjacent Posts. It was fortunate that I recognised him as an officer depicted on a named photograph of Bedford (12 Group) Officers in our collection. The gentleman sitting on his left [Douglas Hopcraft] was the Head Observer with the rank of Chief Observer. He is wearing above his left pocket the (short-lived) insignia of Head Observer. His second in command, his Leading Observer (Post Instructor) is sitting on his right [George Deeley].

This photograph probably dates from 1943-44. As the long-serving members have only four War Service Stripes it is most unlikely to be an end-of-war stand-down photograph. Third and fourth from the left, back row [Arthur Humphries and Arthur

Newell], are wearing the pre “Royal” breast badge which should have been replaced by the crowned badge by then.’

Information provided by Primrose Buckle (née Roberts):

Primrose’s step-brother Lawrence Pyman was a Spitfire pilot who died in 1941 over the Channel and is commemorated on the War Memorial (p.56). Her father, Major Roberts, and family had lived in Deddington House (now Manor) since 1932. Her mother, Freyda, helped with the care of children arriving as evacuees with health problems (p.80).

Primrose became a plotter in the Post in Oxford[1]. She recalls ‘I used to hitchhike every day to Oxford; no one ever told me there was a Post in Deddington! I joined up in Oxford encouraged by our officer Miss Cooper of marmalade fame. On night duty we slept on iron beds in 2 layers - bunks - with huge square mattresses called biscuits - you had to search and search for three the same thickness as if the middle one was too high you were bent up! I once asked (as I was in the Plotting Post in the new Bodleian) what the delicious smell coming from the kitchen was. I got very short change - "that’s for the officers breakfast" - we just got doorsteps.’

[1] The ROC Museum advised that other members of the Oxford Post included:

Louise Andrews
‘Georgie’ Gray
Fred Harris
Sybil Joyce
Ronald Cuthbert Maasz (in C and D Crews),
Ray Maltby
R D T Onions

The Women's Land Army and Timber Corps (WLA & TC)

Land Army cap badge

Timber Corps cap badge

Commemorative badge issued in 2008

With their uniform of green ties and jumpers and brown felt slouch hats, the WLA and TC worked from dawn to dusk each day, milking cows, digging ditches, sowing seeds, harvesting crops and cutting timber. The veterans campaigned for years for recognition and were given considerable help in this by the actress and MP, Glenda Jackson. Her website contains advice on how to apply for the badge.

The words that follow are by Ruth Johnson as published in *Deddington News*. 'For a healthy, happy job, join the Women's Land Army'(1940s slogan). The heroic achievements of British agriculture during the Second World War must not be forgotten. The objective of a plan drafted in 1936-37 was the production at home of as much of the food most needed in war time as possible. Yet, during the war some 98,000 men had left the land to enrol into the Armed Forces. Somebody had to step into the breach and none were better organised than the Women's Land Army colloquially known as the Land Girls. Imagine my pleasure when over a welcome cup of tea, a dear, only too modest, Deddington friend chatted to me about her two years service in the WLA and showed me a letter of thanks signed by the Prime Minister, and her brand new shiny commemorative badge.

This is a long overdue official thank you for war work, to the surviving members of over 80,000 young women volunteer labourers on the land. My friend, together with another Land Girl, shared work on a big estate, tending a large market garden, looking after six Jersey cows, poultry and generally supporting two elderly estate workers, the only regular staff left who had not been called up. The girls were quartered above a stable/barn, did their own cooking on a single electric ring and even had water laid on into their quarters! (the men had to make do with an outside tap). Once a fortnight the girls took turns with weekend leave to visit their parents, but each felt duty bound to return on the earliest milk train on Monday morning to lighten again the on-duty girl's heavy burden. Luckily healthy food was always in good supply which eked out their 7s. 6d a week pay. My friend showed me her original WLA badge worn on her issue uniform of green jumper, beige shirt, tie, hard-wearing trousers, Wellington boots and a warm coat. Sadly, I could not persuade her to dig out some old photos from the attic. She said: I was only one of thousands doing my bit for my country. Yes it was hard work, but we learned a lot and also had some fun. We two Land Girls got on famously and are still in contact with each other to this day. The WLA Badge has been specially designed by the Garter King of Arms and bears the Royal Crown. The commemorative badge shows a gold wheat sheaf on a white background surrounded by a circle of pine branches and pine cones to indicate the work of both the Women's Land Army (WLA) and the Women's Timber Corps (WTC), known as Timber Jills (Lumber Jills was another common sobriquet). The WLA was disbanded in 1950. Land Girls and Timber Jills we salute you.'

A few of those who joined the WLA or WTC were:

Jean CLARKE née Woolley.
Jean lodged with Arthur and Clara Clarke and worked for Mrs Hoare (the Old Farmhouse on the west side of lower New Street) who kept dairy cows in fields on the Oxford road. She married Leonard Clarke, brother to Arthur, after he was invalided out of the Army.

Violet June FRENCH (1928-2003) née Cooper.
She was an Oxford girl who married Gerald French from Clifton.

Dorcas LOVE.
She lived in digs in the village.

Irene (René) O'ROURKE née Sheppard.
She lived at the Paper Mill cottages. Her home town was Bristol.

Enid TURNEY.
She also lived in the Paper Mill cottages. She came from Norfolk.

Diana UNDERWOOD (b 1923) née Fortescue.
She recounts her experiences as a 'Timber Jill' (WTC) on page 186.

Jean GREEN (b 1924) née Walsh.
Jean was born in Wakefield, Yorkshire but was sent as a Land Army girl to the Welford's farm in Clifton in about 1941-42. She would have been about 17. There were two other Land Army girls on the farm. Jean now lives in Brisbane, Australia, with her daughter Merle Langley who provided this information after reading the appeal for information in the *Deddington News*.

The Inland Waterways (I W) Service

One of the smaller wartime organisations was composed of trainee boatwomen for the Inland Waterways. This select band of about 90 women worked on the canals and waterways - but do they impinge on our parish? Well, slightly because the Oxford Canal runs along part of our eastern boundary and it was operational during the war transporting essential supplies and, secondly, because a lady in nearby King's Sutton, Olga Kevelos, was one of their number. Olga later became landlady of one of the pubs in the village. She died in October 2009 and it was her obituary which drew this organisation to our attention.

Those women who answered an advertisement in the national press in the early 1940s found themselves, after six weeks' training, operating narrow boats which each carried up to 50 tons of essential supplies. The so called 'idle women' derived their nickname from the initials 'IW' on their badges. This stood for Inland Waterways, but the territorially jealous boat people - born and bred to the canal system - called them 'idle women.'

Between 1943 and 1946 some 45 women, aged from 18 to about 35, worked on the canals and waterways replacing men who had joined the services. They transported aircraft parts and machinery from the London Docks to Birmingham; then collected coal and took it to London. After a round trip of some three weeks transporting these and other vital supplies, they had the option of a week's unpaid leave.

Teams of three women managed a pair of boats and, unlike the Land Girls, they didn't get any extra rations. They lived on cocoa with condensed milk, national loaf and peanut butter and, when possible, they scavenged swedes and potatoes from the fields as they passed. It was essential to be able to accept living rough. Many women weren't used to it, and it was very hard ... lighting fires, using buckets for loos, cooking on black ranges, sharing a tiny back cabin. In addition to living in very cramped conditions, the girls had to load and unload the cargo, repair the engine, navigate locks and tunnels, empty the bilges, scrub hatches, chop firewood and prepare meals - 'idle women'?

Olga KEVELOS (1924-2009) was a war-time volunteer living in London who was in the IW. She travelled regularly along the stretch of the canal linking London and Oxford to the Midlands. In 1983 she returned to the area to help her younger brother, Ray, run the Three Tuns Pub in Kings Sutton. She was also a leading lady motorcyclist. Emma Smith wrote about her experiences in her book, *Maiden's Trip*, as did Susan Woolfitt in her book, *Idle Women*.

The Emergency Services

Air Raid Precautions Service (ARP)

This photograph of Deddington's wardens is courtesy of Geoff Todd. We have yet to put names to all the faces but one of them is **Laurence Wallin**, the 14-year-old son of one of several village bakers. **Sidney Rule** (front row, sixth from the right), County Surveyor, was in charge. **'Herbie' Callow** is on his left. Most of the ARP wardens worked for the council and several were also in the Home Guard.

The Fire Service

The Deddington Fire Brigade was called to Coventry on the night of 14 November 1940 when a major German air raid destroyed much of the city. The name of **Ben KERRIDGE** is the only brigade member we could establish.

The Police Service

William Charles WEST (1901-52) was a War Reserve Policeman and stayed on as a Special Constable after the war.

His daughter, José, married Leading Aircraftsman Bob Stevens. Her childhood memories of wartime Deddington can be read on page 184.

The Women's Voluntary Services (WVS) and Evacuees

The WVS was established in 1938 to encourage women to join the Air Raid Precaution Service (ARP). They were given national responsibilty for evacuation and eventually moved some 1.5 million people (primarily children) out of cities in the early days of September 1939. Many evacuees subsequently returned to their homes, preferring the danger of bombs and the company of familiar neighbours to living in a strange area. However, a considerable number stayed on in their new homes and were integrated into the community - as the list on the next page shows.

By 1941, 1 million women belonged to the WVS. It was a voluntary organisation in which no one held a specific rank. It had a uniform but it was not free so many members simply wore the badge on their lapels.

The casualty rate was high: 241 members of the WVS were killed during the May 1941 Blitz alone and many more were wounded.

In due course this largely unsung, but increasingly vital, organisation took on many other varied roles. They collected clothing for evacuees, the bombed out and other needy people. They helped with the distribution of food and drink to troops and to victims of bombing; over 10,000 people were fed by them over the 57 nights of the Blitz and the people who survived the bombing of Coventry received some 14,000 meals. After the 'All Clear' was sounded Incident Inquiry Points were established and manned to help people find out about relatives and friends in areas that had been bombed. On a wider and more general basis they educated everyone in not wasting what they had and assisting the authorities with food rationing. There was a Salvage Officer and Food Leader in every WVS centre. To help with this they ran a series of campaigns such as 'Salute the Soldier', 'Wings for Victory', 'Spitfire Funds' and 'Warship Week.'

Two key people in the Deddington WVS responsible for evacuees were:

Helen LOVEDAY who lived at Castle End. It was her job to devise and manage the processing system for receiving and allocating billets to those arriving by train at Ayno Halt Station.

Freyda ROBERTS was the wife of Major Reginald Roberts and lived in Deddington House. She had been a Voluntary Aid Detachment (VAD) nurse in WWI and so was given responsibility for caring for evacuee children arriving with ailments. The children were first given a medical examination in Foresters Hall in the Tchure.

Those who were identified as having impetigo or scabies were initially sent to stay with Mrs Roberts at Deddington House. She soon had to start a hospital at the Old Vicarage because the number of children arriving with medical problems could not be accommodated in her own house. Healthy children were interviewed in a room on the top floor of the British Legion building[1] and allocated to foster parents. The weekly amount paid by the Government for an unaccompanied child was 10s 6d,[2] with an additional 8s 6d for a second child and a further five shillings if a parent had to be accommodated as well.

Some of the evacuees who came to Deddington

Doreen ASHTON née Stewart.
She was at Campbell School in Beacontree, Essex, with Pauline Savill and was evacuated to Deddington with her mother. Doreen stayed on after the war and married Ken Ashton and now lives in Kidlington.

Ada BLISS née Sorrell (D).
She was sister to Henry Sorrell (Royal Corps of Signals) who is named on the War Memorial (p.56). Ada married Sergeant Arthur Bliss.

Pauline FRANKLYN née Savill.
She married Lance Corporal Peter Franklyn. Their story is on page 131.

Ronnie HALE.
He was cousin to Derrick Robbins.

Edward LLOYD.
He was the son of a London docker. Lived with the Harper family (Harry and Daisy and nephew Albert) in what is now Quinque House on New Street. Teddy's older sister Rosie was lodged across the road with Sybil French. Both children went to the Primary School.

Derrick ROBBINS (D)
He arrived by train from London on his own to stay with his relatives, the Ells, who lived at Tower View. His extensive recollections (p.168) give a fascinating insight into Deddington during the war years.

Jonny RYAN.

Dorothy (Dol) TARLING, née Sorrell.
She was Ada's younger sister. She married Ken Tarling who was in the Navy. After the war Ada and Dol were joined in Deddington by their mother Eva.

[1] Now the 'Royal' British Legion and occupying the same building - see page 38.

[2] Ten shillings and six pence - there were 20 shillings to the pound and 12 pence to the shilling prior to decimalisation on 15 February 1971.

Airfields near Deddington

One of the major changes inflicted upon the area was the creation of 12 airfields. Suddenly there was an influx of servicemen and women and aeroplanes flying overhead.

Barford St John
Built in 1941 and still open.
An RAF station which was, initially, a Relief Landing Ground for 15 Flying Service Training School, Kidlington.
In April 1942, it was used by Bomber Command as a satellite airfield for Upper Heyford.
Gloster Aircraft Company used part of the airfield to develop the Meteor fighter.
The units stationed there were 16 Operational Training Unit (OTU) and 1655 Training Unit. The aeroplanes involved were mainly Wellingtons and, for a short time, Mosquitoes.
It was bombed on 24 August 1941.

Barton Abbey
Opened on 30 September 1941 and closed in early 1945.
It is recorded that it was used by the RAF as a storage area by 8, and later 39, Maintenance Unit. The aeroplanes involved were mainly Wellingtons. José Stevens worked there as a typist in 1944-45 and recalls that it was 6 MU supporting Brize Norton and Little Rissington. More of José's memories can be read on page 184.

Chipping Norton
It was opened by the RAF in July 1940 and closed in December 1945. The first occupants were 15 Service Flying Training School equipped with the North American Harvard. Later 6 Service Flying Training School took over the airfield.
It was bombed on 29-30 October and also on 18-19 November 1940.

Croughton
It opened in 1940 and is still operated by the USAAF.
Initially it was a satellite airfield for 16 OTU at Upper Heyford, part of Bomber Command, the main aircraft being the Handley Page Hampden and the Avro Anson.
In July 1942 it became a Glider Training School flying the Hotspur Gliders and then in March 1943 became a satellite airfield for Kidlington. When the forces ran short of trained glider pilots, it reverted briefly to being a Glider Training School.
Number of known air accidents in the vicinity is 12.
The airfield was bombed on 20 September 1940.

Edgehill
It opened in October 1941; in 1949 it was placed under Care and Maintenance and eventually closed in 1954.
It was used by the RAF, 21 OTU initially then, in the spring of 1943, 12 OTU moved in and then in 1945 it became 25 Maintenance Unit.
It was briefly re-opened during the Korean War as a satellite station to Moreton-in-the-Marsh.
It was the airfield which hosted the first test flight of the jet engine in February 1942.
In the autumn of 1941 there were at least three air accidents.

The OTUs were teaching the crews to work as a team within the aircraft but also as part of a larger attacking force. They were therefore involved in missions over Continental Europe and suffered casualties.

Enstone
This RAF station was opened in 1942 and closed some time after 1946. It was initially a satellite station for 21 OTU who were at Moreton-in-the-Marsh. More intriguingly, it was also the base for a very secret unit of which nothing is known except that its six Lancaster bombers were painted black and without squadron markings and at all times these aircraft were either flying or hidden from the view of everyone on the airfield.
In 1944 a flight of six Tomahawks was used for training.

Eynsham
In 1939 this airfield was also known as No. 6 Ammunition Park where thousands of tons of ammunition were stored. It then became a Maintenance Unit which it remained until it closed in 1948.

Hinton-in-the-Hedges
This airfield was opened in November 1941 when it was used by 13 OTU who were followed by 16 OTU. It ceased military operations in July 1944.
The other major user of the airfield was 26 Signals Group whose work involved developing aerial systems.
There are known to have been five accidents, one in 1941 and four in 1942, including one on 24 July 1942.

Kiddington (Glympton)
It opened in 1941 as a Relief Landing Ground for its larger neighbour, Kidlington, where 15 Service Flying Training School was based.
Later it was further involved in the training of Glider Pilots.

Kidlington
This was a civil airfield that was requisitioned in September 1939. In the rapidly changing world at that time it became a maintenance facility, a satellite airfield for Abingdon and an RAF Code Training Centre and the base for 6 Service Flying Training School, then 15 Service Flying Training School. All within a year.
In 1942 it became the 101 (Glider) OTU and later 102 (Glider) OTU was added. All training activity ceased in June 1945 and gradually the airfield ceased military operations.
The airfield was bombed on 3 November 1940, when one airman was killed. Further attacks were on 27 February 1941 and 12 August 1941 but without any fatalities.
One of the unsolved mysteries of the war is that Amy Johnson died *en route* here.

Upper Heyford
It was originally a WWI airfield which reopened in 1927 as a bomber station. At the outbreak of WWII it became 16 OTU. This involved flying Hampdens, Wellingtons and eventually Mosquitoes. It was also the base of a secret unit involved in radio countermeasures.

The airfield, like most military sites, attracted the interest of German intelligence; this extract from a German map identifies buildings and munitions dumps - Item 5.

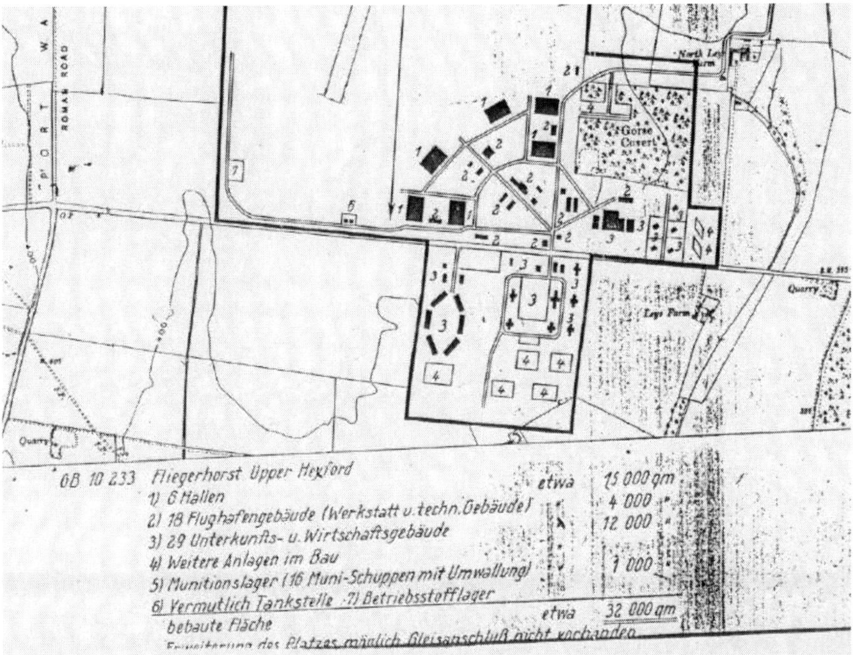

It was attacked by bombing on 12 March and 9 May 1941.

The level of activity was so high that concrete runways were laid in 1942 which closed the airfield from March to December and flying transferred to Barford St John.

In 1951, the airfield was handed over to the USAAF and continued to be operational up until 1994. It was an important part of the US Forces' quick response to possible Soviet aggression during the Cold War. US airmen were a common and welcome sight in Deddington but the recreational facilities on base were so good that there was little need to visit the village; in fact Deddington Tennis Club used the base courts in the 1980s prior to building the present courts at the Windmill Centre.

Wykham Hill
This airfield was briefly used in 1944. It was used by spotter aircraft attached to 6 Field Artillery Battalion which was part of the US Army's 5th Artillery Group whose headquarters were in Banbury.

Photographs and illustrations

Soldiers billeted at Deddington House marching out of the courtyard

Pilot Officer Lawrence Pyman RAFVR (*far right*) with 65 Squadron Spitfire

Compton Bassett Radio School, Wiltshire, June 1943

(Standing l to r) **Daphne Tucker , others unknown**
(Seated l to r) **Lily Pringle, Margaret Morton, Joan Pittaway, AN other with dog**

'Nobby' Clarke

Pam Dance

Leslie Drinkwater

Fred Ellis

Ron Harper

Walter Hayward

Bill Ivings

Harold Pratt

Tom Pratt

Bill Spiers

Bob Stevens

Bernard Sykes

Frank Tarling

Joe Tarling

Ken Tarling

Len Tustain

HRH The Duchess of Gloucester inspecting the WAAF contingent at Chicksands Priory when Michael Allbrook's mother, Squadron Officer Gwenda Allbrook, was stationed there

Stoker Edward Bostock Dumbleton

Edward died on 24 March 1941 in a dockside accident while serving on *HMS Manchester* which was being refitted after its role in the Norwegian Campaign.

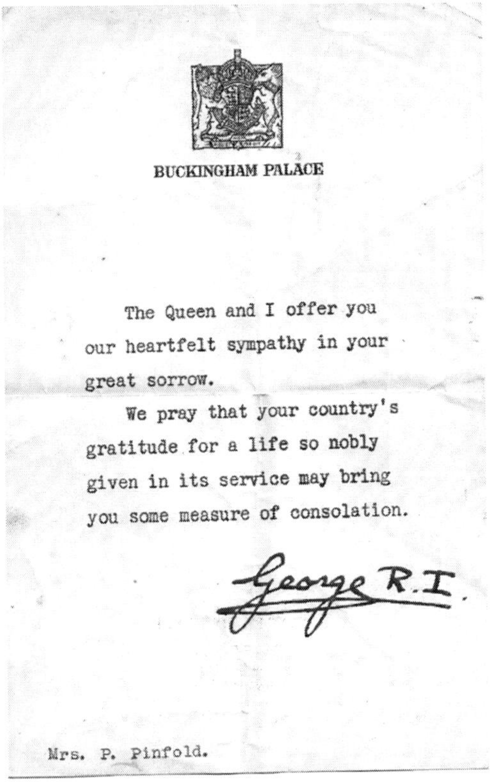

BUCKINGHAM PALACE

The Queen and I offer you our heartfelt sympathy in your great sorrow.

We pray that your country's gratitude for a life so nobly given in its service may bring you some measure of consolation.

George R.I.

Mrs. P. Pinfold.

This letter of condolence is now in the possession of Marguerite Weigand, née Pinfold, who is the granddaughter of Elizabeth Pinfold - mother of Percival Pinfold killed in action in 1917 (p.28). She was listed as Edward's next-of-kin.

Marguerite recounts 'My Dad, Frederick, went to his funeral and on the way back the train had to stop in a tunnel all night because the Germans were bombing Coventry.'

Bicester airfield - 2001
WWII Control Tower and Gun Emplacement

Photograph courtesy of Robert Truman

The airfield was first opened in 1917 for the Royal Flying Corps

The Post-War Years
(1945-2010)

Key to entries

If known by other than the first forename or (familiar) name
then the <u>used</u> name is underlined

* denotes has brother(s) or sister(s) who also served

D denotes deceased, but the year is unknown

The names in this chapter of those who served

Anderson
Bell
Berry
Bolton
Bouverie
Bowler
Bradshaw
Brain
Brearley
Burdon
Cheney
Clarke
Clinch
Cosgrove
Cousins
Davidson
Drake
Farley
Flux
Forsyth
Franklin
Freeman
French
Frost
Fullbrook
Gardner
George
Gibbs
Gines
Green
Hall
Harper
Hart
Hirons
Holiday
Holt
Hood
Lewis
Malcher
Marmion
McCutcheon
Morris
Packard
Parkinson
Read
Robbins
Shepherd
Smith
Sykes
Wallin
Westbury
Wheeler
Wilkinson
Wilson

See the note on page 6 for a further explanation about names

The name on the War Memorial

1950

Robin Lovenden HALL (1931-50) Private.
The King's Own (Yorkshire Light Infantry).
He was conscripted for National (compulsory military) Service in October 1949 and was serving in Malaysia when his patrol was ambushed by terrorists on 10 June 1950 and he was killed age 18.[1]
He is remembered on the Roll of Honour in Batu Gajah, known as 'God's Little Acre', and his grave is also there.
He was the son of Richard Stanley and Edna L Hall, the landlords of the King's Arms, (now the Deddington Arms) Horsefair.

The following additional information has been provided by Robin's sister, Pat Colegrave, and from John Scurr's *Malayan Tales of The Yorkshire Light Infantry* published by Pentland Press (ISBN 10 1858214750). John was a fellow infantryman of Robin Hall.

Robin was a member of a platoon under the command of Sergeant Phil Hogan. They were scouting at the head of D Company near Ampang (vicinity of Ipoh) when they came to a fork in the track. Sergeant Hogan decided to split the Platoon into two sections. He took one section of 10 men down one fork and his second in command, Sergeant Cookson, took the second section down the other fork.

Almost immediately Sergeant Hogan's Section was ambushed by a large group of communist bandits hidden in scrub and grass both on high ground and at ground level. The leading scouts - Privates Harrison and Gough - were killed at point blank range by a Bren gun; four others were killed almost immediately - Privates Boden, Hall, Hudson and Jones. The remaining four were all wounded. Despite his wounds, Lance Corporal Vernon Brown had the presence of mind to keep one hand on his rifle and, as one bandit came close, Brown shot him dead. The remaining bandits quickly disappeared back into the jungle.

Sergeant Hogan was shot through the legs and was found by the second section crawling back up the track for help. Private Storey had his kneecap blown off and Private Daniels later had to have his right hand and wrist amputated. Lance Corporal Brown died of his wounds one week later.

Private Horace French served in the same regiment and company as Robin and had just returned with the patrol prior to this one. Photographs of them both can be seen on page 107.

[1] Robin's sister was presented with the Elizabeth Cross (p.109) on 10 June 2010. The Elizabeth Cross and Memorial Scroll are granted to the Next of Kin of UK Armed Forces personnel who have died on operations or as a result of an act of terrorism in national recognition of their loss and sacrifice.

The men and women who served and returned

Since the end of WWII British Armed Forces have been involved in at least five wars and some 50 different conflicts. During the period that it was in force (1948-63) those called up for their National Service often served - and died - alongside regular servicemen and women in these conflicts.

Royal Navy

Alan ANDERSON National Service.

Ernest (Ernie) ANDERSON National Service.

John William Waller BURDON (b 1930) National Service. Sick Berth Attendant.
He served from 1948 to 1950. His basic training was carried out at *HMS Royal Arthur* in Wiltshire (a 'stone frigate') with specialist training at the Royal Naval Hospital, *RNH Haslar,* in Gosport. He served most of his two years at *RNH Stonehouse* in Plymouth but latterly was attached to the Royal Marines at their infirmary. He has happy memories of being in the Devonport Divisonal team for RN athletics, playing rugby for the Royal Marine Barracks and, in particular, the music of the RM Band.

Terence (Terry) Henry CLARKE (b 1940) Chief Petty Officer.
He served in the Navy from 1955 as a boy seaman at the shore training establishment *HMS Ganges* where tradition required all boys to climb the 142 foot high mast. He subsequently served in submarines.

Robert (Rob) Stanley FORSYTH (b 1939) Commander.
He served from 1957 to 1980, mainly in submarines, including the Polaris Force and command of a nuclear attack submarine. His story can be read on page 128.

Anthony (Tony) HARPER National Service. Steward.

John HOLIDAY National Service.

Martin Henry PACKARD MBE (b 1931) Lieutenant Commander.
He joined the Navy aged 13 as an Officer Cadet. His career included some experiences more unusual than most. While serving as a Midshipman on the aircraft carrier, *HMS Triumph,* he was a passenger in a Firefly V off the coast of Korea which came under 'friendly fire' from US/South Korean forces who mistakenly assumed them to be the enemy on what transpired to be the first day of the Korean War. He later served in *HMS Pincher* in 1953 during a mission to the Arctic to monitor fall-out from Soviet nuclear tests.

Notwithstanding his earlier disastrous flying experience - including a crash landing on the carrier after being shot at - he joined the Fleet Air Arm as a pilot, but his flying career came to an end with a car crash in 1959 following which he spent two years on *HMS Blake* and became a Greek interpreter. Because of his language skills he was appointed to Malta in 1963 as a Naval Intelligence analyst. He was sent to Cyprus to lead a mediation process to resolve the intercommunal Turkish/Greek violence. Despite the apparent success of this mission it was abruptly halted and he was sent back to the UK. A request for transfer to the UN mediating section led to a year studying Arabic at Durham University but he was drawn in by his Greek friends to help with opposition to the 1967 military dictatorship. The Foreign Office, who became aware of this, called for his Court Martial; this was rejected by the RN but he was allowed to resign his commission. Martin's own book *Getting it Wrong* (Authorhouse ISBN 978 1 4343 7065 51) and Brendan O'Malley's book *The Cyprus Conspiracy* (IB Taurus) both provide interesting insights into the highly charged politics of the Cyprus dispute.

He moved permanently to Greece where he continued supporting opposition to the regime. He also set up Levi factories in Greece and Malta and developed business in the USSR, which attracted the unfavourable attention of the CIA and led to media headlines.

His father, a Church of England vicar, was the incumbent from 1950 at Fenny Compton, Lower Heyford and Sandford St Martin in turn. His mother spent the last years of her life in Deddington; one sister lives in Deddington and another at Duns Tew.

John PARKINSON (b 1942) Petty Officer Mechanical Engineer.
He ran away from home in 1959 to join the Navy as a Junior Stoker. Life in his training establishment, *HMS Raleigh*, was tough; instructors still used 'starters' (short sticks) to enforce discipline on the boys, many of whom deserted 'over the wall' at night. After a short sea qualification period in *HMS Roebuck* he joined *HMS Lion*.The first six months were a 'flag waving' tour of the Mediterranean when *HMS Lion* escorted the Queen in the Royal Yacht, *HMY Britannia*. This was followed by a year showing the flag round South America - joining the Navy was clearly a good decision! At the end of 1962 he joined *HMS Belfast*. The ship received the Freedom of the City of Belfast on his 20th birthday. He recalls celebrating both occasions with a memorable (or possibly not!) run ashore. He left the Navy in 1964 to get married.

Ronald (Ron) SHEPHERD National Service.

David (Smudge) SMITH* (b 1941) Able Seaman, Gunnery Branch.
He was a Boy Seaman entry in 1958 to *HMS Raleigh*. He served on *HMS Loch Fyne* (Frigate), *Apollo* (Minelayer), *Adamant* and *Ausonia* (Depot Ships), *Letterston* (Minesweeper) and *Delight* (Destroyer). There were several Deddington men in the Royal Navy; himself, Terry Clarke and Alan Anderson all met up in Malta on one occasion. He left the RN in 1968 and joined the Merchant Navy working for BP tankers including manning the river boats going up the Amazon and Congo in pupose built, shallow draught, River class petroleum carriers.

Herbert John SMITH*(b 1938) Able Seaman, Gunnery Branch.
He joined in 1955 and served successively in *HMS Theseus* (training ship), *Bulwark* (aircraft carrier), *Excellent* (gunnery school), *Crane* (a sloop on Far East station), *Troubridge* (frigate on West Indies station), *Tenby* (frigate in Dartmouth training Squadron) and *Phoebe* (frigate on Far East station). He was landed at Mombasa, East Africa, from *Phoebe* and made his way back to UK and civilian life in 1968.

Gerald SYKES National Service.
He served on *HMY Britannia*. [Editor's note: service on the Royal Yacht was by special selection and required well above average ability].

Women's Royal Naval Service

Barbara FROST née Lewis* (D) Wren.
She served at *HMS Merlin* a Naval Air Station near Donibristle in Fife. She enjoyed her time so much that she named her house 'Merlin' after it.

Army

Leslie (Les) BERRY (D) National Service.
Horseguards.

Simon Pleydell BOUVERIE (b 1928) National Service. 2nd Lieutenant.
The Life Guards. He served from 1946 to 1948. After 14 months training he spent six months with his Regiment in Palestine on peace-keeping duties. He was in the leading armoured car when the British Army pulled out on 15 May 1948. Fifteen miles inside the Palestine border they encountered the Egyptian army; they were, he says, very 'trigger happy' and planning to attack and eliminate Jewish settlements. This never received any publicity for whatever reason - perhaps to avoid hostile Israeli reaction? - and the invasion was aborted quite quickly. The Egyptian army then withdrew behind its own borders.

John Leslie BOWLER MC (b 1932) National Service. Lieutenant.
The Welch Regiment. He served from 1950 to 1952. In 1951 they were deployed to fight in Korea; he was decorated for his actions. His story can be read on page 117.

George Henry BRAIN* (b 1935).
The Royal Army Service Corps, 16th Field Ambulance Division, 63rd Infantry Brigade of Gurkhas. He served from 1953 to 1957, mainly in Malaya. He had a brother who did his National Service in the army, but no details are known.

John CHENEY (b 1929) National Service. Bombardier.
He joined the Royal Artillery in 1949 and trained at Park Hall, Oswestry. He had been sent off to boarding school aged seven so was quite well used to living away from home. He therefore found himself in the slightly unexpected role of 'mothering' other recruits in his unit who were away from their families for the first time and suffering badly from homesickness.

He recalls little of note livening up his two years of National Service other than being inadvertently shelled in an Observation Post on Salisbury Plain by his own gunners. Most of his time was spent on clerking type duties at the Royal Artillery Depot in Woolwich. He finished his service in 1951 then joined the Queen's Own Oxfordshire Hussars (TA) until 1955. He points out that this did not involve learning to ride.

Jack BREARLEY National Service. Corporal.
The Royal Army Ordnance Corps. He served from April 1947 to June 1949.

Terence (Terry) CLINCH (b 1936) National Service. Corporal.
Royal Electrical and Mechanical Engineering (REME) Corps. He served from 1952 to 1954, starting at Blandford Forum, then Barton Stacey, followed by Gosport where he did his clerk's course. Then on to HQ of Ack-Ack [anti-aircraft] command in Aldershot where he was in charge of distribution of 'Emers' (electrical and mechanical engineering regulations) to all depots. This meant collecting the Emers

once a month and taking parcels to the railway station and sending them on their way. Ack-Ack command was closing but he remained on with the Adjutant until the last base closed. His reward was a posting to Woolwich, London, which he recalls as being the worst barracks he was in. He formed a small band for dances whilst at Gosport. In Terry's own words 'I was summoned by the RSM to play at his pub club in Gosport, earning quite a lot of tips not to mention drink each evening. It meant I got back after lights out in company with the RSM and was never taken to task about my untidy state on parade the next morning - but then it was the RSM who inspected us!' He sums up his NS experience '... like most National Servicemen, I went nowhere exciting but made the most of it as one does.'

Donald DAVIDSON National Service. Lance Corporal.
The Oxfordshire and Buckinghamshire Light Infantry.

Norman DRAKE (b 1939) National Service. Sergeant.
The Royal Army Educational Corps. He served from 1959 to 1961, largely in the Far East. His story can be read on page 126.

Peter FARLEY (b 1937) National Service. Bombardier.
He served from 1959 to 1961. He trained in guided weapons and served with 23rd Gibraltar Battery in Gibraltar, the Benbecula Missile firing range in the Outer Hebrides and in Dortmund, Germany.

Arthur Frederick Francis (Jim) FLUX MBE (b 1934) National Service. Captain.
Royal Artillery. He was called up in September 1953 and was selected for Officer Training at Mons where RSM Brittain was the senior NCO - notorious for having the loudest voice in the Army. On passing out he was appointed as a 2nd Lieutenant in 15 Medium Regiment as part of the British Army on the Rhine (BAOR) whose role was to oppose the Soviet Army should it try and roll forward over the German plain. He was the only NS officer in his regiment to be given charge of one of the four troops of 4 x 4.5 inch guns. He also learned to drive Matadors (gun towing vehicles) and Bren Gun Carriers and to sail on the Mohne See where repairs to the dam (breached by the Dambuster's raid) could be clearly seen. He completed his service in 1955 when he joined the Territorial Army as a Lieutenant in 257 County of Sussex Regiment RA until 1960 then, as a Captain, at 133 Infantry Brigade HQ. He left the TA in June 1963 when his job took him overseas.

Brian FRANKLIN* (b 1928) National Service.

Dennis FREEMAN (b 1929) National Service. Rifleman.
The Oxfordshire and Buckinghamshire Light Infantry. He served in the UK from May 1947 to mid-1948 and then was transferred to the Duke of Cornwall's Light Infantry serving in Greece - where the British Army still had a military presence - until he finished his National Service in May 1949. He was Standard Bearer for the Deddington Branch of the the Royal British Legion from 1993 to 2005.

Horace FRENCH (1931-99) National Service. Private.
The King's Own (Yorkshire Light Infantry). He served in Malaysia and was involved in the same action in 1950 in which Robin Hall was killed (p.95).

Victor (Vic) FULLBROOK National Service.

Roger GARDNER (1931) National Service. Private but qualified for 2nd Lieutenant.
He served with the The Oxfordshire and Buckinghamshire Light Infantry from 1949

in Cyprus and later in the UK with the Duke of Cornwall's Light Infantry, 6th Armoured Brigade until 1951. He did TA service until 1954.

Leslie (Les) GEORGE (D) National Service.
The Oxfordshire and Buckinghamshire Light Infantry.

Geoffrey GIBBS (b 1933) National Service. Private.
1st Battalion, The Devonshire Regiment. He served from 1951 to 1953, mainly in Libya based at Derna (alternative Darnah) in North Africa which they reached via Tripoli and Tobruk still showing signs of the wartime siege.

Roger Leonard GINES (b 1939) Corporal.
The Houshold Cavalry (Royal Horseguards). He served from 1956 to 1959 and spent two years and four months of his time in Cyprus fighting the EOKA terrorists.

Andrew Fleming GREEN KCMG MA (b 1941) 2nd Lieutenant.
He was a short service officer in the 1st Royal Green Jackets from 1962 to 1965. After Mons Officer Cadet School, he joined the regiment in Penang in 1963. Having trained in jungle warfare, he served two tours in Borneo as a Platoon Commander. The first tour was on river patrols based in Lutong and the second in a fort deep in the jungle, right on the border with Indonesia, south of Mirri. Apart from defending the fort, their task was to patrol the jungle border to discourage infiltration by communist irregulars from Indonesia who were seeking to de-stabilise the new state of Malaysia which had just been formed to permit Britain to disengage from her colonial responsibilities in the region.

In 1965 his regiment was posted to Berlin as part of the garrison. The task of his platoon was to blow up two bridges over the Havel if the Russians should ever attempt to take over the British sector of the city.

On retirement from the army he joined the Diplomatic Service. He spent half his career in the Middle East. The remainder of his service was divided between London, Paris and Washington. His last post was as HM Ambassador to Saudi Arabia. He retired in June 2000.

David G HOOD MC (b 1933) Major.
The Nottinghamshire and Derbyshire Regiment (Sherwood Foresters). He served from 1951 to 1977 in Germany, Malaya, Norway, Libya, Cyprus and Northern Ireland. His MC was awarded whilst serving in Malaya. He is currently President of the Deddington Branch of The Royal British Legion.

Arthur LEWIS* (b 1927) National Service. Sergeant.
The Oxfordshire and Buckinghamshire Light Infantry. He was called up for National Service in April 1945. He joined at Goojerat Barracks, Colchester. While he was still training, the war with Germany ended but the war with Japan continued. He expected to be posted there; however, the Americans dropped the atom bomb on Japan and on 15 August 1945 the conflict ended. He was selected to be a weapons training instructor for platoons of 33 men as they were called up for National Service, with a Platoon Officer, two Corporals and a Lance Corporal. He was then given the job of training 33 Danish men who had joined the regiment. He was demobbed in 1948.

Ian Gordon McCUTCHEON* National Service. Private.
The Parachute Regiment. He served from April 1946 to July 1948.

James (Jim) Henry MORRIS (1929- 2004).
The Grenadier Guards. He served as a regular soldier from 1946 to 1952 as part of the British Army on the Rhine and was then a reserve for a further seven years. In 1958 he married Mary Malcher whose three brothers all served during the war, one in each of the services (p.161), and whose father, Jack, was in the Royal Observer Corps (p.72). He was a King's Sutton man.

Patrick READ National Service.

Derrick ROBBINS (1928-2010).
He served from 1946 to 1948 and was stationed at Brentwood, Aldershot, Exeter and Stockbridge. Unfortunately he did not tell us which regiment he served in but his extensive wartime memories of Deddington as a young boy can be read on page 168.

John Russell WALLIN* (b 1928) National Service. Lance Corporal.
7th Battalion, Light Infantry (Parachute Regiment) which became the 3rd Battalion in 1948. He was called up in 1947 under the war time system prior to the start of National Service. He served for two years as a National Servicemen thereafter. Training was carried out at Upper Heyford - four jumps from a balloon then the real thing. His battalion was posted to Hildesheim in Germany not far from Hamburg. He recalls that the city was still completely devastated. While carrying out a major exercise parachuting on to Luneberg Heath they had to abandon the exercise and go on full alert because the Russians had closed off access to West Berlin leading to the period known as the Berlin Airlift to keep Berliners supplied with food and essentials.

Thomas (Tommy) SMITH National Service. Sergeant.
Air Gunner/Wireless Operator.

Edmund WHEELER National Service. Private.
The Royal Pioneer Corps. He served from January 1950 to February 1952.

Milson WESTBURY (1930-2002) National Service.
He was an Aynho man who served in Royal Electrical and Mechanical Engineering Corps from 1948 to 1950 and went to the Suez Canal Zone where the British Army had a standing presence. He was Standard Bearer for the Deddington Branch of The Royal British Legion from 1960 to 1993.

Timothy (Tim) Robert WILSON OBE (b 1962) Colonel.
The Queen's Dragoon Guards. He is still serving having previously served in Germany, Northern Ireland, Bosnia and Iraq. His story can be read on page 190.

Royal Air Force

James (Jim) BELL (b 1939) Corporal.
He was born and grew up in Oxford. He joined in 1957 rather than waiting to be called up for National Service. He served three years as a regular in the RAF Police based at RAF Brampton, Huntingdonshire, where he met his wife Barbara who was an Aircraftwoman at the time, working in the Station Headquarters.

He recalls that one of the buildings they had to guard contained German WWII aerial reconnaissance photographs of Russia that were, of course, very valuable in the Cold War. However, they were also extremely inflammable and needed to be stored under refrigerated conditions as they were a constant security and safety hazard.

Another memory is of the time that all the local recruited staff in Cyprus had to be replaced, almost overnight, by UK servicemen and women because of bombs being placed in British bases by EOKA sympathisers.

On completion of his service in January 1960, Jim joined Oxford City Police, which in April 1968 amalgamated with other local forces to become Thames Valley Police. He worked in a wide range of Police posts and on retirement he was a Detective Sergeant on the Serious Crime Squad.

Anthony (Tony) BOLTON (1920-2010) Squadron Leader.
He joined the Royal Navy on the outbreak of war in 1939 (p.59). He remained in the service until 1955. After a brief spell in commerce he re-enlisted in the RAF in 1957 as a Flight Lieutenant. In the UK he served at Hucknell, Northolt, Marby, Old Sarum. Sealand, Abingdon, Uxbridge and Little Rissington. Overseas he was based in Singpapore (Seletar) from where he went to Hong Kong and Kuala Lumpur. His last overseas appointment was in Washington DC, USA. He left the RAF in 1973.

Roger Lovell BRADSHAW (b 1932) National Service. Leading Aircraftman.
He served from 1950 to 1952 in the administration branch of the RAF Medical Service stationed at Freckleton near Blackpool. His father (a Bloxham man) had served in WWI with Maurice French in D Company of The Queen's Own Oxfordshire Hussars.

Brian COSGROVE MBE (1926-2010) Flight Lieutenant.
RAF Volunteer Reserve. He had been a Meteorological Air Observer in the RAF from 1943 to 1947 (p.65). Having been demobbed and got a job with Spillers, he joined the RAF Training Branch in 1948 where he continued to pursue his love of flying by becoming a gliding instructor. He retired from the RAF a second time in 1964 as a Flight Lieutenant. By 1981 he had given up his main job and become secretary of the British Microlight Association. He subsequently became its Chief Executive and set up the present office in the Bullring in Deddington from whence, almost single handedly, he turned micro-lighting from an aerial 'Hell's Angels' into a fully competent authority authorised to administer air worthiness. He retired in 1993 and was awarded the MBE for his services to microlighting.

Terence (Terry) COUSINS National Service.

James (Jim) Percy FRANKLIN (b 1930) National Service. Leading Aircraftman.
He served from 1951 to 1953 in Egypt in the Canal Zone. From 16 October 1951 to 19 October 1954 troops were in an 'Active Service' situation; it was a dangerous time and many lives were lost through terrorist attacks on camps and vehicle convoys, sniping, abductions, murder and sabotage etc. It is estimated that around 70% of the British Armed Forces stationed in the Canal Zone during this Emergency period were conscripts completing their National Service and were not fully trained in anti-terrorist fighting.

Frederick Kenneth (Ken) HART (b 1927) Squadron Leader.
Engineering Branch. He served from 1952 to 1987.

John HIRONS National Service.

Stephen (Steve) George MALCHER* (b 1928) National Service. Leading Aircraftman.
The story of the Malcher brothers is on page 161.

James Carlyle MARMION OBE (b 1924) Group Captain.
He had previously served in WWII (p.66). His post-war flying career took him to USA, Canada, the Middle East, Africa, India, Singapore, Australia and Germany. From 1945 to 1953 he served a ground tour with a Fighter Group then operational flying on a Lincoln Squadron. From 1953 to 1957 he was responsible for the conversion of bomber aircrews to jet engined aircraft including training in the nuclear role. He advised on anti-Mau Mau operations in Kenya and during the Suez Crisis. He was awarded the OBE in June 1957. Between tours on 138 Valiant Squadron and the Vulcan wing, he was assigned to the Skybolt air-launched ballistic missile project In Dayton, Ohio, until its cancellation under the Macmillan/Kennedy accord on the Polaris submarine-launched system. His later and more senior staff appointments were increasingly in Air Reconnaissance and Intelligence in which he became a specialist. He retired from active duty in 1979 but served a further six years on special duties in Whitehall. He and his wife Stella lived in Deddington for many years before they moved to the West Country in 2006.

Alistair John McCUTCHEON* National Service. Leading Aircraftsman.
He was based at Moreton-in-the-Marsh from November 1952 to November 1954 so he was - very conveniently - able to cycle home at weekends to play for Deddington Town Football team.

Kenneth Dogson (Ken) WILKINSON (1934) National Service. Senior Aircraftman. 208 Squadron RAF Regiment. He served from 1953 to 1955. His six months basic training was carried out at Padgate, Cheshire, followed by anti-aircraft training on the Bofors gun at Watchet, Somerset. His squadron was sent to carry out the RAF Regiment's role of airfield protection in the Suez Canal Zone. This encompassed the period known as the Suez Crisis for which participants received a campaign award only in 2003.

The Venerable John Hewitt WILSON CB MA (1924-2008) Air Vice Marshal.
He became an RAF Chaplain in 1950. For the first 10 years of his service he served on flying stations, most notably in Aden and Germany. He then served as the staff Chaplain to the RAF's Chaplain-in-Chief, the Venerable Frank Cocks, before being appointed in 1963 as senior Chaplain at RAF Cranwell. This was followed by Assistant Chaplain-in-Chief at the HQ Far East Air Force, and in 1969 he filled a similar appointment at the Strike Command at High Wycombe. In 1973 he was appointed Honorary Chaplain to the Queen and the next year he was made Chaplain-in-Chief to the RAF and remained as such until 1980 when he retired - the longest serving of any in that post.

He was appointed Archdeacon Emeritus and Canon Emeritus of Lincoln Cathedral and Chaplain Emeritus to the Worshipful Company of Coachmakers and Coach Harness Makers.

In 1991 he was appointed Rector of Somerton, the Heyfords and Rousham where he formed a close relationship with the USAAF personnel at the nearby Upper Heyford airbase.

Hewitt and his wife Joan's youngest son, Tim, was commissioned into The Queen's Dragoon Guards (QDG) in 1984 (p.190).

Women's Royal Air Force

Barbara Mary BELL (b 1940) née Holt. Senior Aircraftwoman.
She joined the WRAF in September 1957 following a visit by an RAF recruiting team to her school in Kendal, Westmorland. To a 17-year old, in the 1950s, it seemed to be a much more exciting thing to do than what were, at the time, other quite limited opportunities for women. Following three months of basic training at RAF Wilmslow, Cheshire she was posted to RAF Credenhill in Hereford for trade training as a typist. She was then posted to RAF Brampton where she met her future husband, Jim, who was serving in the RAF Police.

A highlight of her time in the service was taking part in the 1958 Festival of Remembrance at the Royal Albert Hall. This requires each service contingent to march down steps onto the arena floor, keeping in step as they transition to marching forward across it, then marching up the steps of the stage - not at all an easy thing to do in the presence of the Queen and senior members of the Royal family! The following day she took part in the Service of Remembrance at Westminster Abbey.

Barbara and Jim married in 1961, lived in Oxford until 1971 when they moved to Banbury and where they brought up two sons - Andrew (1963) and Chris (1966). The family moved to Deddington in 1981. Andrew served as a volunteer, manning the Royal Observation Corps nuclear war monitoring post at RAF Barford St Michael (see article overleaf).

Royal Observer Corps' Nuclear Monitoring Bunker

Deddington's WWII Observation Post (OP) (see map p.73) was only equipped for aircraft spotting. In the late 1950s at the start of the Cold War, a new underground bunker was built at RAF Barford St John airfield, equipped with nuclear radiation monitoring equipment, in location P451345 and was renamed Bloxham, OXF/17.

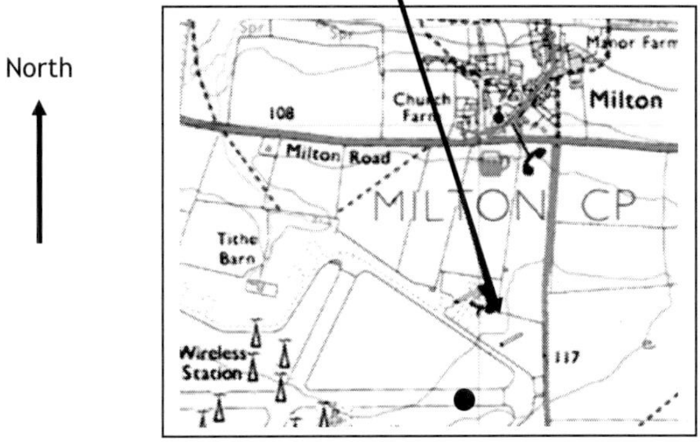

RAF Barford St John

Access was via a metal hatch lid set in concrete then down a vertical ladder in a narrow concrete shaft that led to the bunker about 100ft down. There were two small rooms about 20 x 20 ft square - each with a bed - and a small kitchen and chemical toilet.

Room 1

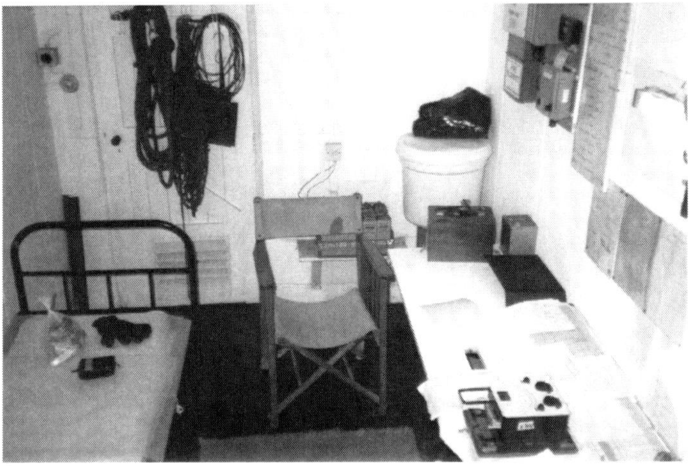

Room 2. The white-faced instrument on the desk is a meter to measure gamma radiation levels.

The bunker was linked to a secret underground location in Wiltshire created for the purpose of providing a nuclear shelter for the government in case of all-out nuclear war. There were 25 Observer Groups in the UK at that time and over 800 monitoring positions. The Bloxham one came under No 3 Group HQ based at Cowley Barracks in Oxford. The crew's main role would have been to report the extent of devastation in the north Oxfordshire area in the event of an exchange of missiles with Soviet Russia - always supposing any one was left alive to report this!

One of the crew who manned the bunker was Andrew Bell. He enrolled for duty in the rank of Observer in July 1982 and served until 1989. This photograph was taken in 1986.

He recalls that local training evenings were held regularly and weekend exercises took place on a national scale. A highlight of the annual programme was attending a voluntary training camp for a week at a selected RAF Air Station.

Andrew Bell

Photographs

Barbara Bell on the left

Terry Clarke

Horace French beside Robin Hall's gravestone in Batu Gajah
14 June 1997

Robin Hall

Arthur Lewis

Jim Morris

John Parkinson

Hewitt Wilson

The Elizabeth Cross - presented to Mrs Pat Coleman (née Hall)

10 June 2010

Private Robin Hall was killed in action in Malaya 10 June 1950

Personal stories

This chapter provides just a small small cross-section of the experiences of the men and women – in one case a child -in and out of uniform, of the people in this book but everyone, of course, has their own similar personal story if space allowed.

Familiar names - rather than formal ones and rank - have been used in the manner in which they are known in the community. Details of rank and service can be found in the records in previous chapters.

SID BERRY

Rob Forsyth

Sid proudly wearing the white beret of the Arctic Convoy Association

Sid was born on 28 April 1920 in a small cottage in Hudson Street, Deddington and lived in the village all his life except for his five years in the Royal Navy during WWII. He started his working life as an apprentice to a baker - of which there were at least eight in the village - so it was no surprise that he was made a cook on volunteering for the Royal Navy in September 1940. Nothing in his life to date could have prepared him for the four years of near constant warfare at sea that followed.

His first experience of this was on board *HMS Mashona which* took part in the Lofoten Raid in March 1941. In May of the same year *Mashona* was ordered to join the hunt for the *Bismarck* in the Atlantic. He recalls seeing shells from *HMS Rodney* destined for the *Bismarck* passing overhead. Shortly after this *Bismarck* was sunk and *Mashona* was ordered back to Plymouth. While en route she was attacked and sunk by German Focke-Wulf aircraft. Sid told the story that when he came to the surface after jumping overboard, he thought he had gone blind but in fact his cork lifejacket had ridden up over his head! He was not rescued until after dark and then spent six weeks in hospital with an injured leg.

He then served on *HMS Ashanti* which, throughout the rest of 1941 and the first half of 1942, carried out escort duties for numerous Arctic Convoys bound for Russia. He had many memories of the atrociously cold, bad weather and the frequent attacks by aircraft; on one occasion off Bear Island they withstood an attack from 50 Heinkel 111s which carried two torpedoes each. On another occasion Sid volunteered to man an ASDIC (submarine detection) set. The submarine was successfully sunk by another ship but Sid felt he should have had the credit for finding it in the first place. East-bound convoys arrived in Archangel which had little to offer by way of recreation except joining their Russian hosts in heavy drinking competitions. He still had a Soviet Navy rating's hat won as a prize.

In August 1942 *Ashanti* was sent to the warmer - but no less dangerous - waters of the Mediterranean to take part in Operation Pedestal. This was an attempt to run some 50 merchant and naval ships past a gauntlet of German and Italian aircraft, E-boats, minefields and submarines in an attempt to bring much needed relief to beseiged Malta. It has gone down in military history as one of the most important British strategic victories of WWII. However, it was achieved at a cost of more than 400 lives and the loss of nine (of the original 14) merchantmen, one aircraft carrier (*HMS Eagle*), two cruisers (*HMS Manchester* and *HMS Cairo*), and a destroyer (*HMS Foresight*) but it saved Malta. It was on this same operation that Lt Robert (Buster) Churchill died in action (see p.58). *Ashanti* was constantly in the thick of it and became Convoy Commodore for the merchant ships when the previous ship was sunk. Sid recalled that at Action Stations, when there was no cooking to be done, he helped out with ammunition supply to an anti-aircraft gun in a very exposed position on the upper deck; from here he could clearly see the pilot of a dive-bombing Stuka as it made its attack - which fortunately missed - in its near vertical dive.

Malta was under near constant air attack so there was no run ashore in Malta and it was back to UK waters for further convoy screening work. The war diary of the ship refers to constant submarine and air attacks and taking a badly damaged sister ship, *HMS Somali,* in tow. One can hardly imagine the tension there must have been on board *Ashanti*, crowded with survivors, dragging *Somali* at about 5 knots towards home, concerned as to how easy a target they both must be. In the end, after some 400 miles, the tow parted in bad weather, *Somali* sank and they could proceed at a safer speed.

In November 1942 they were back in the Mediterranean as part of the support group for the Allied Force's North African landings known as Operation Torch. They were then pretty much constantly involved in hostile activities in the western Mediterranean until the ship returned to the UK for a much-needed refit in June 1943. In November they were back at sea on escort duties which included escorting the battleship *HMS King George V* on passage from Gibraltar to UK with Prime Minister Winston Churchill embarked.

His captain on *Ashanti* was Captain Richard Onslow who, Sid believed, was a relative of Dr Jones of Deddington. This local connection may account for why the Captain once advanced him some pay from his own pocket against his next pay packet.

In early 1944, Sid volunteered for the submarine service thinking this might be safer! In May he joined *HMS Selene* in the Far East where she sank five Japanese sailing vessels and three coasters, and damaged another sailing vessel by ramming it and a coaster. He transferred to *HMS Vivid* in July 1945 to return to the UK and left her to be released from the Navy in March 1946. He was still on the Fleet Reserve list for training in 1956.

In 2004, sitting at home in his favourite (and audibly squeaky) armchair, Sid made some audio recordings of his naval experiences and recollections of village life. These recordings can be down-loaded from the Deddington OnLine website (www.deddington.org.uk).

He took part in every Remembrance Day march past through the Market Place until 2005. He died in December 2006.

THE 'BOWLER BOYS'

Rob Forsyth

The account that follows draws heavily on a privately published book written by Leslie Bowler's son, John. I strongly recommend reading his book *Leslie William Harold Bowler* (available from the Library) because, apart from containing many more details, it also contains a mass of information about life in the trenches in WWI and quotes extensively from war diaries. These provide a most interesting insight into the small detail of day-to-day life in one of the bloodiest wars in history.

In his book John acknowledged his indebtedness to Christopher Bowler and Audrey Cox (née Bowler) for information about their parents (Geoffrey and Frank respectively). I also thank all three of them for this information.

How the Bowler family came to Deddington

At the turn of the last century Thomas William Bowler was the Managing Director of the family business, Victor Jay and Co. in Southwark, London. The 1901 census records that he and his family lived in Wandsworth. The company were felt and straw hat manufacturers and are attributed with the development of the original bowler hat. In 1891 Thomas had married Alice Turner of Deddington. The Turner family[1] lived at The Poplars now known as Castle End. Thomas and Alice, with their growing family, moved to Deddington in 1909 to live in what was then called Eastleigh but has since been renamed Bowler House. They had six children - Leslie (b 1893), Geoffrey (b 1895), Frank (b 1898), Kathleen (b 1900), Cyril (b 1903) and John, known as Jack (b 1906). All five boys went to Bloxham School. The two youngest children, Cyril and Jack, were drowned in September 1917 in the River Cherwell near Clifton while swimming. Their graves are in the churchyard.

[1] The Turner family had lived in Deddington for many years. Briefly:

The Reverend Edward Turner (1752-1836) had 12 children and was uncle of the famous engraver, Charles Turner.

Thomas William (1800-63) was the Reverend's 12th child and a GP. He was the first Turner to occupy The Poplars in 1825 when it was then known as The Green. He married Elizabeth Newman (1799-1878).

Edward William (1834-89) was their second child. He also became a GP and married Louisa Ann Colman (1838-1930) from Norfolk (one of the Colman's Mustard daughters). Louisa was reputed to be quite a formidable character, featuring large in parish affairs and lived to the age of 92. Edward and Louisa also lived at The Poplars, where they had nine children.

Their third child, Alice, married Thomas Bowler. Their only son, Thomas William (1871-1933) continued the family tradition by becoming a GP. NB: Although she coincidentally bore the same surname, Mary Vane Turner - author of *The Story of Deddington* - was not related by marriage to this branch of the Turner family.

The Poplars was sold some time between 1930 and 1939 and later renamed Castle End.

LESLIE BOWLER

Leslie was born in Islington. After school he joined his father in the family business. War broke out in August 1914 when he was 21 years old and he enlisted as a Territorial soldier. He joined the 16th (Public Schools) Battalion, Middlesex Regiment whose part-time training was conveniently carried out near to the Victor Jay factory. The photograph is of Leslie as a Captain wearing his MC decoration with bar and also the laurel sprig of his two Mentions in Despatches.

Photograph taken circa 1919

He was commissioned as a 2nd Lieutenant on 9 June 1915 into the 22nd Battalion, County of London Regiment (The Queen's). He arrived in France on 11 November. He was now a full Lieutenant and was Platoon Commander for the next 15 months. His Battalion was stationed at Allouagne 10kms west of Béthune. There is insufficient space here to recount his experiences in full but what follows will give some idea of his very busy war.

1915-16

On 15 December he went into the front line trenches at Vermeilles for the first time. This section was only 20 yards from the Germans. From then until February 1917 his platoon was involved in battles for Vimy Ridge and the Somme offensive - particularly the attack on High Wood in September 1916 during which, in one company, all the officers and sergeants were killed. He received a flesh wound affecting his ability to sit.

1917

In March he became Acting Adjutant to the 21st Battalion. Having survived some 16 months at the front, this HQ appointment improved his chances of surviving the war but nonetheless he and his Battalion continued to be frequently in action in the Ypres salient. In July he was gazetted Captain. He had a few days leave in the UK in October but was back in action by beginning of November and was Mentioned in Despatches on 7 November.

The major attack on the Hindenburg Line commenced 20 November. Massed tanks were deployed and an advance of an incredible four miles achieved. Leslie's Division captured Bourlon Wood in an engagement in which he received the first of his MCs. However, nearly all this ground gained was subsequently lost at a cost to the 141st Brigade of 69 officers and 1939 men. Gas attacks were a particular feature ... 'The Division casualties were enormous. The 19th Battalion suffered particularly heavily. 15 Officers and over 600 men took up position ... of these only one officer and between twenty and thirty of the men remained a few days later, the remainder being in hospital from gas.' At year end they were dug in back on the Hindenburg Line - again.

1918

The pattern continued in the New Year with sporadic attacks and patrols. On 15 March Leslie received the MC he had been awarded at Bourlon Wood. The citation stated that 'in a wood ... heavily shelled and gassed ... he went ahead and recce'd the whole position under the most difficult situations. It was largely due to his determination and skills that the Battalion succeeded in occupying the position.' Fighting was particularly fierce throughout March with attack and counter-attack in the Somme area moving the front line backwards and forwards. The defence of Highland Ridge and the retaking of High Hill stand out. The success of the German offensive led to massive reinforcements being sent from UK - mostly boys of 18.

7 April. For a second time the diary records 'Capt. Bowler was awarded a Mention in Despatches.' Shortly after this he became Signals Officer; this was a particularly important and dangerous position as it entailed maintaining miles of telephone wire intact and frequently while under enemy fire.

On 13 June Leslie took over command of B Company. He was 25 years old. The battle for the Somme continued. Records are unclear but it is probable that he won the bar to his MC on the night of 22-23 August when, without orders, he countered a flanking move by the enemy (who had overrun units either side of him) by moving his company to 'straighten the line'. The citation reads in part '... led his company in an attack with conspicuous gallantry and skill, exposing himself under intense fire with a total disregard of danger ...'

In October he was wounded a second time. A bullet passed through both legs leaving a small exit wound but missed arteries and bones. He walked two miles to the regimental aid post. As a consequence he was invalided home and the war finished while he was convalescing.

Post-war he helped his Battalion Commanding Officer form a Territorial Battalion and only resigned his commission in 1921. He married, became MD of the family firm, a keen gardener and, despite his leg wound, an athlete (Ranleigh Harriers) and rower (Vesta RC). At some stage between the wars the family moved to London.

WWII and Deddington Home Guard

In 1940, in order to avoid the London bombing, he took his young family to Deddington where his mother's family lived. After a brief stay in lodgings they rented the wing of an old monastery (now demolished) named Boulder Dyke in Clifton. However, he still had to keep the family business running during the week and so only returned to Deddington at weekends. He became the Platoon Sergeant of Deddington Home Guard and was then promoted to Platoon Commander when the incumbent (Lt Morris) was promoted to Major. He used to say that he hoped that if that dreadful man, Hitler, did invade he would do so at the weekend! Photographs of him can be seen in the Home Guard section on pages 69 and 70. Leslie took his family back to London in 1946 at the end of hostilities.

JOHN BOWLER

Leslie's son, John, also served for his National Service from 1950 to 1952.

He was commissioned into the Welch Regiment and went with them to the Korean War. He arrived in Korea in 1951 on the same day his father had arrived in France in 1915 and, like his father, he was a Platoon Commander and was also wounded twice. He won an MC, aged 19, through patrolling against the Chinese.

Buckingham Palace 1953 where he has just been decorated by HM The Queen

GEOFFREY BOWLER

Geoffrey was the second of the three 'Bowler Boys'. At the end of 1914 he joined the 5th Battalion, Dorset Regiment and was commissioned into it. The Battalion joined the 29th Division destined for Gallipoli.

In the uniform of an Air Commodore during WWII

They arrived at Gallipoli and on 7 August 1915 they invaded Suvla Bay on the west of the peninsular. The bay, which was about a mile across, was ringed by mountains containing fiercely determined Turks well armed with machine guns and field guns but, above all, enjoying excellent visibility of the invading troops on the beach below.

The Dorsets made three determined uphill assaults through dense, troublesome undergrowth which readily caught fire - frequently burning men alive - without capturing the heights. Geoffrey's ankle was shattered by a bullet and he, along with some 300 other wounded in the assault, were shipped back to the UK. This took many weeks and the conditions on the so-called 'hospital' ship were appalling. The bad medical conditions allowed a widespread increase in gangrene and by the time he arrived at a hospital in England it was necessary to amputate his wounded leg just below the knee.

Many would have thought the young Captain, as he then was, had done enough for King and Country, and the Army had little use for him now. So he joined the newly formed Royal Flying Corps and volunteered for balloons - a particularly hazardous activity in those days - where he became an instructor.

At the end of the war Geoffrey was demobilised and discovered, like many others, that it was particularly difficult to find suitable employment. He joined the recently formed Royal Air Force which had evolved from the Royal Flying Corps and trained as a pilot, gained his wings and became a Flight Lieutenant.

He was rapidly posted to Mesopotamia (now Iraq) to support the Army in their battles against determined and effective tribal attacks. The RAF was able to provide rapid communication, valuable information about enemy movements and give effective support for the defence of isolated British camps, if necessary, using airborne gunfire or even bombs.

About to take off in a Bristol to take part in a Hendon Air Display - probably in 1922

Geoffrey had an illustrious career in the RAF becoming an Air Vice-Marshal towards the end of World War II. His final appointment in 1944 was Deputy Commander of Maintenance Command, a most important post in view of the large size of the RAF at that time. He had a Mention in Despatches but the family are not sure when he was awarded this, maybe at Gallipoli. He retired in 1949 and had been made a CB (Commander of the Bath) and a CBE (Commander of the British Empire).

FRANK BOWLER

Frank was the youngest of the surviving 'Bowler Boys'. He joined the Royal Flying Corps, became a 2nd Lieutenant and commenced his flying training at 7.15am on 20 April 1918.

In the uniform of a 2nd Lieutenant in the Royal Flying Corps

His log book says his first flight was for 15 minutes at a height of 500 ft and 'No Control landing'. The family are not sure what this means. The training appears to have been extensive and included 'landings, low flying, formation flying and stunting, firing, cloud flying and aerial fighting.' He appears to have flown three types of aircraft - a de Havilland, an Avro and a Sopwith Pup - before he became a qualified pilot and received his wings on 12 September 1918.

2nd Lieutenant Frank Bowler was then posted to an aerodrome in France named Fienvillers which is 12 miles north of Amiens in the Somme. His first flight was for 25 minutes on 5 October 1918, during which he carried out three landings. The squadron was flying S.E.5As. They were designed and built by the Royal Aircraft Factory at Farnborough. The armaments were a .303 Vickers machine gun firing through the propeller arc and a .303 Lewis heavy machine gun mounted on the upper wing. It was capable of a maximum speed of 138 mph and could operate up to 19,500 feet.

An S.E.5A aircraft

During October he explored the front line at Bouvincourt, 16 miles south of Cambrai and he noted in his log book that he collected a bent axle on landing. He went to the front line at Le Cateau, 10 miles south east of Cambrai, flew formation with the squadron to the front line, fired on targets and 'scrapped' at the aerodrome, flew 1½ hours cross-country and was lost once on his return. On another sortie to Bouvincourt one of his fellow pilots was killed. This is the sector where the 22nd Battalion, County of London Regiment (The Queen's) were holding the final German offensive, and then drove them back, but it is unlikely that he flew over his brother, Leslie, as he was wounded early in October.

His duties also included flying damaged, but still airworthy, aircraft across the Channel to a particular airfield in Kent, to be repaired and later returned to active service in France.

The day came when Frank reported to the aerodrome workshops as usual and was told that there was just one aircraft needing to be flown back to 'Blighty' but its compass was not in working order. The sky was clear and Frank overcame his own and the workshop's misgivings and took off towards the nearby French coast. With the Channel below him he now had fewer than 30 miles to fly but before long he could see that there was thick fog ahead.

With the happy optimism of youth he decided not to turn back but once in the fog he hoped to gain better visibility by losing height. He was well aware that if he lost course he might even miss Kent altogether and fly northwards out of the Channel eventually to run out of fuel over the North Sea. He had been revving his engine intermittently as he caught glimpses of the waves below and then he saw something as he flew almost right over it - a small English fishing boat with its crew of two on deck, both looking skywards and both with outstretched arms pointing to the north. Frank waved in gratitude as he made a considerable correction to his course. The fog was lifting when he flew over Dover's white cliffs. He never forgot the experience of that day.

Frank later served in WWII and was promoted to acting Wing Commander in South Africa where he was the Transport Officer.

RON AND DAPHNE CANNING

Rob Forsyth

Ron lived in Deddington as did his father. At the outbreak of war (see page 123) he was farming for his uncle Sid.[1] This was a reserved occupation but Ron wanted to enlist so, in 1942 aged 18, he forged a letter in his uncle's name saying that he was willing to release him and Ron was duly accepted by the RAF as a volunteer wireless operator. His uncle never did understand how Ron managed to enlist.

Daphne Tucker was a London girl who also joined the RAF in 1942. She did her six months' initial training as a high-speed morse operator at Compton Bassett Radio School in Wiltshire where this picture of her group was taken in June 1943.

(*standing l to r*) **Daphne Canning Tucker - remainder unknown**

(*seated l to r*) **Lily Pringle, Margaret Morton, Joan Pittaway, unknown with dog**

Daphne then moved for further training to a radio school in the Science Museum in London where she remained until her very comfortable digs in luxury flats called Thurloe Court were hit by a V1 'doodlebug' in mid-June 1944[2] which killed some and injured many of the service women accommodated there. The flats had six floors. Girls on the top three floors had evacuated to shelters on hearing the air raid alarm but the bottom three were deemed to be safe and not required to be evacuated. Daphne was on the third floor. Daphne heard the rocket coming during the middle of the night. It exploded in a gap between the two blocks comprising the flats and pushed the front of the buildings into the road.

[1] Sid Canning's farm was a collection of fields around the village in the vicinity of Daeda's Wood, the Pest House field, Field Barns and Plumden Lane.

[2] The first salvo of V1 'doodlebugs' were fired at London on 13 June 1944. By 16 June, 73 bombs had hit London. Although they were commonly referred to as 'rockets' they were, in fact, drone aircraft driven by a pulse jet engine.

She had to be rescued by fireman using ladders to bridge the gaps across stair wells and where stairs had been demolished.

She lost everything except the pyjamas she was wearing. She was 'walking wounded' and was sent to recover at her parents' home for a few weeks. She did not return to the Science Museum but was sent to the RAF station at Chicksands Priory, Shefford in Buckinghamshire. This was an outpost of Bletchley Park, famous for the Enigma code-breaking activities during the war. Much of the work was highly classified of course and required a high degree of skill. Daphne can still read and send morse and on a recent visit to Bletchley demonstrated this by hand keying a message for a radio ham who was working there. Daphne's father was also a signals officer at Chicksands.

Another person serving at Chicksands was ... Ron Canning ... and the two of them became engaged just before Ron was posted to the Far East in June 1945.

When the atom bombs were dropped on Japan Ron's troopship was diverted to India where he served for the rest of the war. One might have thought that communication between the couple would have now become somewhat sporadic and entirely dependent on the speed of sea mail; however, Ron was working in the signal centre in New Delhi which contained a very new and secret high-speed radio teleprinter linked of course to ... Chicksands! In order to test the service and keep the line 'open' (so that other units did not steal the frequency) continuous transmission was needed. While some of this consisted of real traffic, a lot of it at night was just a tape of garbled transmissions. Ron recognised an opportunity and he and Daphne spent many hours talking, quite illegally, through the night instead of running the tape. They must have been one of the first couples to experience what we now take as a matter of course with internet chatrooms and emails.

Both of them left the service after the war and were married in 1947. In later years Ron worked as a nurseryman in Ascot, before returning to Deddington to help establish the agricultural side of the Windmill School. The RAF connection led to him taking a commission in the Air Training Corps. Various jobs followed as the family moved to Banbury and then to Heythrop Park Estate. Ill-health meant Ron retired at 60. Ron and Daphne came back to Rose Cottage in The Stile as neighbours of Rob Forsyth. He became a Parish Councillor. In the words of Reverend Hugh White 'While Ron declined physically ... he remained courteous and generous, courageous and uncomplaining under his afflictions. Those who visited him enjoyed his immense knowledge of Deddington past and his sly, gentle, well turned wit. He liked to bemoan the performance of the England Cricket Team and the inability of people to mow lawns properly; however, he was a radiant not a grumpy old man.'

Editors' note:

Ron's memory of hearing of the start of the war was published as an article in the *Deddington News* in July 2003

'It was Sunday 3 September 1939. The Vicar of Deddington, the Reverend Dr Maurice Frost had come to the end of his sermon preached from the pulpit. The choir boys in the stalls, by now a bit fidgety, suddenly heard the heavy oak door, leading to the South porch, creak and slowly open. That event alone, happening in the middle of a service would enthral the most pious of choristers. But greater things were to happen. There, in the open door, stood Police Constable Reg Butler with his helmet tucked reverently under one arm. Hardly daring to breathe the boys watched him slow march along the centre aisle towards the chancel. He seemed to will his big boots to tread as noiselessly as possible, not wishing to disturb the sanctity of the church. On the steps to the chancel, priest and policeman met and exchanged a few whispered words. A deadly hush hung over the congregation while the policeman almost tiptoed back down the aisle to the door which he closed with the greatest of care. Congregation and choir now turned their full attention to their vicar who stood head bowed for a moment, then stepped to the centre of the nave to inform his parishioners that "Great Britain is at war". Ron hardly remembers singing the closing hymn, but to this day he remembers clearly the moment in church when war was declared, and he still sees his elders who at close of service stood together in little groups fearfully speculating on a future that would change most of their lives.'

BILL COWLEY

Wendy Burrows

Bill was born in Deddington in 1925. His parents' home was in The Stile. He volunteered for the Royal Marines at the age of 17 and was called up at the end of 1942 and sent to Lympstone Barracks, near Exmouth, in Devon, where he distinguished himself by being the best all-round cadet in the squad and was presented with a red diamond-shaped badge to put on his left shoulder.

He was sent to Deal Barracks on an NCO's course where he was promoted to full Corporal, then to Towyn in North Wales, a holding camp.

Bill was selected into the Commandos and was sent to Achnakerry, near Fort William in Scotland, an estate owned by Lord Lovat, where he went through very rigorous and intensive Commando training. He was trained to look after himself.

He then went to 46 Commando Royal Marines in civilian billets in Ramsgate, then to Sandown in the Isle of Wight, where he trained for the D-Day landings and the capture of six German batteries of coastal guns at Merville, Normandy. On landing, he was up to his neck in the sea, carrying all his heavy equipment, as the landing craft could not get close enough for a dry landing. Even his cigarettes got soaked!

The German guns were captured by the 6th Airborne Division, so the change of plan was to clear the German fortifications at Luc-sur-Mer, attacking houses full of Germans. The flushed-out Germans were then escorted to the beach and sent to England as prisoners-of-war.

Bill's Division was then joined up with the Canadian 3rd Division and were sent to capture the village of Rots. They advanced at 5am and cleared the Rue river valley of Germans, suffering no casualties, fought through a wood and came to a cornfield in front of Rots. The Germans had machine guns along a hedge the far side of the field in front of houses. The order came to fix bayonets and to advance through the cornfield, firing rifles. Twenty-two men died in this action and many were wounded and taken prisoner by the Germans. Those left held the village all night and were 7 miles in front of everyone else. Next morning they were told to retreat, to prevent being cut off. They lost their second-in-command, Major John Lee.

The Canadians buried 122 Germans. Bill took two prisoners: Hitler Youths of 17 or 18 years. They withdrew back to the original front line, not having eaten, washed or slept for days. They were then ordered to join the 6th Airborne Division, holding the left flank of a bridgehead against Germans for two to three weeks. Canadians and Americans were on the right flank. They fought their way down to Trouan, which they held for a few days, being shelled each day and night.

It was at Trouan that Bill's luck ran out and he was badly injured. This was in August 1944. He was put on the top of a jeep on a stretcher and taken to the Trouan Casualty Clearing Station. He had seven pieces of shrapnel in him, one of which lodged in his brain. His right shoulder and right hip were shattered and a knee and forearm were badly wounded. He was taken to a Field Hospital near the beach, a large marquee with a red cross on the roof. He was flown to Benson and taken to the Radcliffe Infirmary in Oxford, but there were no beds, so he was taken in an ambulance train to Bath Royal United Hospital for an operation to remove the shrapnel from his brain. He was in a coma for seven weeks and was invalided out with a pension of £2 per week.

He was on crutches for three years. He worked at Wells and Son (Ticky Wells') draper's shop in the Market Place for 30 years, then in Field's, a draper's shop in Banbury. He was the caretaker at Deddington School for the 15 years up to his retirement.

NORMAN DRAKE

Norman Drake

Norman is in the centre row, sixth from the right

'My call-up papers stated that I should report to Whittington Barracks near Lichfield on 3 December 1959. I was to join the Worcestershire Regiment as Private 23755030 Drake N. As I was Welsh, and Welsh rugby was quite good at that time, I was immediately recruited into the camp rugby team. This was a bonus as it saved me from many tedious marches and cross-country runs. In addition I was also asked to play for Lichfield Town Rugby Club which went down well with my superiors.

Halfway through the 10 weeks' basic training the whole intake was transferred to the Staffordshire Regiment, which meant that, when we had completed the basic training, the regiment was to be posted to Kenya. I was fortunate to be transferred to the Royal Army Educational Corps and was sent to Beaconsfield, the headquarters of the Corps, for a further six-week course. When we completed the course we were all promoted to Sergeants and given our postings. I volunteered to go to Malaya even though it was still under a State of Emergency.

My transfer to Malaya was very interesting as I was to travel by ship. The *SS Nevasa* was a cruise ship and it was with the wives and children of commandos, who were travelling ahead of us on the commando carrier *HMS Bulwark*, that we were to make the journey. An added attraction was that I was invited to join the Entertainment Committee which helped to lighten the nearly four weeks we were at sea. The route took us through the Suez Canal stopping at Aden and Colombo on the way to Singapore.

My posting in Malaya was to Ipoh, close to the Cameron Highlands, a hot-bed of communist terrorists. When the British Government declared that the emergency was over, a large passing-out parade was arranged to take place in Kuala Lumpur, the capital of Malaya. However, it was still felt by the military that the terrorists would attempt a major attack to prove that they were not beaten. The result was that the Ipoh garrison was put on full alert to repel any such attack. Fortunately it never came.

I was then posted to the Army Boys' Trade School at Nee Soon Barracks in Singapore to teach military map reading. It made a pleasant change to teach boys who wanted to learn, compared to the hardened soldiers I had taught in Ipoh. The time in Singapore proved very interesting with little sign of any unrest amongst the population, although there were occasional outbursts. To ensure the safety of the women and children living in married quarters outside the camp, we carried out manoeuvres at night practising their safe removal into the camp.

On Saturday mornings we had the RSM's drill parade. This included all ranks from Sergeants to 1st Lieutenants. For those of us who were quite good at drill it gave us opportunities to impress the RSM, which certainly came in handy from time to time.

Once a year for two weeks the school was moved to an island off Singapore where there was no running water or electricity. As I had been given medical approval for shaving only with an electric razor, I did not shave for the whole two weeks; this photograph was taken during this period. However, as soon as we returned to Nee Soon, the RSM made it very clear, in a one-to-one brief conversation, that I should enter the sergeants' mess only when shaven.

The main event of my stay in Singapore was meeting a young woman called Joy Poole, who subsequently became Mrs Joy Drake.

I returned to the UK and Beaconsfield on 1 September 1961 and was demobbed one week later. I still keep in touch with the Royal Army Educational Corps and am listed in the bi-annual journal *Torch* as the only sergeant retired member.'

ROB FORSYTH

Rob Forsyth

'When I made a decision, aged 16, to apply for entry to Dartmouth, it was only 10 years from the end of WWII, two years from the end of the Korean War, National Service was still in force and bookstalls were still full of war-time stories. I could not think of anything more exciting than to join the Senior Service. I was right. The Cold War became very "hot" for the submarine service in which I was to spend nearly my entire naval career.

I first went to sea in *HMS Appleton*, a coastal minesweeper. I then joined *HMS Chichester* which was an air defence frigate destined for the Far East station but the 1961 Kuwait/Iraq crisis intervened and we were dispatched to the Gulf. My career path changed completely after four months because my Captain had decided that my character and skills were well (better?) suited to the submarine service and I was to start training in September 1961. This was a bit of a surprise but sounded exciting. In any case there was no room for objection - once you received the Queen's shilling you did what you were told! I was landed in Mombasa to make my own way to Nairobi to catch an RAF trooping flight home a week or so later.

The training school was located at Gosport in Fort Blockhouse, originally built during the Napoleonic wars. It became the home base for submarines when the first RN submarine, *Holland 1*, entered service in 1901. It is now a museum.

My first submarine was *HMS Auriga* (March 1962) attached to the 6th Submarine Division in Halifax, Canada. *HMS Auriga* had just completed a refit in UK so the first few months were spent "working up" in the Clyde, Scotland, before deploying to Halifax. Nonetheless I managed to find time to get married before we sailed.

This period marked the real start of the Cold War. The stand-off between the USSR and USA over the installation of Soviet missiles in Cuba occurred just before we sailed across the Atlantic. It was to affect all our lives from then on. During the two years of being based in Canada we would regularly go north to practise patrolling beneath the arctic ice where the Soviet submarines often operated.

1965 to 1968 was spent serving in *HMS Sealion* based at Faslane in Scotland, taking a specialist sonar course in Portsmouth and then back to Scotland on the shore

responsible for the operational efficiency of all submarines. With Russian ships and submarines passing our front door, so to speak, every day we were very pre-occupied in tracking their movements around the Atlantic seaboard.

Hong Kong: traditional farewell to our Captain, in a rickshaw pulled by his officers

In 1968, after barely a year in Scotland, the family (two children by now) and I had to pack our bags to fly to Singapore because I had been appointed as the 1st Lieutenant of *HMS Cachalot*. These were the dying days of Empire before the services pulled out of their East of Suez bases. Although the Indonesian Confrontation had ceased three years previously the emergence of the Chinese Navy as a major force gave us new intelligence tasks.

In 1969 I was selected for the Submarine Commanding Officers' Qualifying Course - aka "The Perisher". This six-month course is a prerequisite for command of a submarine. Failure means your submarine career "perishes". I was appointed in command of *HMS Alliance* in January 1970 at Devonport. One's first command is a daunting experience but we were too busy chasing Russian submarines or practising attacks against our own forces for me to have much time to think.

Periscope photograph showing the track of a torpedo heading for the target.

The target ship is 2 ½ nautical miles (nm) away but the visible bubbles extend only a few hundred yards. The target and torpedo tracks co-incided at 1 nm and were assessed as a 'hit'. The torpedo was set to run about 25 feet below the keel of the ship to avoid a real hit!

Two years in command was followed by nuclear training at the RN College in Greenwich to prepare me for joining *HMS Repulse* (1972). This was one of the four Polaris missile-carrying submarines based on the Clyde. The Polaris Force was required to have one submarine at sea at all times, ready to launch its 16 missiles within 15 minutes of receiving the order to fire. This required each submarine to have two crews (Port and Starboard) alternately taking it on patrol. I was to be the Executive Officer of the Starboard crew. A patrol lasted from four to eight weeks and during that time there could be no contact of any sort between the crew and their families, other than that each crew member could receive a short weekly message (known as a "family gram") of 40 words. It was a very difficult existence for the crews' families who did not know when the submarine was sailing or would return. No outgoing signals of any sort could be made even for, say, a death on board. This is still the case today with the Trident Missile Force.

I was promoted to Commander in 1974 and appointed to run the "Perisher" for two years. Being a student on this course five years previously had been a challenge; being in charge of it as 'Teacher' was even more so.

In April 1977 the family (now three children) came to live in Deddington which is not very far from Priors Marston, Warwickshire, where I had grown up. The original plan was to stay here for a few years during my next appointment, which was to command a nuclear "Hunter Killer" submarine *HMS Sceptre,* but somehow we never found any reason to move away.

I joined in time to see *HMS Sceptre* launched. The two years that I then spent at sea on her I can only describe as exhilarating. All I can disclose at present is that we were a very fast, deep diving submarine designed specifically to counter the Soviet submarine threat at a time when the Cold War was at its height.

Barrow-in-Furness 20 November 1976

Bigger and better Russian ships and submarines were appearing in the Atlantic every year. Our task was to track them so that we could counter-attack immediately if hostilities started. We therefore spent a lot of time trailing very closely behind them wherever they went to observe how and where they operated; this included such exciting manoeuvres as passing under Russian ships' hulls to take periscope photographs of propellers and other underwater equipment.

At the end of my command time I was sent to a desk job in the Ministry of Defence (July 1979). Everyone has to do their penance time here and I was no different. While I found it interesting, I was fretting to get back to sea but my chances of doing so were going to be much reduced because the Navy was about to lose a large number of ships; and so I decided to opt out before it became a sad place to be. In January 1981 I stepped "ashore" for the last time as a serving officer and embarked on a commercial career which led me to Ferranti, Racal and Westland before retiring from corporate life in 2000.'

PETER AND PAULINE FRANKLYN

Rob Forsyth

25 March 1944 on the occasion of their engagement

At the outbreak of war, Pauline Savill was a 13-year-old at Campbell School in Beacontree, Essex. Pauline and her 10-year-old brother Terry, together with a large number of pupils, were evacuated to Deddington in 1939. Her parents had impressed on Pauline that she should ask for both of them to be billeted together. She tried her best to convey this to the billeting officer, Helen Loveday, in the evacuee reception room on the top floor of the British Legion building, but Terry was still sent to live with Mr and Mrs Finch near the library while she was sent to stay with Mr and Mrs Course; it was thought that Pauline could help them with their three children. They lived at the Nook on Victoria Terrace. Alan Course was the brother of 'Doughie' Course whose bakery was at the corner of The Stile and New Street - and was where Sid Berry worked before the war. Within a short while Alan moved to Oxford so the billeting officer had to find another home for Pauline. In the event she thinks this was one of the best things that happened to her as she went to live with Mr and Mrs Shirley in Philcote Street. They had no children but clearly loved having Pauline as a surrogate daughter for the next few years. Uncle Harry and Aunty Carrie's house became her second home for the rest of her life.

Pauline went to school first in the village and then walked or cycled to the College for Further Education which had been evacuated to North Aston Hall. The College lent pupils a cycle which they could keep after two years; sadly the College went back to London three months short of Pauline's two years!

She was not short of friends because so many others from Campbell School were in the neighbourhood - some in Deddington and others in outlying villages - but she developed new friends through a club for young people that was run at Forester's Hall in The Tchure and the Holly Tree Club owned by Mrs Collins, where she met a young Hempton lad called Peter Franklyn who was 16 and working as a butcher's boy at Boltons opposite the British Legion building. They clearly hit it off from the start and quickly became sweethearts. In July 1942 Peter was old enough to enlist. Pauline, accompanied by her visiting father, walked with Peter to Aynho Halt to wave him off to join the Royal Armoured Corps. For the next two years they met only when he came home on leave. Pauline's parents got to know him quite well because her mother had come down from London with her other younger daughter, Diane, and they lived with the Shirleys as well for 18 months.

Peter went to France with his tank regiment after D-Day and moved with it through Europe into Germany with the advancing Allied Forces as they liberated Europe.

Peter 'somewhere' in France or Belgium

This carefully posed photograph shows him with his tank crew and some very relieved (literally) locals - including children on top of the tank. Peter is third from the right, kneeling. He obviously could not write in detail or very often but did send regular messages on Army Field Service postcards ...

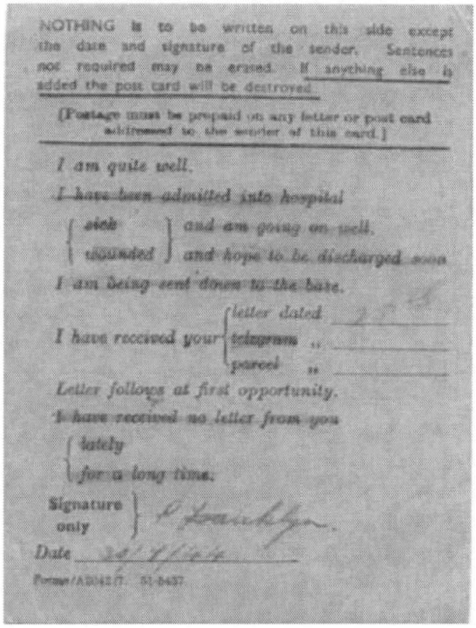

NOTHING is to be written on this side except the date and signature of the sender. Sentences not required may be erased. If anything else is added the post card will be destroyed.

[Postage must be prepaid on any letter or post card addressed to the sender of this card.]

I am quite well.

~~I have been admitted into hospital~~

~~sick~~ / ~~wounded~~ ~~and am going on well.~~ ~~and hope to be discharged soon~~

~~I am being sent down to the base.~~

I have received your letter dated ~~telegram~~ ~~parcel~~

Letter follows at first opportunity.

~~I have received no letter from you~~ ~~lately~~ ~~for a long time.~~

Signature only

Date

... which told Pauline that he was alive and well, but not a lot more.

After she left the College, Pauline went to work in the Fire Guard office in Banbury. This office had the responsibility of managing the fire watchers who were on duty every night in case of air raids. Terry went back to London in 1944 aged 14 to get a job; most evacuee boys did the same thing because 14 was the normal school-leaving age as their parents generally needed the money. Terry then worked for the same company – Mercantile General Insurance - for the next 44 years.

Three weeks before the end of the war Pauline went home and immediately got a job in the Treasury in Whitehall working in the office that awarded honours and medals – many of them (too many) posthumously. Because of where she worked she was able to witness the Victory Day parades from Earl Mountbatten's offices looking on to Whitehall which was an enormously exciting place to be. She lived at home for the next two years until Peter was demobbed in early 1947. They were married on 22 March 1947 and came back to Deddington to live with Uncle Harry and Aunty Carrie again. Peter got a job in Tucker's grocery store (now Otters Restaurant) and their married life continued happily with he and Pauline running Mr Bolton's newspaper business from New Street. Peter went back to butchering after a while but Pauline kept the newspaper business going for 16 years. Mr Bolton owned the Post Office which was subsequently bought by Ken and Edith Garrett.

After some years they moved to Aynho then again to Banbury where Pauline now lives; however, Peter's family are still represented in Deddington by his niece, Mary Tompkin, and her family who continue to be a great help to Pauline to this day.

THE GARRETT FAMILY

Rob Forsyth

Home Farm, Clifton: late 19th century photograph

Home Farm was the family home of Francis Beesley Garrett (1843-1912) and his wife, Mary, with their children, Ruth (b 1886) and their son Frank (1891-1955).

Son Frank served with The Oxfordshire Yeomanry (Queen's Own Oxfordshire Hussars) during WWI. The Hussars were a volunteer cavalry with a large number of recruits from farms recruited specifically because of their ability to ride.

A Field post card from France on 9 April 1915. Francis is on the right

In 1914 he married Florence Rose Walker (b 1889 in Islington) who was a nurse at the John Radcliffe hospital. She was known as Rose.

During WWII Frank was in the reserved occupation of farming and so he joined the crew of the Deddington Royal Observer Corps post (see photograph p.72).

In his ROC uniform

Frank and Rose had four sons and a daughter. The eldest children - Frank, Tom, Ken and Mary - all went off to the war. John, who was the youngest (b1923), was categorised as in a 'reserved occupation' running the farm with his father. He continued to do this after his father died in 1955 in a tractor accident. Tragically John died aged 50 in a car accident

FRANK GARRETT

Frank and Rose's son, Frank, was a tail gunner in 467 Squadron, Royal Air Force Volunteer Reserve (RAFVR), based at Bottesford. He died on 18 August 1943 age 26 on a raid on Peenemunde (p.55).

A relative of one the other crew members recounts 'The crew came together in March/April 1943 and were involved in 19 major, highly dangerous, operations during that summer. They were all to meet their fate at Peenemunde on the night of 16-17 August. Several of their bodies were recovered from a lake at Peenemunde, although the body of Adam Brand, the air gunner aboard, was washed up on the shores of Poland, 20 miles away.'

Frank Garrett

MARY WEBB (née Garrett)

Mary joined the RAF in 1942 and trained and worked as a telephonist at RAF Honiley, at Wroxhall in Warwickshire.

TOM GARRETT

Clifton School 1926. Tom is in the front row, third from the right

Tom joined the local regiment, The Oxfordshire and Buckinghamshire Light Infantry, in 1939. He did not like talking about his war experiences - which he said were pretty tough - so his family have no knowledge of his own involvement other than they know he served in the Far East. Records show that it was the 6th Battalion that went to the Far East and subsequently served on the Arakan front during the advance down the west coast of Burma in 1944-45, fought at Akyab in 1944 and at the main Japanese base at Tamandu in 1945. How much of this Tom participated in himself we do not know but, as all of these engagements involved very fierce fighting, one can fully understand and respect his reticence.

Tom 'somewhere' in the Far East

KEN GARRETT

Ken served in the RAF Volunteer Reserve from 1942 to 1946 driving low loaders (known as 'Queen Marys') which recovered crashed aircraft. From 1943 to 1946 he was stationed overseas in Alexandria, Egypt and Basra, Iraq. He met his wife, Edith Minty, who was a WAAF, while they were both doing driver training.

In Amyra Egypt 1945

EDITH GARRETT (née Minty)

Edith served in the WAAF from 1942 to 1945. She trained as a driver at Morecambe where she first met Ken. She then deployed to a Beaufighter airfield in Lincolnshire as an ambulance driver. She has very clear memories of the sky being packed full of aircraft for the 1,000 aircraft bombing raids. She also recalls seeing a Beaufighter burst a tyre on take-off and cartwheel exploding into a hangar. Despite the ever-present sadness of death and injury, she nonetheless remembers her time in the service as being exciting and great fun; youth had the ability to rise above the terrible circumstances that surrounded air and ground crew equally. After a couple of years she moved to York to Command HQ driving staff cars.

Ken and Edith were married in Chesterfield then came to live in Deddington where they ran the Post Office store for many years until they retired in October 1985.

The occasion of Ken and Edith's retirement from the Post Office store with sons Andrew (*l*) and Peter (*r*)

TED HARPER

Rob Forsyth

Albert Edward (Ted) Harper was born on 13 September 1920 in New Street, Deddington. He was brought up by his grandparents William and Alice Harper.

William Harper

Alice Emily Harper

He attended the local village school, followed by a place at Banbury Grammar School. On leaving he went to work in the office at the Shell Mex depot in Banbury.

When World War II broke out on 3 September 1939, he was eager to enlist. He went along with Clive, a close friend since childhood, and they both enlisted with the Royal Warwickshire Regiment. He became Private A E Harper, No. 5383360.

He carried with him a miniature leather-bound *Book of Common Prayer* and a picture of his grandmother, Alice Emily, whom he always referred to as mother.

After the completion of basic training, his regiment was part of the ten infantry Divisions which made up the British Expeditionary Force deployed to the Franco-Belgian border, following the invasion of Poland.

In May 1940, his regiment was amongst the troops which were cut off, forced to retreat and ultimately trapped on the beaches at Dunkirk. During the evacuation of

Dunkirk between 26 May and 4 June 1940, when every available ship and boat was utilised, 330,000 men were rescued. The larger ships were unable to anchor too close to the shore, so soldiers would swim out to them. He was swimming out to one of these ships with Clive, who was not such a strong swimmer, when they were captured by a German U-boat.[1] They were landed and then forced marched into Germany, being ill-treated en route by beatings and starvation.

The soldiers were sent to Prisoner of War (PoW) Camps by railway. He and Clive were sent to Stalag XX-B PoW camp in Malbork, Poland. His family received a postcard from him, confirming he was a PoW, that his PoW number was 50404 and that he was in Stalag camp No XX-B - and nothing more.

Ted is marked with an X in this very rare camp photograph taken in Stalag No XX-B

During his period as a PoW he was part of a work force doing agricultural work on local farms. Whenever possible he would take the opportunity to steal and eat raw eggs for the protein, not forgetting to hide the shells. He tried to smuggle eggs back into the camp for other PoWs but rarely succeeded.

[1] U-boat or E-boat? Ted's recollection was that he was captured by a U-boat i.e. a submarine; it is arguable, however, whether Admiral Doenitz would have risked one of his valuable submarines to be on the surface in shallow water and so unable to dive to evade attack. There are no records of such in the RN Submarine Museum or in the Royal Warwickshire Regimental Museum. However, there were a number of German high-speed, motor torpedo E-boats operating in the area throughout the evacuation. Dare one suggest that, to an army man, the distinction between a small surfaced U boat and an E boat may not have been absolutely clear. But this is not to state that his recollection is incorrect and it has sparked off further research into this interesting event.

When it became evident that he spoke German fluently he was used as a translator. Over time his health, along with others, deteriorated badly: partly because the Germans withheld Red Cross parcels. He was admitted to the camp hospital with a severe case of pleurisy, the treatment for which included using leeches, and gave him a life-long phobia of hospitals.

In late 1944, the British and American Allied Forces advanced through Europe. The Germans retreated and evacuated PoW camps in the East, including Stalag XX-B, in order to take the PoWs away from the advancing Allied Forces. These enforced marches have been labelled the Death Marches. The PoWs were weakened and emaciated by ill-treatment and poor diet. Many were forced to march for 86 days covering 500 miles, dressed only in rags against bitter winter weather and with virtually no food. Stragglers were shot. He was one of the lucky survivors; however he was devastated that his friend, Clive, died on this march. It was reported that when the Allied Forces rescued the PoWs, they resembled those liberated from concentration camps.

After being liberated, he was flown back to England and was admitted to Walton Hospital in Liverpool as a patient – he is marked by a cross in the photograph below. It was during this time, that he met, and would later marry, Staff Nurse Ceridwen Jones (on his right) who had trained and then qualified as an SRN at Walton Hospital during the war.

When he recovered he was assigned by the army to be a military presence on hospital wards where German PoWs were being treated.

After he was demobbed from the army, he returned to Deddington and resumed employment at the Shell Mex depot, where he was promoted to foreman. He married Ceridwen Jones on 13 July 1946. They were allotted the first post-war council house built in Deddington (No.1, The Paddocks) because of the number of points they were awarded for their war service.

He bore no ill-feeling towards the German people, in fact Hermann Kruse, who was a German PoW, used to do some gardening for him at No.1. Their two children, Michael and Marian (who provided me with most of this information and the photographs) were born while living in Deddington. A work promotion meant the family moved to the outskirts of Coventry in October 1955 where their second son Graham was born in 1956.

Ted worked for Shell Mex for most of his working life before taking voluntary redundancy in 1969. He spent his last few years working for the Standard Triumph Motor Company in an administrative capacity. He died on 1 April 1976. Ceridwen is a resident in a home in Coventry.

DENYS HEYWOOD

Denys Heywood

1966 Hawaii - embarking in a Vulcan bomber for the next leg of a round the world operational sortie

In March of 1944 I was in my last year at boarding school and asked permission to go and volunteer for flying duties, my intention being to join the Fleet Air Arm. I went to Burton-on-Trent but, after a fruitless search for the Royal Navy's Recruiting Office, I came across the Royal Air Force's Recruiting Office and volunteered for aircrew. Having been put on the Reserve I entered Caius College, Cambridge, as an undergraduate in the autumn of 1944. I was called up in March 1945 and started training as a pilot, flying Tiger Moths and Harvards.

I got my 'Wings' in 1946 and then went to an Operational Training Unit flying Spitfires. A posting followed in 1947 to 32 Squadron flying Spitfires in Palestine, our main role at that time being to search for Jewish illegal immigrant boats trying to get to Palestine.

In the cockpit of a Spitfire

After the Mandate ended, the Squadron moved to Cyprus and I was posted to Habbanya in Iraq, where, after a short spell as an ADC I joined 249 Squadron flying Tempests. At the beginning of 1949 the Squadron moved to Egypt to join the two other Tempest Squadrons forming 324 Wing.

Tempest Mk VI

Another pilot and I were detailed to fly the Squadron Harvard aircraft from Habbanya to Deversoir in the Canal Zone in Egypt. However, we had engine problems en route and eventually crash-landed on a lava-coated mud flat in Transjordan.

We were then surrounded by fierce-looking armed tribesmen who turned out to be members of the Transjordan Frontier Force, and who were happy to guard the badly damaged aircraft. We were taken to a nearby oil pipeline station manned by English engineers, and were very well looked after by them until we were picked up by an aircraft and flown on to Deversoir.

20 May 1949

A little later in 1949 I had brake problems on landing, the Tempest somersaulting and landing upside down just after touch down. My left hand was crushed between the windscreen and the gunsight and I lost some fingers plus other minor damage. Surgery and a brief spell in hospital at Fayid followed, after which I returned to flying duties on the Squadron.

In the middle of 1950 I was posted back to the UK and joined 247 Squadron at Odiham in Hampshire flying Vampire fighters.

The Venom was developed as a fighter/bomber from the Vampire which was the RAF's second jet aircraft. The first was the Meteor which carried out early test flights from Enstone and Barford airfields near Deddington.

Venoms in aerobatic formation

Later in the year I completed a course to become an instructor on gunnery and bombing. A posting followed in April 1952 to the Operational Conversion Unit at Stradishall, Suffolk, as a Flight Commander Instructor on the Gunnery Squadron flying Meteor fighters. During this period I had a brief detachment to the Fleet Air Arm flying Sea Furies on *HMS Illustrious* and also two Light Fleet Carriers, *HMS Triumph* and *HMS Glory*. A further detachment followed to 56 Squadron flying

Meteors from Waterbeach, near Cambridge, to assist them with some flying problems they were having. Then another brief posting to another staff job at Headquarters Fighter Command at Bentley Priory.

In May 1954 I joined 112 Squadron at Bruggen in Germany as a Flight Commander flying the Sabre which was an American aircraft and the first operational supersonic aircraft in the Royal Air Force. This period was the beginning of the Cold War. In April 1956 the Squadron was re-equipped with the Hawker Hunter (background).

In June 1956 I was promoted to Squadron Leader and posted to Celle in Northern Germany to command 94 Squadron flying Venom fighters. Celle was only about 20 miles from the East German border, and Communist MIG fighters could be seen patrolling their side of the border – a very hot Cold War. In September 1957 94 Squadron was disbanded in company with many other squadrons when the then minister decided that manned aircraft were not the right way to go, with emphasis being put on rockets.

After a Staff Course in 1958 I was posted as the Staff Officer responsible for Flight Safety at Headquarters 13 Group, which controlled the northern fighter group. This posting lasted until the end of 1960 and I then attended Staff College at Bracknell during 1961, followed by three years at the Air Ministry in London. During this time a very good friend, who trained with me, was the Chief Instructor at the Empire Test Pilot's School at Farnborough, and he arranged for me to fly many interesting aircraft.

Vulcan bomber

In the middle of 1964 I was promoted to Wing Commander and started refresher flying via Jet Provosts, Meteors, Canberras and finally the Vulcan at the Operational Conversion Unit at Finningley in Yorkshire, followed by a posting to command 617 Squadron,the Dambusters, at Scampton in Lincolnshire. It was the height of the Cold War, and we carried the Blue Steel Ballistic Missile with a megaton warhead. At that time every V-Bomber squadron had one aircraft permanently ready to go, and frequent Quick Reaction Alerts (QRAs) were practised by the stand-by crews.

Our operational target was Leningrad, now called St Petersburg, and our route would have taken us north to near the Arctic Circle and then south at low level through the northern end of Norway and across Finland. We would not have had enough fuel to return home after the attack but this fact was not really an issue because there would have been nothing to return to. Some rather vague survival areas were designated, but I do not think any of us really considered this fact seriously for obvious reasons.

A 'Lone Ranger' training sortie over Labrador and Alaska. Blue Steel weapon is in the bomb bay but it is fitted with a dummy warhead

In 1967 I was appointed as the Supreme Allied Commander Europe's (SACEUR) representative on the Joint Strategic Planning Staff, which was located at USAF Strategic Air Command Headquarters at Offutt Air Force Base, Nebraska, USA. Whilst there I was promoted to Group Captain but remained in America until the end of 1970.

The first half of 1971 was taken up with the Air Warfare course at Manby in Lincolnshire. Then some refresher flying on the Vulcan and a conversion course to the Hercules prior to an appointment as Group Captain Flying at Akrotiri in Cyprus. This was the biggest flying base the RAF had in the world and was home to six squadrons - two Vulcan, a Lightning, a Canberra, a Hercules/Argosy and a Whirlwind Helicopter Squadron; this was a super flying time in a super location.

The appointment ended in August 1973 and a posting home followed, with a course lasting five months at the Royal Naval College, Greenwich. At the conclusion of this Senior Officers' War Course I was supposed to remain at Greenwich as the RAF Director. However, a difference of opinion with the naval element of the Directing Staff resulted in the cancellation of this appointment and a posting as the Senior Officer in charge of Administration at the Bomber Group Headquarters at Bawtry, near Doncaster. And there I remained until I retired in September 1976.

The following is a list of the 44 different aircraft I have flown. Many aircraft had variants of the same type so I have put the number of variants flown in brackets.

Ansons (3), Argosy, Auster (2), Balliol, Beaver, Canberras (2), Cessna 410, Cherokee, Chipmunk, Comanche, Dakota, Devon, Harrier, Harvard, Hercules, Hunters (4), Hurricane, Javelin, Jet Provost, Lancaster, Lightning, Lincoln, Lockheed T33, Lodestar, Meteors (6), Mosquitos (2), Oxford, Phantom, Piston Provost, Prentice, Proctor, Sabres (2), Sea Fury, Sea Prince, Spitfire (2), Sycamore, Tiger Moth, Valetta, Vampires (3), Venoms (2), Ventura, Viscount, Vulcan, Whirlwind.'

Editors' note:

Denys died in October 2010. At his funeral his brother-in-law recounted that his peers gave Denys the nickname of 'Heinz 51' because of the very large number of aircraft he had flown. In fact he flew 62 different aircraft including variants. Flying a 'variant' was, of course, not just a matter of climbing into a cockpit and looking to see where the handbrake was; it required the pilot to be formally trained and qualified before he flew it. From my own discussions with my contemporaries who were naval airmen we think that this very extensive list of aircraft flown has to be some sort of peacetime record - if one can call the Cold War peaceful.

STEPHANIE HIGHAM

Stephanie Higham

Third Officer Pigott and Buster

'When I was nine my father resigned from the Army[1] and decided to live on the Continent because of my mother's poor health. We went to Vienna for two years where we had governesses and then moved to Rome and always went to Carinthia in southern Austria for the long summer holidays. As children we spoke German rather than English - much to the annoyance of our parents. In those days, girls were not supposed to have careers so that when war broke out, my only qualifications were fluent German, Italian and French.

When there was an appeal by the Admiralty for German speakers I enlisted and was sent to Queen Anne Mansions for an interview. After a German test I reported to the Royal Naval College, Greenwich on 11 May 1941. Our course lasted two weeks and we had to learn the English and German naval ranks, parts of ships and other naval subjects. As well as this, we did squad drill, kitchen fatigues and learnt naval history and organization. This was the time of the fire raids on London and we had to spend every night in the cellars, sleeping on mattresses on the floor packed in like sardines. We were then kitted out and sworn in as WRNS.

[1] Stephanie comes from a military family. Her grandfather was Lieutenant Colonel Charles B Pigott CB DSO (1859-97), 60th Rifles and 21st Hussars. He was in the column sent up the Nile to rescue General Gordon but it arrived too late. He died age 40 of yellow fever. Her father was Major Berkeley Pigott (1894-1982) 17th/21st Lancers. She was married to Commander Walter E Higham (1897-1990) who served in the RN Submarine Service from 1918 to 1933.

On 16 May 1941 I was posted to Winterton on the east coast with two other Wrens. We were billeted in private houses and our landlord and his family slept in their Anderson shelter whilst we had their room. Everyone except me passed out as an Acting Petty Officer, Special Duties,[1] but I had to return to Greenwich on 19 June and retake the test which, luckily, I then passed.

Our social life was hectic and we seemed to go to parties every night, often coming back to go on night watch. Our job was to listen for E-boats that might attack our convoys. Unfortunately we did not hear much but during the day time we picked up a mass of German radio transmissions (R/T) coming from the Russian front which we took down and sent to the War Office. The locals thought that we projected pictures of ourselves on to a screen to lure the E-boats ashore. On 1 July the First Officer in Charge visited us and read the riot act; in future we must wear uniform and be in early. I don't think this had much effect on our life-style!

All the parties and boy friends came to an end when I was transferred to Fairness, North Foreland, Kent, on 3 December. I arrived with five pieces of luggage and a dog to a decidedly frosty welcome. What a change it was - just like going back to boarding school. No late nights, no parties and no social life - apart from a game of golf with the other Wrens. We had to spend a night on duty in an isolated tower on the cliff edge, at the end of a phone, so that if any traffic was picked up by the watch keeper, we could swivel our aerial and take a bearing and thereby, with a cross bearing, fix the location of the transmitter. My little dog Peter was in great demand to spend the night in the tower as it was really quite frightening being by oneself and not knowing if the approaching footsteps were a German Secret Agent who had scaled the cliff from the sea or an amorous Home Guard! The dog always remembered his time with the Wrens and greeted anyone wearing black stockings with great joy.

On 4 January 1942 I was sent to Greenwich for a refresher course and then to Dover where we worked under the castle in a tunnel next door to the plotting room, and lived in Dover College. Dover was shelled throughout my time there and the siren would not sound until after the first shell dropped - all a bit nerve-wracking especially when a large piece of shrapnel came through the wall of our brick shelter just above our heads. Luckily no one was hurt but the shelling did mean our off-duty nights were often disturbed. The work was much more interesting and we could always look into the plotting room and see what was going on in our area. One summer's day two of us went for a bathe at Abbotscliffe. There was no one else there and it was not till later that we were told that the beach was mined.

[1] The WRNS Special Duties (SD) Service was created in the summer of 1940. Its task was to intercept enemy naval wireless traffic and to pass the information to the Naval Intelligence Centres. It formed a part of the larger 'Y' Service providing an enemy signals interception network serving the Royal Navy, Army and RAF. The SD Service was set up and guided by Lieutenant Commander Frederick Marshall RNVR. Serving Wrens, with knowledge of German, were called upon to volunteer and were trained by Marshall and his staff at Greenwich Naval College and later at RNTE Southmead, Wimbledon. Most of the Wrens were then posted to wireless interception stations along the south and south east coasts of England. Approximately 400 Wrens passed through the naval 'Y' Service during the course of the war.

On 25 October 1942 I was transferred to Command HQ in Portsmouth. Our quarters then were in the lovely old Manor (now Council Offices) in Fareham. We had our own panelled mess room and a lovely garden to relax in. Every day we went to Fort Southwick on the top of Portsdown Hill with a view of the whole of the Solent and then proceeded to descend a flight of a hundred steps into the underground tunnels in the chalk. We worked 24 hours on and 24 hours off which meant that for one of the duties we were on duty in the office all night and the other time we did the afternoon, then went to bed about 9pm in a bunk in one of the tunnels and after breakfast we did the morning watch and then changed over at lunch time. Whilst on duty we came up for a breath of fresh air and had our meals in a Nissen hut inside the walls of the old fort. Our office was just one door away from the main plotting room of C in C Portsmouth - the next door office being occupied by a Staff Officer, Commander Peter Scott, who allowed us the use of his bunk in his cabin when he was not there and, in exchange, we sewed his buttons on for him! The tunnels were cut into the chalk and lined with corrugated iron which made them very damp and when the ventilation broke down it was very hot and airless.

We received traffic intercepted by Ventnor and Portland Bill stations. This mainly consisted of reams of four-letter code which we had to send to Station X (Bletchley Park) by teleprinter. There was also a certain amount of three-letter code which was a straight substitution code and I spent many an hour trying to break it and send the results to Station X who then sent us the correct decode. This code was used by the local naval establishments, harbour masters and lighthouses in the Channel Islands and on the French coast. They would ask for the lighthouse to be switched on and off at set times from which, according to which lighthouse it was and what time, we could deduce if E-boats were planning a sortie or a coastal convoy was expected. Very occasionally R/T traffic emanating from E-boats was picked up. It is only now when the secrecy period has ended that I realise that the four-letter codes were the naval Enigma code. It was a great disappointment to us all when the two German battleships, *Gneisenau* and *Scharnhorst*, steamed up the Channel in complete silence and undetected.

In January 1944 I went before a selection board for a commission. As it turned out I was not allowed to leave Portsmouth to go to the Officers' Training Class until after the invasion had taken place. I was sent to Ventnor and Portland Bill to meet the Wrens we talked to daily on the phone and to see how their stations worked. I was also sent for a week's course to RAF Kingsdown where we learned about German aircraft R/T from our WAAF counterparts. When we saw the conditions they lived in - a Nissen hut with 20 beds, one iron stove to heat it and the loo two huts away - we were glad to be Wrens.

In April the troops started to arrive along the coast and soon every verge and lane was crammed with men and vehicles. From the beginning of April not one of us working in the Portsmouth Command was allowed to leave the area and no one was allowed in.

On 9 May I was told that I would be going to Officers' Training Course the following Saturday. This was, not surprisingly, cancelled on the Friday. The invasion night proceeded, from our point of view, peacefully with no R/T or three-letter code messages to tell us that the Germans knew what was happening. When we came up to the top of the downs after the night watch the sea was empty instead of being tightly packed with ships. The traffic we picked up became more interesting with reports from the local garrisons, harbour masters etc. and long messages of exhortation from Hitler for all to die at their post for the Fatherland!

On 12 August 1944 I was sent to the station at Southwold where I promptly went down with tonsillitis and was more of a nuisance than a help to them. I was just about well enough to get to my Officers' Training Course at Framewood Manor, Slough. The course successfully completed, I was sent to Greenock as Assistant Admiralty Berthing Officer - a job I knew nothing about and had to be taught by the duty Wren. The living conditions were terrible; a Victorian villa with 12 of us in one room and, as I was the only watch keeper, I could never get any sleep in the day time.

After having had my tonsils out, I was sent as Assistant Duty Staff Officer to C in C Western Approaches at Derby House, Liverpool. This was a very interesting job as all the Atlantic convoys and naval ships were controlled from this HQ. We were visited by Churchill and the King and Queen. I was then drafted to Freddy Marshall's establishment at Wimbledon (footnote p.150) and met many of my old friends there. We were given the job of translating captured German documents - highly technical ones such as the working of the V1 and V2, the effect of frostbite and medical experiments, etc. We used large technical dictionaries to look up all the unknown words and only hoped that if there was a choice of words we picked the right one and that the scientists, engineers and doctors, etc. could make more sense of what we wrote than we did.

We heard that some of us would be able to go to Germany as interpreters and I applied to go and was sent on an interpreter's course for four weeks. Then, after a medical examination, I was given numerous inoculations and kitted out as if I was off to the North Pole. We flew to Hamburg and then proceeded by car to Flag Officer Schleswig-Holstein's HQ at Plon. The Royal Navy had taken over a very modern German training barrack situated on a lake. One block was the Wren Officers' Mess. I shared a large room with another Wren Officer and our two large dogs. We were thoroughly spoilt being about one girl to four men and a choice of parties to go to every night with champagne and caviar!

I worked in the Admiral's interpreter's office where we translated messages to and from the German Admiral who had been left in charge of the German fleet in Kiel harbour. There was one day when things nearly went wrong. Under the peace treaty, a third of the German Navy had to be handed over to the Russians and when the time came to do this, the German sailors mutinied and refused to go. Our Admiral had to send some of our own sailors with the German ships to guarantee that all their crews would be returned to Germany.

I was able to act as interpreter at one of the War Crimes trials and at various meetings. Life was hard work during the morning with riding, sailing, shooting or skiing most afternoons and parties at night. Unfortunately this came to an end on 23 April 1946 when I had to return home to be demobbed.'

JOHN HODGES

Wendy Burrows

1943

John volunteered for the Royal Armoured Corps in June 1941, aged 19. After six weeks training at 57th Training Regiment he joined the Royal Armoured Corps at Warminster, where he was promoted to Lance-Corporal. He was one of four who went to Sandhurst in February 1942, was commissioned into the East Riding Yeomanry, and underwent further training at Newmarket, Bovington Camp and then East Lulworth, Dorset, a holding camp, before being sent to Egypt. He was given command of 30 men, all available for posting to active service. About 4,000 men left Liverpool, taking three months to arrive at Twefik, Egypt, via Bahia Blanca, South America, and Durban, South Africa.

He was installed at RAC Base Camp at Abassia Barracks, near Cairo. After an interview he was accepted into the 3rd King's Own Hussars, which were then recovering from taking part in the Battle of Alamein in October 1942, and were now re-forming at Aleppo, 300 miles north of Cairo and a three-day train journey away. He was sent on a series of courses back at Cairo in tank management and gunnery. On the train journey back to Cairo, the train in which John was travelling was hit head-on by a train heading in the opposite direction on the single track. The carriages were telescoped and many men were killed.

John, near death, woke up in the wreckage and called for help. A rescuer eventually found him and he was taken back to Aleppo, badly injured with a crushed chest and broken leg. He somehow pulled through and spent six months in the British Hospital at Sidon.

In September he rejoined the regiment which was now fully trained and waited to go to Italy. He was sent in an advance party of 20 men to Italy, landing at Taranto. He was given command of a troop of three tanks and started the trek up through Italy. The Germans were employed in defending, so it was all-out fierce fighting for

200 miles all the way up past Monte Cassino to the Northern Line close to Arezzo. Many men were killed, including Germans. John was the only officer in the squadron of 12 tanks who had not been wounded or killed. In July 1944 he was awarded the Military Cross for his actions.

From September to the end of 1944 he was non-operational and the regiment was withdrawn from Italy in January 1945 (some men had completed four years service) and sent to Palestine. John was sent to Syria on patrols in Homs, a town where local Arabs were engaging the French. He then returned to Palestine. In November 1945 his patrol car, on duty late at night in teeming rain during a riot in Tel Aviv, hit a concrete road block. John was in the back of the vehicle and was thrown violently forward, but his right foot was caught and he suffered such a severe ankle dislocation that his foot was facing backwards.This terrible injury caused him to be invalided out of the army and he was eventually treated at Cardiff Hospital, near his home at Abergavenny.

John came to live in Deddington in July 2006 having been diagnosed with Parkinson's disease. His son, Christopher, had lived at Aynho for many years and wanted him to be nearby. John previously lived in Yorkshire and, prior to that, he was Deputy Head of King Edward's School, Birmingham.

Editors' note:

John has recently written a book *An Account of the Wartime Experiences of John Henderson Hodges,* which has been privately published with the assistance of Wendy Burrows and is now available from Deddington Library.

LES LEGERTON

Wendy Burrows

Les was one of two Deddington men (Len Plumbe was the other) to serve with the 14th Army in the Far East - the 'Forgotten Army' as it was known. He served in the 7th Battalion, The Worcestershire Regiment. His war experiences - including having only one pair of glasses for the whole of his time in India and Burma - were recorded in two articles.

The Soldier**:** This extract is quoted from *The Soldier* magazine, May 2004, and is in Question and Answer style. It is reproduced here by courtesy of the magazine.

How did you arrive in Burma?

'After training in Bombay we arrived at Dimapur where we could see all of the parachutes that had been dropped to keep the Royal West Kents supplied.'

Did you have any close shaves with the enemy?

'On one occasion in the jungle I heard some chickens and I thought I'd have one and went towards the sound. It wasn't chickens at all, but Japanese soldiers. They nearly caught me - there was always the danger of Japanese snipers who would hide themselves up trees.'

What was the food like?

'We lived on ration packs, usually tins of beef or mutton, and bars of chocolate. We ate whatever we were given.'

Was the jungle tough?

'It was hard. In a place nicknamed Death Valley there were huge mosquitoes and biting flies.'

Banbury Guardian: This second extract is quoted from an article dated 4 March 2004 'Heroes of Kohima recalled' and is reproduced courtesy of the *Banbury Guardian*.

'Leslie Legerton, 87, of Levenot Close in Banbury was a Private with The Regiment. He was told before Dunkirk that his eyesight was too bad for him to fight, but afterwards was called to go to India.

He said: 'I thought to myself: If I lose my glasses I've had it, because I couldn't see anything without them. Then when we went to Dimapur the first thing that we had to do was have a shower and I stepped on my spare pair of glasses and broke them. So all through the conflict I only had one pair of glasses.'

Les's machine gun carrier

Les left the Army in 1946 and moved to North Aston and later to Banbury. He died in 2005.

THE BATTLE FOR LEROS - TED JOHNSON AND BILL MINNEAR

Rob Forsyth

Following the capitulation of Italy as an Axis power, the Dodecanese island of Leros was occupied by British forces on 15 September 1943. The Battle for Leros began with some 50 days of continuous daylight German air attacks from September until German air and sea landings took place on 12 November. The battle ended four days later with the capitulation of the Allied forces to a numerically superior enemy on land and, more critically, in the air where no fighter cover to counter the Stuka bombers was provided. The occupation, then loss, of Leros was heavily criticised at the time as a poor strategic decision by Churchill. A list of those RN ships and Army units lost in the battle appears below.

The majority of the surviving British Forces were taken prisoner. They faced the grim prospect of spending the rest of the war in a German PoW camp. Senior officers were taken off the island by flying boats; more junior officers and their men were crammed into ships and taken to the Port of Piraeus on the mainland of Greece and then marched through the streets of Athens - the Greek crowd were largely sympathetic to the British - before being tranported in cattle trucks some 1,400 miles to Germany by way of the Balkans with very little food and no sanitation facilities - and in winter.

Naval ships lost or damaged

6 destroyers sunk: *HM Ships Dulverton, Eclipse, Hurworth, Intrepid, Panther, His Hellenic Majesty's Ship (HHMS) Olga*
3 submarines sunk: *HM SMs Simoon* and *Trooper, HHMS Katsonis*
10 lesser warships sunk, including six motor launches and two landing craft
1 cruiser crippled beyond repair: *HMS Carlisle*
3 cruisers heavily damaged: *HM Ships Aurora, Penelope* and *Sirius*
4 destroyers heavily damaged: *HM Ships Hursley, Penn* and *Rockwood, HHMS Adrias*
4 submarines heavily damaged: *HM SMs Torbay, Unseen, Unrivalled* and *Unsparing*

Army units involved and subsequently captured

234 Infantry Brigade HQ
4th Battalion, Buffs (Royal East Kent Regiment)
1st Battalion, King's Own Royal Regiment (Lancaster)
2nd Battalion, Queen's Own Royal West Kent Regiment
2nd Battalion, Royal Irish Fusiliers (Princess Victoria's)
3 Battery less one Troop 1 Light Anti Aircraft Regt RA
Troop of 25 pounders. These guns had been captured once before at Dunkirk and had been given to the Italians. They were later found again on Samos
Detachment 9 Field Company Madras Sappers and Miners
47 Defence Issue Depot (DID) Royal Army Service Corps (RASC)
161 Field Ambulance Royal Army Medical Corps (RAMC)
570 Advanced Ordnance Depot Royal Army Ordnance Corps (RAOC)
Detachment Long Range Desert Group (possibly squadron strength)
Detachment Special Boat Squadron

TED JOHNSON

Ted as a PoW

Ted enlisted in the Royal Ulster Rifles (RUR) in September 1940. He was commissioned in June 1941 and posted to the 2nd Battalion, The London Irish Rifles, who were then in the 47th London Division defending the beaches in the Littlehampton area. In June 1942 he was posted to the Middle East where he arrived just prior to the Battle of El Alamein. Being of Irish nationality, he was further posted on to Malta GC where the 2nd Battalion Royal Irish Fusiliers (The Faughs) needed officer reinforcements. As an RUR commissioned officer, he was attached for all purposes to the Faughs, a nickname in use since the Napoleonic Wars deriving from their unpronouncable Gaelic motto "Faugh-a-Ballagh" meaning "Clear the way". They were part of the Allied forces that occupied Leros.

Ted's platoon had faced a counter-attack and beach landing by German troops. In the subsequent action the platoon had to retreat in the face of an overwhelming force; for his part in this Ted was awarded the Military Cross. In the end the Germans overran all the Allied troops who were forced to surrender. This was largely due to the lack of air cover which allowed the Germans to bomb the island every day for several weeks largely unopposed. The whole British force were made PoWs. Ted published a book, *Island Prize, Leros 1943* (Kemble Press) in January 1992 and has also recounted his PoW experiences in an article in the December 2007 edition of the *Deddington News*:

'Christmas 1943: We, a group of prisoners, had recently completed a 14-day cattle truck journey from Athens to Moosberg, near Munich, where the touring accommodation was not ideal (40 hommes - 8 chevaux was the sign on the outside of the wagon). Now, on 23 December, I was one of a random selection leaving Moosberg for another camp. We were told journey time would be two days but at the end each prisoner would have his own room! Travel accommodation improved to a train of hard seat coaches. During the usual body search before we left I lost my issue field dressing to the "ferret". I hope the small compass hidden in it was of use to the eventual finder. Our guards for this journey were more amiable than those we had known before and I was able to buy a loaf of bread from one of them for 10 cigarettes (Red Cross, no doubt). We arrived at our end station Lukenwalde, near Berlin, having come via Leipzig and Halle in the late evening of Christmas Day.

After the usual "Raus, raus, schnell, schnell" we marched through the snow towards the lights of a camp on the horizon. The welcome we got was no different from any other prison we had so far encountered: wire, grim-looking Wehrmacht soldiers and the predictable rough-looking German Shepherd dog with handler. The inevitable body search took place again. This time all personal possessions were taken and with Teutonic efficiency were listed in detail. Toilet articles were given back and we were permitted to keep the clothes we wore. We were all issued with a palliasse cover, two wood pulp blankets, one bowl, one knife and one spoon. By now the outlook was worrying! Next, we were moved into a long low building which contained individual cells. I now saw the truth behind the news about each officer having his own room! No explanation was given as to why or for how long one was being given such personal attention, but by now, since capture, we were becoming used to the devious methods of the "detaining power". It dawned on me that I was in solitary confinement and that this was a novel way to celebrate Christmas.

There was no meal that evening but a redeeming feature was that my cell was warm. This personal hovel in which I spent the next 10 days measured 15ft x 7ft 6 inches (5 paces by 2½ paces) and contained a bed with straw palliasse, a table and a stool. The metal door had the traditional peep hole, the small window was barred and high out of reach. Twice daily, what passed for food and drink was brought into my cell by a Russian slave labourer under armed escort. It was from one of these unfortunate walking skeletons that I learned why I was incarcerated - interrogation. As the days went slowly by, I thought a lot about my predicament and the events which led to this situation, and how only three years ago I was a schoolboy enjoying the freedom of my native Ireland. I sang a lot to keep my spirits up and tried to keep fit by pacing up and down my cell and running on the spot. I devised a game by rolling up my socks into a lump and playing catch against the cell wall. My release came during the tenth night at about 2am when I was taken under escort to confront a smooth-talking German officer in a brightly lit office. He spoke good English with a Canadian accent. The gist of the questioning, which was conducted in a calm conversational atmosphere, was to get confirmation of facts he already knew. I hope the answers to his questions added little to his already detailed knowledge of the events leading up to the recent operation in the Aegean, in which we had come off second best. During the interview he noted that as a citizen of a neutral country I was in the British Army - why? Finally he suggested that I help myself to be released by agreeing to join a German Free Irish Battalion which, he said, already included some of my comrades. He did not look surprised when I declined. Later I found very little evidence that such a unit ever existed. At the end of this very mild session I was released from solitary confinement into a barrack room where I met some of my colleagues whom I last saw on Christmas night and who had gone through a similar experience. A day or two later, when our whole group had been through the ordeal, we were escorted to a more permanent abode: Offlag VIIIF in Czechoslovakia.'

After the war, Ted elected to stay in the army and obtained a regular commission in the Faughs. He was adjutant of the 2nd Battalion in Palestine 1945-46 and later Adjutant of the Army Apprentices School at Arborfield 1948-50.

He spent three years on secondment to the Gold Coast Regiment in West Africa and later became Adjutant to the Queen's University, Belfast, Officer Training Corps from 1954-56. He retired from the army in 1958.

BILL MINNEAR

Bill was a Company Quarter Master Sergeant in The Duke of Cornwall's Light Infantry. He served in Crete and India before being part of the force that occupied Leros. Following the surrender of Allied Forces, Bill and his unit were, like Ted Johnson, transported to Germany to be incarcerated in three different prison camps (Stalags VIIA, XVIIA and VIIIA) over a period of 15 months. Finally, in the early months of 1945, they were force-marched across Germany from east to west at the hands of German guards as an evacuation manoeuvre from Stalag VIIIA which lay directly in the path of the rapidly advancing Russian armies. Despite being told by their German captors that there would be rail transport at the end of a two-day march to the rail junction of Bautzen, it did not happen. The march then became a long struggle for survival for over 400 miles. This was in the worst months of winter, with cold winds, privation and hardship taking their toll. Some died. Some tried to escape and at least one prisoner was shot dead doing so.

Two months later they arrived in the western zone of Germany with everyone in extremely poor condition. The war, however, was drawing to a close with Russians approaching from the east and Allied forces from the west. The column then arrived in the vicinity of units of the American 9th Army as they drove towards the River Elbe - the last natural obstacle before the final drive to Berlin. Overnight the German guards disappeared - although some were captured quite quickly by the Americans. Most of the prisoners were in a dreadfully emaciated state which was not improved by too much rich food eaten too quickly. Repatriation to England followed in two stages via Brussels. Bill finally reached home in late April 1945 in a physical condition from which he took a very long time to recover.

THE MALCHER FAMILY

Rob Forsyth

William John Eide Malcher and his wife Mary came to live in Deddington in 1910 to look for work on the railways.They had a large family from which two sons, Henry (b 1878) and Jack (b 1898), served in WWI.

HENRY MALCHER

He enlisted as a Private in The East Yorkshire Regiment. He was discharged wounded and awarded the Silver War Badge on 13 July 1915. This badge was intended to absolve the wearer of any possible charge of 'shirking' military service.

JACK MALCHER

He enlisted as a Private in The Gloucestershire Regiment in August 1916 as soon as he turned 18. He went with them to France. He was full of stories about the front - including shell holes big enough to lose a gun carriage and its horses in and keeping his food in a billy can to stop the rats stealing it. He was similarly full of stories about his posting to India on re-enlistment in the Regiment on 16 June 1919 - which was the day after he was discharged from war service. He spent some time in the Khyber Pass which was the source of many of his stories! His birth certificate, service documents and a few of the postcards that he brought home from India can be seen in the gallery on Deddington OnLine. His volunteering to re-enlist may have been because his father had returned to London after his wife died and Jack had no real home to go to. He was discharged for the second time in June 1921 when he returned to Deddington where he worked for the rest of his life in Hopcraft butchers,which subsequently became Powells.

In 1922 Jack married Mary Smith of Deddington. Mary's two brothers, John and William Smith, had served in WWI (p.49). The family lived in 'Sunnyside' on Castle Street which is still called by the same name. During WWII Jack was a member of the Royal Observer Corps and he can be seen in a photograph in the article about the ROC on page 72. Jack and Mary's daughter, Mary, married Jim Morris from King's Sutton who joined The Grenadier Guards (p.101). They had three sons who served - Bill, Denis, and Steve (in order of age).

Bill **Steve** **Denis**

BILL MALCHER

Bill was the same age as, and a good friend of, Bill Cowley. They both tried to sign up together while under age but were sent home until they were 17. Bill Malcher then joined the Royal Navy as a Telegraphist while Bill joined the Royal Marines.

He served on *HMS Hargood* which was a US Lend Lease destroyer employed on Atlantic convoy escort duties much of the time. His widow, Edna, says that he talked very little of his experiences but she recalls him mentioning that when Action Stations were set the Telegraphists were locked into the wireless office. He saw a lot of ships torpedoed in the Atlantic and men in the oily burning water and also had terrible memories of D-Day when *HMS Hargood* assisted with the landings on Omaha Beach; here they saw hundreds of bodies floating out to sea from the beaches.

At the end of the war he spent time at *HMS Merlin*, a Fleet Air Arm airfield at Donibristle in Fife, Scotland until he was demobbed.

In 1948 he married Edna whom he had met while dancing at the Dome in Brighton in 1944. They lived in Deddington and Bill worked for the Council. Edna became the librarian three months after the Library was opened in the presence of J R Tolkien in 1956. They moved to live in Banbury shortly after their third child was born in 1967.

DENIS MALCHER

At the outbreak of war Denis was only 13 but joined the Home Guard until he was 18 (1944) when he signed on for the Royal Army Ordnance Corps in which he served until he was demobbed in 1947. Most of his time was spent at Donnington in Shropshire but latterly he was closer to home at Bicester.

STEVE MALCHER

Steve was just too young to serve during the war like his brothers but he wanted to join the RAF so joined the Air Training Corps and the Royal Observer Corps. He then became a National Serviceman from 1946-49 serving in the RAF Regiment which was charged with defence of airfields and became a Leading Aircraftman (Ground Gunner). He was stationed in Hamburg, Germany throughout his time. He was seconded for some of the time to Berlin as an aircraft loader during the Berlin Airlift.

PEGGY PACEY

Rob Forsyth

Peggy joined the Territorial Reserves in 1938 and transferred to the RAF in 1939 until war end. She worked her way up through the ranks via administrative duties then trained in vehicle maintenance. She took a more advanced course while a Corporal to become a fitter and an instructor. She recalls frequent air raids and, on one occasion, of diving into a trench with a couple of friends. An unexploded bomb fell into the far end of the trench and one of her friends said 'I think it must be a gas attack bomb' but the other friend said 'the gas is entirely human and let's get out of here!' She then became a staff car and despatch motorcycle rider while with 3 Group Bomber Command in East Anglia.

Escorting (l) and meeting (r) HRH The Duchess of Gloucester on a visit to RAF Feltwell in 1941

Peggy in a DUKW amphibious vehicle crossing the Severn

Peggy also helped with the water testing of the DUKW[1] which was a British design that had been rejected by the UK armed forces; however a prototype, while being displayed to US forces, rescued some coastguard men from a sandbank in bad weather and was instantly put into production in the USA and then supplied to the British under the Lend-Lease agreement.

On another occasion she was required to collect Flying Fortress spare parts on her motor cycle from London and deliver them to an air base in East Anglia in February - a trip she remembers very clearly. On arrival she was called in to meet Winston Churchill who was visiting the base and had heard of her winter journey. She was later apppointed as Transport Officer in command of a large depot at Hartlebury in Worcestershire. Peggy's sister, Elizabeth Maud, was also in the WAAF and became a cypher officer stationed in Washington, USA, for most of the war.

Peggy has lived on Park Farm since she bought it in 1961 and is well known as a breeder of thoroughbred horses as was her uncle, John Bletsoe of National Hunt fame, who farmed it as a previous owner.

[1] DUKW is not an acronym but the manufacturer's code for a type of Military wheeled amphibious landing-craft: D means 1942, U means utility (amphibious), K means all-wheel drive, W means two powered rear axles.

LEN PLUMBE

Rob Forsyth

Len is second from the right, 'somewhere' in the Far East

Len did his training as a flight mechanic (engine fitter) in Bristol specialising in Bristol 14 cylinder radial sleeve valve engines. His first appointment was to Bomber Command air station RAF Stradishall in Suffolk where he worked on Wellington (two-engined) and Stirling (four-engined) aircraft. He then moved many times around 3 Group Bomber Command airfields - Waterbeach, Wratting Common and Marham amongst them.

It took 50 ground crew and seven aircrew to turn round a bomber returning from a sortie early in the morning to have it airborne for the next night's sortie over Germany. The top of a Stirling's engine was 22 feet from the ground and, in winter on an east coast airfield, this could give you frostbitten fingers working on cold metal. Sometimes they hardly slept for days at a time when big raids were in progress.

Many aircraft were badly damaged and could not make it back to base; in which case Len would be part of the support team that was dispatched to find, recover or salvage them. Len recalls that the racecourse at Newmarket was a favourite place for belly landing aircraft with damaged undercarriages. No doubt race tracks were similarly useful elsewhere across the country.

In 1944 he embarked on *SS Athlone Castle* and spent six weeks travelling to Bombay in convoy. The ship was crowded with troops and clearly was not much of a pleasure cruise. He does not know which route they took because they did not call in anywhere and every time they looked at the sky the sun was in a different place due to the zigzag courses they steered as an anti-submarine measure.

His unit went by train to Chittagong in East Bengal (now Bangladesh) and from there they set off down the east coast of Burma as a mobile Beaufighter support unit in a variety of places as far south as Cox's Bazaar.

Admiral Mountbatten had decreed that, in order to defeat the Japanese, Allied Forces would fight through the monsoon period - previously it had been thought too wet to do this. Len's unit was flown into small strips cleared in rice paddy fields which would be a runway for one or two days before they moved on. They were a long way from any civilisation and never quite sure on which side of the front line they were, and so supplies were dropped in canisters kicked out of the doorways of low-flying Dakotas operating out of Dum Dum in West Bengal, India. A very important part of the supply was cigarettes; not so much for Len and his mates to smoke but because they were the only 'currency' that villagers valued in return for good information on the whereabouts of Japanese army units.

Mosquito aircraft suffered from being made of wood. Termites could eat them and wood rot quickly set in in the monsoon rains. Wings sometimes fell off because of the combination of both!

The standard practice in the UK had been for support parties to be dispatched on trips of up to six days to find crashed aircraft; in the jungle the same routine was followed with the addition of compasses in their kit together with silk maps (paper maps were useless in rain) and 'compo' rations for food. The latter were almost inedible once you had consumed the bar of chocolate and the small can of bully beef; the rest was sawdust. So they also had to learn what was edible from the forest. All the usual jungle problems existed - getting lost and very small snakes being the worst. When an aircraft was found it had to be destroyed by fire and all sensitive instruments removed to stop the Japanese getting them.

Nearly everyone contracted malaria at some time or other and it took Len several years to get over it on his eventual return to the UK.

Len remembers that finding clean water was a major problem because the Japanese had poisoned the water in surrounding villages and even the drinks in shops and bazaars. The problem was solved by using Japanese PoWs to drink the water first!

Len with Abdul the water fetcher

When Rangoon fell to Allied forces his unit was brought back to Madras in India were they were re-outfitted in new 'jungle greens'. There were two sizes - big or bigger! They embarked on a New Zealand ship, *SS Tamaroa*, and carried out a beach landing on 5 August 1945, rifles at the ready, at Port Swettenham on the east coast of Malaya. The first atom bomb was dropped on Hiroshima next day and Nagasaki three days later.

The long road home began with a move to Kuala Lumpur, then to Singapore after its liberation. Some of the Japanese aircraft remaining on the base were those used for Kamikaze missions.

Len finally went back up into Malaya to the RAF camp in Butterworth before returning home by ship to be demobbed in 1946.

He continued using his engineering skills in civilian life; working at Hopcroft Holt Garage until he opened the Archway Garage (now Deddington Dental Practice) on New Street in 1957. He ran this until he retired in 1991. He also provided his expertise to a private collection of vintage cars.

DERRICK ROBBINS

His recollections of being evacuated to Deddington

Derrick Robbins

Derrick Robbins' 'Recollections' were originally published as a series of articles in the *Deddington News* and subsequently on Deddington OnLine. We are indebted to him for this unique and fascinating addition to the history of Deddington. What follows is almost verbatim with some additional editorial comments by Rob Forsyth in square brackets.

'I was born 6 October 1928 in East Dulwich, South East London. An early memory is of an evening in November 1936 when my mother got me out of bed and we walked a short distance to the top of Forest Hill to watch the Crystal Palace burn to the ground.

My mother was called Edith and my father Frederick. I had two sisters older than me, Constance and Lillian. I started school at age four and attended the same building, Friern Road School, until Friday 1 September 1939. I had a happy childhood - but all of this changed with the outbreak of the war.

I was at the tender age of nine on 1 September 1939 when at exactly 11am on that fateful Sunday morning the Prime Minister Neville Chamberlain spoke those unforgettable words "I have received no such undertaking so a state of war exists between Great Britain and Germany". So began the phoney war. Immediately afterwards, the "take cover" warning sounded and my father, mother, two sisters and I stood around the kitchen table with our gas masks in our hands waiting for whatever was about to happen. The all-clear sounded shortly after and I remember thinking "Oh well that's it, it's all over thank goodness." The Sunday roast was forgotten and was burnt to a cinder.

Evacuation to Deddington by train. Next morning we were all up early and I packed my little suitcase with my prize possession, my bus conductor's outfit, one set of change of clothes and Dad took me to Paddington Station in Praed Street, bought me a ticket and put me on the 9am Bicester slip train on platform 1 and off I went alone in the world to Aynho high level station. There, the guard blew his whistle, waved his green flag and off puffed the little push me-pull me train to Banbury, leaving me standing there with no one, not even a dog, in sight.

No porter, so what to do with my ticket? Oh well, down the sleep slope to the roadway and off through Clifton. I knew the way I had done it many times alone without any trouble to my aunt and uncle's home [the Ells], Tower View in the Bullring. So began my stay in dear old Deddington.

Market Place in the 1940s

School. The next morning I was taken to the house next door, to the post office where kindly Mr Harmsworth lived, the headmaster, and registered to attend the local village school on the corner of Banbury Road and Earl's Lane. Life there was good, easy-going, but my bubble was burst when I was informed that I had passed the scholarship exam and had to transfer to Banbury County School across from the Horton General Hospital, now Sainsbury's, I believe. So, equipped in my maroon blazer, cap with real silver badge and school tie, I joined others on the Oxford bus each day, boys upstairs, girls downstairs, never the twain must meet. Each lunchtime we would walk down town to a building in the Market Place where we were given a hot meal. After we would walk down to the station where a train carrying wounded troops would stop on its way somewhere up north. One Thursday, market day, an unannounced German bomber made its appearance and rudely dropped a bomb near the main signal box. War had come to Banbury.

Life at Tower View [now Wirral House] was so different from at home in London. In those days most folks would bathe once a week in a tin tub, usually Friday evening, and change their clothes. Here, every evening I had to jump into the largest bath I had seen. I should mention that Uncle Chris Ell had lost a leg in WWI and was now one of the finest boot and shoe repairers anywhere. Consequently, my weekday black boots and my Sunday brown boots were always in good repair.

One thing folks today would notice was the complete lack of motor vehicles. Dr Frost had his little Austin 7 which he always drove flat out, Johnsons had their lorry, and Arthur Canning his delivery van. Every one else walked, took the bus or if lucky had a horse, or horse and cart. Even the local bobby had to pedal a pushbike around his patch. I'll never forget though the fish and chip van which toured the local villages and stopped outside Tower View every Thursday and Saturday evening. Oh the great smell, the great taste, nectar for the Gods wrapped in newspaper! No rules and regulations in those days.

Aunt Emily - companion to Lady Bowes-Lyon. Aunt Emily Tooth [sister to Uncle Chris Ell] was educated at a prestigious school where she became very friendly with a girl of her own age. When they left school Emily went to live with her friend, Lady Elizabeth Bowes-Lyon [later to be Queen Elizabeth] becoming her paid companion. Also in the employ of Lady Elizabeth's father, the 14th Earl of Strathmore, was Arthur Horace Tooth, the family's chauffeur. Emily and Arthur fell in love and married. They enjoyed living in many lovely homes generously supplied by the Earl. Before WWII they lived in a Chelsea mews flat, but when WWII started they moved to a large house in Dartmouth. While I was stationed in Exeter in the Army after the war I would visit them. Arthur was a born prankster. When I arrived at Dartmouth station he would be waiting there beside the Earl's old Daimler resplendent in his old-fashioned uniform. He would call out so that everybody could hear: 'Over here, my Lord; her Ladyship has tea ready on the lawn!' We would then drive off and he would burst into fits of laughter. The old Daimler, by the way, was one of those cars where the passenger seats in the back were enclosed, while the driver sat in the open. I imagine there was some form of protection against wet weather. Communication between front and back was by way of a speaking tube.

Food was rationed, just enough to survive. Luckily living in a farming community had its benefits such as a large allotment up the Hempton Road. Also most folks had chickens and some had pigs as we did. The Ministry of Food and Agriculture kept a sharp eye on the limited amount of animals you kept, or thought they did. A large percentage of the animals had to be sold to the government at rock bottom prices. However there were ways around that rule and I for one never went hungry. In fact when I went home for short periods I would be carrying black market food. Who would suspect a schoolboy of breaking the law? Tower View had a large cellar and my uncle was an avid home wine maker. There sat very many barrels of wine and all sorts of wine was bubbling away in cauldrons all around. Ten o'clock every morning we would gather around the kitchen table and drink the health of the service men. Even me at my young age.

Air Raids. Not to forget the dreaded black-out. No lights to be shown after dark. 'Put that light out' became a famous cry especially when the drunks were being thrown out of their local boozer. Also we had *double* summer time which meant that on a clear evening during the summer months it could be almost daylight at midnight. Never could understand why they screw around with nature. With great forethought my uncle arranged for an air-raid shelter to be built in the back kitchen garden. This was a great playhouse for my cousin Chris and me. My aunt, being a glutton for punishment, took in two boy evacuees but they did not stay long. Country life was too quiet for them. The government paid 4s 6d each week per evacuee [Government records say 10s 6d]. In autumn, school would be closed to allow us kids to help with the harvest or whatever. I would help my Uncle George

Clark's father who had a small-holding up the Hempton Road. Potato-picking was back-aching work for £4.

I was woken up one late evening and we all rushed off to the air-raid shelter. What was going on I know not but we sat there for about 20 minutes before going back indoors. Next morning I found out that two bombs had been dropped in a field just south of Deddington but they had failed to explode. What happened to them I do not know but they could still be there.

Uncle George was in the Royal Observer Corps which had a look-out post in the middle of the allotments off the Hempton Road. Sometimes I accompanied him and I became quite proficient in aircraft recognition. Although I was under age I joined the Air Force Cadets. We met once a week either in the village school or in a large barn-like building behind the big house in the Bullring. In charge of us was a fiery Scot by the name of Jock McCutcheon who lived next door to Miss Weaver in the Market Place. [There is no record of a Jock McCutcheon serving in WWI but two McCutcheon men did post-war National Service in the Army and Air Force.]

Church. My aunt never went to church but insisted that I did. Church to a young lad was boring, so I played hooky. She found out and took me to the Reverend Dr Maurice Frost and I became a reluctant choir-boy. We were paid one half penny for every time we attended church and that is how I became a millionaire. I was chosen to attend a two-week voice training course at the College of Church Music at Tenbury Wells, Worcestershire, under the tutelage of Sir Sidney Nicholson. It was somewhat monastic but I enjoyed it. I went with Mr Coles' (known as Lamby Coles) son. Dr Frost was a kind gentleman but if he thought that we boys were not giving his sermon our complete attention, he would march us out of the choir stalls and sit us in front of him with the congregation. I took piano lessons from the wonderful Miss Lilian Weaver who lived next door to the Co-op in the Market Place. That house was full of cats. I would do work for her in her back yard. I loved her.

The Army came to Deddington and were billeted all over the village. Some moved into the block in the Bullring and is now, I believe, apartments. The Bullring was made to be a perfect barrack square and drill took place every morning. This corresponded with an imitation battle dress my mum sent me. Uncle Chris made me a wooden replica of a Lee Enfield rifle complete with detachable bayonet. I used my little pocket money and bought a tin hat from Woolworths in Banbury for three shillings and six pence and made belt, puttees and ammunition pouches out of stiff brown paper. So dressed I would stand outside the house and copy the commands of the Sergeant Major, much to the amusement of the troops. This was too much for Sergeant Major smarty pants, and he yelled as only a Sergeant Major can "go away you 'orrid little man" or words to that effect. This I reluctantly obeyed like any British soldier would.

The Home Guard on parade: is Derrick the small boy in the background?

Family. My grandmother, Sarah Bull, was a rum one. She always wore a black dress down to the floor and as a child I thought she had no legs because I never saw them. She wore a man's flat cap and an apron at all times, even when out shopping or going to church. Granny Bull used the daily newspaper as a tablecloth, it saved washing and could be used each morning to light the cooking range. On my visits to her I was delighted to read *Rupert Bear* from the tablecloth. Grandma died just before war broke out at home in the Horsefair and Grandpa moved into a room at Tower View. Also Joe Ell, Uncle Chris's father, moved from Oxford into another room. I never gave it a thought at the time but both gentlemen kept to their respective rooms and never joined the family for meals, not even on Christmas Day. They both spent every day at their beloved allotments, come rain or shine. Each smoked a tobacco called thick twist which had to be cut up with a very sharp knife. When lit it smoked and smelt like hell. Each evening Job Bull would join Joe Ell in his room and they would put the world to rights as the whole room became thicker and thicker with the evil-smelling tobacco. I had to take them each a bowl of soup at supper time and could not get out of the room quick enough.

I mentioned the air-raid shelter my Uncle Chris had built. Well he also had a smaller and less luxurious shelter built for the two elderly gentlemen, his logic being that we might very well survive a near miss from a bomb but would be asphyxiated in a confined space if they joined us, puffing away on their foul pipes which hardy ever left their lips. These two gentlemen were as different as chalk and cheese but they got on famously. Grandpa Bull was rough and ready and he and I would kick a ball about in the large back yard. Joe Ell however was refined, smartly dressed and when indoors always wore a scull cap. He paid me a penny to clean his boots once a week. Grandpa never cleaned his boots. He was kind to me and I loved him. Thinking back before the war I would go with him, during the summer break, to work and sit on his lap and guide the horse pulling the binder, or reaper, at harvest time. Then we would go gleaning to help with food for the chickens.

Each of the two elderly gentlemen had an oil-burning stove in his room. One extra cold night Grandpa Bull pushed the stove under his bed to warm it up. Beds were higher in those days. Fortunately my aunt came in or else the whole house would have burnt down. My Aunt Win worked at the Banbury aluminum factory as a cook. My cousin Chris Clark, who lived at Tower View, needs some explaining. He was the son of George and Win who lived just down from the then police station on the High Street. Two rooms up and two down and each one was no more than six feet each way. Tower View was a better environment. Their landlord was Tom King who charged them two shillings and sixpence rent. Each Sunday young Chris and I would go with Uncle George for a long walk around Deddington. I learnt a lot about nature that way and of course it was good exercise.

Other evacuees. The two boys who stayed at the Ells for a short while were cousins and also evacuees. One was about my age and the other younger. I do not recall the name of the young one but the other was Ronnie Hale. They came with a large group from East London but were tidy and well cared for. For what it is worth, there was a mother and two young girls who came from London and lived in a cottage in Clifton. I do not remember names but they were the only ones in that village. The girls went to Deddington School and would bring their packed lunch meal and picnic at the Ells. We would play in the yard until it was time to return to school. This was early in the war.

Johnson's timber yard fire in 1941. I remember with clarity the night my Aunt Mill Ell got me out of bed and took me down through the Market Square to watch the horrendous fire. Deddington at the time only had a very old hand-cranked trailer pump which had no effect on the fire. I remember vividly going the next day down to the yard to see the utter devastation caused and to witness the horrid smell of burnt timber. The delivery lorry was just a pile of twisted metal giving proof to the great heat that was generated. Some folk said it was sabotage and some, God rest their souls, said it was the only way the man from the Ministry of Labour could move Uncle George to send him to the aluminium factory in Banbury where aircraft wings were made.

[The fire was first spotted and reported by a passing low-flying aeroplane.]

Miscellaneous memories. During the winter, on Saturdays, I would go down to the Castle Grounds to watch a football match played on a very uneven surface. There was also a bowling green immaculately kept by Uncle Chris and Joe Ell. It was laid out with Cumberland turf and you were only allowed to step on it if you had special shoes. Occasionally I was allowed to bowl, wearing the special shoes of course. At the time these were the only sporting activities going on. However at Banbury County School I did get to play rugger, football and cricket. My aunt took me to Oxford on two occasions and we took a tour of the University and along the river to see the house boats.

There were two means of transport during my stay, the double decker bus which ran from Oxford to Banbury without deviation, and the Midland Red which ran from Banbury to Deddington branching off into Adderbury and Bodicote. Of course there was the private bus owned by Stanley Hall, publican of the King's Arms, but he mainly only ran on Banbury market day, one trip there and one back. Later in the war he was given two extra small buses, with hard wooden seats, to run workers to and from the two aluminium factories - one in Banbury and the other beside the railway station south of Adderbury. All day long trailers would pass through Deddington on their way to these factories, carrying parts of crashed or damaged aircraft, British and German. On windy days parts of these planes were blown off the trailers and we children would race each other to see what treasures could be found. My biggest souvenir was a bomb release switch off a German bomber. I believe these two factories built wings for the RAF. One day we came out of school to find a repaired and rebuilt ME109 in the Market Square. We children were allowed to crawl all over it and I sat in the cockpit letting my imagination fly.

Each day a must was to tune into the news at 1 and 9pm, read by Bruce Belfridge, Alvar Lidell or Wilfred Pickles. Also, of course those 'we will never surrender' speeches by the Right Honourable Winston Churchill, Prime Minister. I often wonder what would have happened if he had not been around at the time. I guess we would eventually have won the war but I feel it would have taken longer. Up the Hempton Road beyond those very old cottages known as Windmill Cottages, where Joffer Clark lived, was the village tip smouldering away where we lads would go to throw stones at the rats that lived there. What a way to spend quality time. Somewhere close by in a home-made hovel lived Uncle George's brother who was well over six feet tall and was therefore called 'Titchy'. He had opted out of the world for some reason or other.

One Christmas time a gang of rowdy youths gathered outside Mr ('Doughy' sometimes Dicky) Dodwell's bakery on the square behind the Town Hall. Needless to say he was a little peeved due to the fact that he had to get up each morning to get the bakery going. Unable to sleep he opened his bedroom window and poured a bucket of water down. Unfortunately Uncle George had just turned into the square from the Tchure and caught the lot. What George said was never recorded but a blue cloud was said to be seen hovering over his head. Oh to taste those lardy and dough cakes just once more like he could bake them! I have both their recipes but they are not the same. It's the oven that does it. He also took in folks' Sunday roast which he would cook to perfection for a very small fee while they attended church or goofed off.

One winter, 1941 I believe, it snowed for a week. Uncle Chris made me a sled and off I went to test drive it down the slopes at the Castle Grounds. This was too tame so I joined others and went up the Banbury Road, turned left into a field with a long slope. Banbury County School was closed for the week. Unfortunately tragedy struck one summer. The gentleman [Denis Washington] who owned the fish and chip van also owned a large combined harvester and his son slipped and had his foot amputated in the machine.

Sweet rationing. How I loved to take my sweet ration coupons to the sweet shop of the two Misses French who had their shop on the square opposite the Post Office. Such an array of goodies. Liquorish pipes and boot laces, sweet cigarettes, lollypops etc., all at one penny. Also Smith's potato crisps one penny with salt inside wrapped in a little piece of blue paper. There were two other sweet shops. One in Hopcraft Lane and the other down by the entrance to the Castle Grounds, run by a Clark relative. Once a week I would accompany my aunt around the village when she would collect a small sum of cash for a health club which helped pay for ambulance or hospital fees. No National Health service in those days. That way I got to meet a lot of people. One thing that has changed: dinner was always eaten at mid-day. The evening meal was light and was supper. Maybe this is why obesity was not so prevalent in those days.

The King came to Banbury. One day we were marched out of school and assembled along the Banbury Road by the hospital. On both sides of the road for about a mile were troops standing smartly to attention. A car drew up and out stepped King George VI to inspect his soldiers. I remember saying at the time "he is wearing make up". At the time we did not know he was sick.

The Home Guard. The Local Defence Volunteers (LDV) quickly changed their name to the Home Guard as people were calling it Look – Duck - Vanish but then became known as Dad's Army! It was first introduced by Winston Churchill on 23 August 1940. As a point of interest, my father was in the Home Guard formed by his employers J Sainsbury at their warehouse in Blackfriars. They had a secret weapon: as the German tanks passed by below they were to drop sacks of flour on them. Hope it was self-raising flour, and then the tanks would rise and float away![1]

In case of invasion church bells would be rung and certain officials would run about like scalded cats blowing whistles. I knew nothing of this, it was grown-up business. In the kitchen was a scrubbed table with a large drawer in which every thing that did not have a home was thrown. In there I found a whistle and promptly put it in my trouser pocket. Later in the evening I was playing hide-and-seek with friends around the Bullring area and as nightfall came I realised I was alone so, you guessed it, I took out the whistle and blew. No one came so I went home. Unbeknown to me some thought the invasion had started but by then I was fast asleep and not found out or shot. By the way church bells could ring to bring people to church. Deddington has always had a great bell-ringing team which I for one hope they keep even though I never hear them now unfortunately. Strange as it may seem, Tower View was close to the church and the Westminster chimes would register in my mind even though after a few days they would not register. However, believe it or not, when I returned home I would hear the clock chiming in my mind and if I looked at a clock or watch it was always at the time I heard. One of those unsolved puzzles. I loved to climb to the top of the church tower and look around at the surrounding countryside.'

[1] The idea of dropping flour into an open tank hatch was not as hare-brained as some of the other schemes the Home Guard thought up. Flour dust would have temporarily blinded the crew, giving an opportunity to follow up with a home-made petrol bomb which would ignite the very combustible flour dust and set fire to the inside of the tank. Fortunately the need to test this system was never called upon.

Group outside the Unicorn Commercial Inn (*l to r*) Fred Davis, Nancy Lambert (née Sanders), unknown US serviceman, Queenie Sanders (née Hunt), Alfie Hunt
(courtesy Clive Sanders)

In the lead up to the D-Day invasion, US Army troops were billeted behind the Unicorn, in the British Legion Hall and at Adderbury Hall.

Postscript:

Derrick returned to London in 1942. In 1946 he was called up for National Service and afterwards joined a law firm. He married twice and moved to the USA to Sarasota, Florida in 1977. In our frequent email correspondence he often said how much he would like to see Deddington again but sadly he died in March 2010.

EDNA SEWELL

Edna Sewell

'In February 1943, I achieved my ambition of joining the WRNS and, if honest, it wasn't patriotism but the uniform that seemed more flattering! The sea was in my blood, so I found myself in the RN Recruiting Office in Albert Square, Manchester, with a questionnaire in front of me asking "Why did I wish to join?" "Did I have relatives in the Navy?" and pictures of RN Officers' sleeves from which I had to recognise the rank. I must have done OK as a few weeks later I was sent a travel warrant with instructions on how to get to Mill Hill, North London. My destination was a large new building which the Admiralty had taken over. It is now the Cold Research Institute. For me it was a very exciting journey on my own to London, I'd never been further than Blackpool before. So there I was with what seemed hundreds of girls like myself, putting on uniforms and learning our basic training, such as saying going ashore instead of going out and remembering to look what the dress of the day was. If it was greatcoats and we tried to wear raincoats then there was no going ashore that day, but we learned very quickly. After this training we were posted to various naval bases.

I went to Chatham where I served as a Writer in the Surgeon Commander's office at the Naval Hospital and I loved it. However, after six months this came to an end, when I was drafted to a Convoy Signal Base at Southend-on-Sea. Here, with about 10 other Wrens, we kept the Confidential Signals books up-to-date which were kept in lead-lined bags and issued to the RN signalmen at the conference, before they left on each convoy, going through the English Channel or up the East Coast.

The busiest and most secret time I remember was the build up to D-Day when merchant ships were loaded with army supplies in the London Docks and sailed down the Thames to Southend, where hundreds of ships assembled off Southend Pier and, along with their escort naval vessels, were formed into convoys ready to sail to France.

8 May 1945 was VE Day. Four days later I married and within a month I was discharged from the WRNS as, in those days, married women weren't allowed to serve in the forces during peacetime. I was given a Post Office book containing my

very small discharge gratuity payment. Mine was No.1 so I could possibly claim to have been the first Wren to leave after the war.

All Wrens in WWII were volunteers. There was no conscription and there was no policing. The RN police had no jurisdiction over us and we were very proud of this, but if a Wren went AWOL [absent without leave] or committed a crime, she was immediately dishonourably discharged and, being of conscription age, could possibly be called up for ammunitions or the Land Army. That really was hard work. I only knew of one case during my service.

Editors' note:

Primrose Buckle, who has contributed some of her own memories to the WWII Royal Observer Corps article (see p.75), mentioned to me that she joined the ROC to avoid joining the Wrens because she disliked the idea of perpetuating the wearing of boarding school type long knickers down to the knee any longer! I asked Edna about this and she confirmed that official ones were indeed long, although not made of wool; they were not very comfortable and were known as 'blackouts'.

GEORGE SPENCELEY

George Spenceley

George (far right) with aircrew and ground staff in the Middle East

George Spenceley, a Sergeant Pilot rising to Warrant Officer, joined the RAF in September 1939 shortly after leaving his school's Sixth Form, neglecting plans for higher education. He had earlier been registered for the RAFVR. He was accepted for flying training initially in Cambridge, finally gaining his wings at Advance Flying Training School, South Cerney, flying Airspeed Oxfords. From there he was posted to Operational Training Unit Bassingbourn before joining 214 Squadron Stradishall. Flying as second pilot with a pre-war trained career crew, George flew 20 operations in Wellingtons 1Cs over Germany before being posted to the Middle East flying non-stop to Malta. After loss of aircraft in bombing raids the squadron re-formed in Egypt where George flew a further 20 operations, most with a new crew, the captain being Flight Lieutenant Hammond DFC and Bar, also pre-war trained. George suggests that his survival of 40 operations may be due to flying with a highly-trained experienced crew.

George volunteered to convert to Liberators in readiness for a posting to the Far East. Returning to the UK on a civilian flight via West Africa, George and two others were posted to Liberator Conversion Unit, Polebrook, but while awaiting a vacancy on a course, was sent to Operational Training Unit, Steeple Morden, as an instructor. It was from there that George was shot down on the second Thousand Plane raid returning from Essen. He was the sole survivor and suffered severe head injuries involving a long stay in a Catholic Hospital in Rheinburg. In recent years George, seeking to gain further information, received a translated extract from the diary of a Sister Bernhild. It said 'One night two planes were shot down near the hospital. All personnel died except for one English pilot. He had a gaping wound in his forehead. This one was fed for five weeks by our sisters.'

George was then confined for three years as a PoW, first at the infamous Stalagluft III at Sagan, later at Stalagluft VI at Heyderkrug, now in Lithuania. On the advance of the Russians, the camp was evacuated and the prisoners sent to what has been described as the 'Hell of Fallingbostel'. Red Cross food had failed to reach the camp and German rations were grossly inadequate. For some survival was uncertain and there were several deaths. But even in the midst of war and mutual hatred an act of selfless kindness can bring some enlightenment. It was Christmas Eve 1944. For no particular reason George was standing at the open door of the barracks prior to it being locked when the postern came round to do his nightly duty. With a quick look left and right and with the words 'glücklich Kristmas' he thrust a small parcel into George's hands. It was a piece of home-made cake, the product of wife or mother.

During the three years of his captivity the morale of those in George's camp was kept up by a reading each day of the BBC News taken down in shorthand from a secret radio receiver which, in spite of many Gestapo searches, was never discovered. Particular joy was expressed when, on 25 March, news was received of the British crossing of the Rhine.They hoped that they would be peacefully liberated but this was not to be, at least for the RAF. They were to be marched, rumour said, into a redoubt to be held as hostages. Other rumours suggested that they were to be handed over to the SS for an uncertain fate.

Taking what little comfort then available, and an apology for a blanket, the RAF contingent was marched out in columns of 300 to 500 men, sleeping for the most part in the open, determined to make it the slowest march possible. In their weakened state it could not have been otherwise. Some collapsed on the way. It is difficult to know what happened to them but some found refuge with Russian or French work camps, others managed to cross the British lines. They crossed the Elbe just before the bridge from Luneburg to Lauenburg was blown.

It was on 19 April that tragedy occurred as they approached the village of Gresse when one of two columns marching in parallel lines was attacked by a flight of British rocket-firing Typhoons. Fifty were killed, more injured. This was within two weeks of release. The march continued east until Russian guns could be heard when there was an immediate reversal of direction. George, like many others was suffering dysentery and also had a swollen septic foot.

The war ended for George and his column at the village of Salem when, after a few days of waiting, a British armoured column arrived to the delight of the prisoners and to the relief of the many German women evacuees fearful of Russian rape. With all German discipline and control gone, some of the women had sought protection in their homes from the British prisoners, a strange reversal of loyalty.

George was evacuated to Luneburg for an operation on his septic foot and three weeks recuperation in an RAF hospital.

Full details of some of these events can be found in the book *The Last Escape* by John Nichol and Tony Rannell, Viking, 2002 in chapters entitled 'The Hell of Fallingbostel' and 'Friendly Fire'.

George and his wife Sylvie have in recent years visited the site of Sagan, now in Poland, where there is both a museum and a memorial for the 50 shot after the Great Escape, and also the site of Heyderkrug. They have also retraced as far as possible the line of the march ending in the village of Salem.

KINDERTRANSPORT EVACUEES

Rob Forsyth

FRANK STEINER

Willi, Frank, Paula and Richard Steiner in 1938

Frank was born in Vienna in 1922 into a Catholic family with Jewish ancestors. His father was a High Court Judge and his mother was a linguist. He and his brother went to a school in Vienna which was founded by Benedictine Irish monks in 1158, but was always known as *Schottengymnasium* i.e. Scottish Grammar School; clearly in 1158 one Celt was obviously much like another! The school's alumni included the last Emperor of Austria and the founder of the Austrian Socialist Party. When Nazis closed the school in 1938 Frank's elder brother, Willi, left to study law in England.

Frank takes up the story 'I arrived in this country in early December 1938 on the first train to leave Vienna as part of the *Kindertransport*. This was a very generous gesture on the part of the British government. Preceding this, on 9 November, the so called *Kristallnacht* (night of broken glass) had ushered in a wave of persecution of the Jews and, as a result, the British government announced that both Jewish and non-Aryan children under 17 would be allowed into the UK without passports or visas for education and training prior to emigration to countries of permanent settlement. Given the reluctance of most countries to let in any refugees at all, this was not only unique but the speed of operations was impressive; the system was up and running less than four weeks after the outrage that provoked it. I suspect that the fact that the then Home Secretary was a Quaker may have had something to do with it. The outbreak of war scotched every idea of re-emigration. By the outbreak of war in 1939 some 9,400 *Kindertransport* had arrived of which about 4,000 eventually joined HM Forces. This may have been responsible for the post-war Attlee government deciding to let us remain in the country and eventually qualify for naturalisation. Nearly 90% were Jewish by faith and were adopted into Jewish families. The prospects were less clear for the 12% of other faiths. On arrival we were lodged in holiday camps on the East Coast and gradually placed into families, schools and hostels.'

Of his departure from Vienna Frank recalls 'Like so much of the autumn and winter of 1938-39 my otherwise good memory has left blanks. I can remember only highlights. In a nice old fashioned way I knelt for my Father's blessing the night before and it is probably the only time I could see tears in his eyes. When my parents took me to the station by taxi, they were not allowed on the platform and when the train pulled out of the station I leant out of the window to try and see them. I can't remember if I did, but I do remember calling out into the dark "I am coming back". That was foolish at the time but perhaps I sensed that the Nazi nightmare would not last, and that I would eventually regain a respected position in Vienna as a frequent business visitor, holder of a senior Austrian decoration, and as a member for over 50 years of the *Kathpress*, the press agency owned and run by the Austrian bench of bishops.'

Frank's parents were subsequently arrested by the Nazis and were taken to Auschwitz. They did not survive.

The head of the Benedictine School in Belmont Abbey School, near Hereford, had offered two places for refugees. Frank got one of these places and after five terms at the school, took matriculation by which time war had broken out. Being in the phase between schoolboy and student, he was interned in the Isle of Man for 15 months. The Isle of Man was used as an internment camp for about 70,000 refugees who were technically enemy aliens, but who had more reason to hate the Nazis than even the British. Around 10,000 finished up in the British forces. Frank was released after volunteering for army service, but was found to be medically unfit.

He went to London, joined his brother in digs and enrolled for a part-time course as an external student of London University, where he took a BSc (Economics), the final examination of which was interrupted by a bomb. He became a fire watcher in 1941 and was trained as a fire-fighter. In 2010 he still sleeps with his face under his pillow, a habit acquired when, during air raids, even in houses not hit by bombs, one's face and eyes might get scarred from flying glass from blasts anywhere in the neighbourhood. He also got a job in food distribution as part of the war effort and in 1945 volunteered again for Army service. He was not accepted as he failed the physical and was drafted into the Civil Service instead. He ended up in the Board of Trade. Because of his ability to speak several languages fluently he was seconded in 1948 to the British delegation attached to the Organisation for European Economic Co-operation. The OEEC was an intergovernmental body charged with administering the US initiative, called the Marshall Plan, for the reconstruction of Europe.

After leaving the OEEC he worked in the oil industry for nine years, but when the company folded, he landed a job in the City with what eventually became the largest stock-broking firm in London and in due course became a partner.

Frank finally arrived in Deddington when he married Rosemary Oldham, who was from an old Warwickshire farming family. Rosemary's aunt Vida Stanley (née Oldham) had lived in Deddington for many years on the corner of Chapman's Lane and the main road. After her husband's death in 1954 Vida sold her house but kept part of the property on which she built a smaller house further down Chapman's Lane. Rosemary inherited this property in 1975. Twenty-five years later, after Rosemary died, Frank converted the garage and an extension into his flat and his daughter and family now live in the main house.

Since 1955 Frank had been a part-time journalist as UK correspondent of an Austrian press agency and for over 20 years a member of the Parliamentary and Public Affairs Committee of the Catholic Union of Great Britain. For the former work he received the Austrian Insignia of Honour in Gold, roughly equivalent to an OBE and for the latter he was made a Knight of the Papal Order of St Gregory.

In 1987 he retired from the City and in 2007 he retired from all voluntary and other functions outside 'the village' and retained only two activities based locally. He was one of the committee which took over producing the *Deddington News* when Norman and Angela Stone handed this over, and early in 2010 he received the Long Service Medal as a volunteer with the Thames Valley Police.

Editor's note: Frank's recollections are quoted verbatim from his brother Willi's autobiographical account of his family. I also drew on Wendy Burrow's resumé of his life from the exhibition 'Keeping the Home Fires Burning' held in the Parish Church in June 2010.

MARIANNE ELSLEY

(1923-2009)

Marianne was born in 1923 in Rostock, Germany. She was still only 15 when, in January 1939, her parents, Franz and Edith Josephy, placed their only child on the SS *Manhattan* (bound from Hamburg to Southampton) to seek safety in England. She never saw her parents again because they died in Auschwitz.

On arrival in England she was taken in by Quakers who were complete strangers but took her extremely warmly into their family and cared for her as of their own.

She married and, for ten years, assisted her husband Ralph with his appointment as a Housemaster at Bedford Modern School. They had two children. After the family moved to Banbury in 1970, she was secretary at Overthorpe Hall School for 20 years. After moving to Deddington in 1973 she was President of the Women's Institute and editor of the *Deddington News* amongst many interests. Her articles on both gardening and cooking were a regular *DN* feature.

She wrote three books about her escape from the Nazis: *A Chance in Six Million* (1989); a tribute to her parents by way of a collection of some 80 letters from them, *Voices in the Night* (1995); and, about her life, *Over the Years* (2004).

Acknowledgement: Christopher Hall's 'Well Remembered' obituary for Marianne in the February 2010 *Deddington News*.

JOSÉ STEVENS

José Stevens

'I was 12 years old when war broke out and was at Banbury County School, having attended Holcombe House Preparatory School, Deddington, from the age of 3 to 10 years. The school fees were £4 18s per term and the cost of the bus fare to school in Banbury was 4 pence halfpenny.

I remember evacuees arriving by bus into the Market Place. All the village children went to greet them and I felt jealous of those families who were hosting them, as my family was not to have evacuees but had air-crew families from Upper Heyford.

My parents, Charles and Gertrude West, ran the Post Office in Deddington and for a time the family lived above the Post Office (now Eagles). They moved to Corner House (now the Police Station and the adjoining Corner House). The present police office was our family shop, selling virtually everything for the home except food.

My parents later bought Holcombe House. They had so enjoyed having the families that, after the war, they ran the Holcombe as a guest house. I remember the Local Defence Volunteers (Home Guard) doing drill in the Bullring and school playground and the Royal Observer Corps plane spotting for enemy aircraft on the fields and allotments opposite where the Windmill Centre is now.

Troops were billeted in Deddington houses, the Manor stables and the Council yard (now the Health Centre). The cookhouse was in the Unicorn yard, where the soldiers went for all their meals. The regiments were the Pioneers, the Yorkshire and Lancashire, the Liverpool Irish and Scottish and the Cameron Highlanders, who taught the villagers Scottish dancing in the school hall on Friday evenings. Then came the Americans with the jitterbug.

I was allowed to go to the dances, but regretted being too young to join in much of the fun of having all the troops around Deddington. It seemed to be the regiments' last posting before being sent abroad.

When I was 15 my father asked for me to be off school as he needed my help to look after my two younger sisters when our mother became ill.

After the war, I got a typing job at Hopcroft Holt, part of Barton Abbey Satellite Landing ground (p.82) which was manned by RAF dog handlers. They patrolled the aircraft - Spitfires and Wellingtons - which were there to be checked and serviced. It closed down in 1945. I was then offered a job at Brize Norton.

When the family bought Holcombe House in late 1946, my parents wanted me home to help run the guest house.

Dad was in the police as a War Reserve Policeman and carried on as Special Constable until his death in 1952.

I met my husband Bob in 1948 (see page 67 for his war service); he then worked in Barclays Bank. He gave up banking and trained as a teacher. We married in 1949.'

DIANA UNDERWOOD

Diana Underwood

Diana was born in Deddington in 1923. Her parents were Alexander and Dorothy Fortescue. Her father was a solicitor with the firm Stockton, Sons and Fortescue. Diana had a younger brother, John, and the family lived in Church Street in the house then known as the Fortescue's House but now called the Old Malthouse. This is her story in her own words:

Diana age five on her front doorstep

'I volunteered for the Timber Corps of the Women's Land Army in January 1941 and received notice of the date and time to go by train to Monmouth station, taking a bicycle with me. Several other girls were on the same train and we were met with a lorry which took us and our bikes to Park End, the training school in the Forest Of Dean, near Lydney.

We were given our uniform, two fawn aertex type shirts, knee breeches, a green jersey, two pairs of fawn dungarees, a short overall coat, a pair of either leather ankle boots or leather shoes, two pairs of knee-length socks, a short light brown overcoat, a bright green beret (which I never wore) and a pair of gumboots. It was hostel type accommodation. We spent the first day indoors, learning about measuring timber and the importance of accuracy as the fellers' wages (they were paid piece work) and the amount paid by the Ministry of Supply for all the timber bought all over the country would depend on our figures.

Out in the woods, with notebooks,100ft tape measures, and ¼ girth tapes, we learned the difference between hardwoods, oak and sweet chestnut, and softwoods, larch and pine. We were shown how to measure the felled and cleaned trees (butts) and number the base if the cutters had not already done so, using blue waxed chalk. We had to record the cordwood (branches cut into 4ft lengths and stacked) and the part cords. The brushwood was burned. Some softwoods yielded pit props of a length which we also had to record. We were later able to work out the cubic capacity of each numbered butt with the help of a small calculator book, a Hoppus.

The fortnight of training passed quickly and we were assigned to jobs in different parts of the country. A girl who heard where I was to go, asked me to change with her as my proposed destination was near her home. She was booked to go to the New Forest.

So, complete with bike, I was met at Southampton station by the local officer responsible for the girls and moving them wherever they were needed. She found us lodgings (digs) and was supposed always to check the digs before we moved. We were sometimes able to find our own digs, but it was never an easy job. Workmen were building an airfield for the Americans at Stoney Cross and they were able to pay more for digs so we were unable to get in anywhere for the recommended £1 a week and usually had to pay 25 shillings, sometimes 30 shillings.

We were given breakfast, an evening meal and a packed lunch. Although we had 12oz of cheese instead of the standard 4oz ration, the landladies had difficulty finding filling for our sandwiches. We had our share of beetroot and "pink paste"! Most foods were rationed and we had to make sure of taking our ration books when we moved digs. I must have stayed with 10 or 12 families, mainly in Lyndhurst, Ringwood and Brockenhurst. If we found good digs it was better to stay and cycle further as our jobs changed. My take home pay was £4 7s 2d a fortnight.

I started measuring round timber in Roe woods, near Ringwood, and then moved to other plantations as each was felled. The Ministry of Supply was responsible for the whole operation all over the country. It supplied all the labour and machinery to provide much-needed timber for all government requirements. It negotiated with the Forestry Commission and private estates for plantations which could be felled. Pine cones were collected and bagged up for seed and sent to a nursery somewhere near Ringwood in the New Forest.

Most of the felled round timber was hauled by Caterpillar D2 tractors from the woods to nearby sawmills or to the roadside to be collected by road-going timber carriages. All the machinery was repaired from the main workshop by Lyndhurst Road station. There was also a large sawmill there, the depot for the lorries, sawn timber, pit props, and cordwood were dispatched by train from the station. One haulier, a family called Kitcher from Brockenhurst, was the only one to use horses for hauling round timber from the woods.

When the bombing range between Fritham and Stoney Cross was to be used we were notified in advance to keep out between the hours specified. Sometimes practice parachute jumps took place along the open ridge. We seldom saw deer.

There were seven or eight sawmills in various parts of the forest. We worked in the attached "offices" which were small wooden huts, rather like present day garden-sheds. They contained a bench, shelves, two stools, a telephone and a wood burning Tortoise stove which toasted our sandwiches, dried wet coats and kept us warm in winter.

We kept records of the daily output of sawn timber, details of stock in hand and sizes required for which we received orders from the main office, Red Lodge in Lyndhurst. We passed on the sizes to the sawyer, he knew what he could produce from the round timber delivered and would tell the cross cutters the lengths he needed. They handled the logs on the skids with a peevy, a long-handled implement with a rounded iron hook on the end. Bigger butts might yield railway crossings - 6ins x 12ins x 12ft long or sleepers - 4ins x 8ins x 8ft 6ins long. The other sawyers cut appropriate sizes from the rest of the log. We checked the sawn timber on to lorries and ensured we had enough round timber on the skids to keep going and enough fuel for the engine.

We calculated the wages for the mill men, who worked piece work as a team and kept a close eye on the daily output figures, on which their bonus depended. If one of the team was away, we sometimes helped with stacking sawn timber or crosscutting. I spent several days on one end of a cross-cut saw at various times.

There were also a number of portable “forest benches” consisting of one rack bench driven from the pulley of a stationary Fordson tractor. These cut four sides from the logs, thus making “squared logs”. We sold the off-cut bark to local men as slabwood, by the lorry load. They sold it on for various building jobs, or cut it up for firewood.

One day a lorry load of Italian Prisoners of War were delivered to the mill, without prior instructions or notice. These came from a nearby PoW camp and were used to do labouring jobs around the forest, They were not allowed to work with the charcoal burners as charcoal was used in the making of munitions. We set them to make up the roadway to the woods which was badly churned up by the crawler tractors. It would get stuck on a tree stump in the mud and have to be pulled off by another tractor. We showed the Italians the slabwood and a heap of sawdust, fortunately they had built this sort of road elsewhere and made a good job of it. They brought us each a bowl of coffee at lunchtime and told us they were in North Africa and hid from the Germans but ran towards the British with their arms up to surrender, they did not want to fight!

We always wondered why one of the tractor drivers looked so clean and tidy in spite of all the mud and why he was so polite. We found out later that he had been a butler before the war which was not a “reserved occupation”. He taught me to drive the Caterpillar tractor.

Most mills were driven by oil engines but the one at Lindford had a steam engine, the driver starting an hour earlier than the other men to get up steam. I spent half a day sawing up slabwood for the engine on a small saw bench when they were shorthanded. It was at Lindford that some kind ladies provided individual meat pies for all the workers there on Fridays. I fetched these from a house along the main road. Jolly good they were too!

The Sawyers used plate saws and inserted tooth saws; these were sharpened every morning before work started and the sawdust was dug out and added to the pile outside. On the whole they cut the sizes that were asked of them, but some had a habit of keeping “elbows” which had always been kept for boat building. Any large elm logs they would put to one side for coffin boards. We were told to discourage these practices!

Occasionally two of us were taken to a softwood plantation to mark straight trees for telegraph poles. However straight they appeared from all angles standing, when they were felled, rined and laid out on skids, they seemed to twist all ways. The GPO buyer always complained about them, they were not as good as the ones he used to get from Norway, but he had to take the best ones. His rejects went for Air Ministry or Admiralty poles.

Sometimes I spent a day with two men and a lorry collecting pit props of various sizes. These were loaded into railway goods wagons and I wrote the consignment notes to places in Wales with unpronounceable names.

My last job was on the Norman Court Estate, near Salisbury, measuring round timber sold to the Ministry of Supply. The agent, an elderly man, Mr Woolley came once a week to check the measurements of the timber felled on behalf of the estate. He agreed with my figures and I found him very pleasant. He told me the estate belonged to the Singer family (of sewing machine fame).

By this time I was married and expecting our first child, but I was sad to leave in autumn 1943. I kept in touch with the girl with whom I worked for a time. She went with some others to Germany after the war, presumably to work on timber for rebuilding. I enjoyed my time in the Timber Corps, we cycled many miles in all weathers, sometimes getting lost in unfamiliar places. There were no signposts and lights on dark mornings and dark nights had to be very dim. I enjoyed the variety of the work, the outdoor life and the kindness and good humour of everyone I met.'

TIM WILSON

Rob Forsyth

This final story is, most appropriately, that of a still-serving soldier...

Colonel Wilson briefing a QDG patrol in Basra, Iraq, December 2004

Tim is the youngest son of the late Hewitt Wilson and his wife Joan. His career in the army reflects the frequent deployment of the modern soldier to the various conflicts around the world that have succeeded the Cold War era.

He was educated at Haileybury College and has an MA from King's College, London. He was commissioned into The Queen's Dragoon Guards (QDG) in 1984. Early service included leading reconnaissance troops in UK, Germany and Cyprus (with the UN Force) followed by a tour as ADC to a Major General.

He was then deployed on Operation GRANBY (First Gulf War) as a Battle Captain leading the advance into Iraq from Saudi Arabia with 7 Armoured Brigade (Desert Rats). Post-war he was appointed Adjutant to the QDG before attending the Army Staff College, Camberley in 1994.

Staff tours as a Major included being Military Assistant to the Inspector General Doctrine and Training, and Ops Officer to 3 UK Division; this latter tour included NATO's first deployment out of area to Bosnia charged with a peace-keeping role trying to keep Serbs and Muslims apart in the centre of what was the former Yugoslavia. As a Lieutenant Colonel, he was a member of the Directing Staff at the Joint Services Command and Staff College in Shrivenham and at its equivalent in Kuwait. He also served in the Ministry of Defence with responsibility for Nuclear Policy and Special Forces.

As a commander, he has served in the Reconnaissance, Armoured (Challenger 1) and Infantry roles in Germany, Canada, Northern Ireland and Iraq. He was Commanding Officer QDG from 2003-05 and led his regiment in Northern Ireland and on Operation TELIC 5 (2004-05) in Iraq in the Formation Reconnaissance role. He commanded the Border Battle Group in Iraq where, in addition to peace-keeping duties, he was given the responsibility for re-forming and re-training the Iraqi Border Police which had ceased to exist. To the amazement of his General, he achieved this within four months. His reward was to be given the further major task of setting up and commanding a new Task Force responsible for security throughout the province of Al Muthanna (west of Basra). Taking over from a Dutch Battle Group, he strengthened the security of the Province by developing the indigenous security forces and by building relations with the provincial government, tribal elders and international aid agencies

Colonel Wilson at a tribal elder meeting, Al Muthanna Province in January 2005

In recognition of his outstanding leadership and contribution to security during both these major tasks, he was awarded an OBE in September 2005 on relinquishing command.

On promotion to Colonel in February 2006, he became Commander Armour Centre at Bovington. He was Deputy Chief of Staff and Garrison Commander Land Warfare Centre 2008-2010 and became Deputy Chief of Staff for the Royal Armoured Corps in June 2010.

He is married to Alexandra Davis and they have three sons.

Postscript

Some names that we were given were just that, without any detail and no mention even of the Service involved. When there was insufficient detail to research further with any degree of certainty, we simply recorded the information that we were given. This problem has been exacerbated by the passage of time and having millions of records destroyed in a bombing raid in WWII. Then, of course, there is that often-mentioned reluctance by so many to reveal their wartime experiences.

So we have placed on record the information that we have been able to discover, not only of those who died, but also those who returned and who, in all too many instances, bore the scars of their service. It is inevitable that we will have not included every one and we do ask that you tell us any missing or incorrect information. We would particularly welcome the names and stories of those who remained at home.

We will, in due course, compile any such new information (including corrections of errors) into a booklet of which we will advise you when it is available; we will also place this information as an addendum to the existing article on the Deddington OnLine village website (www.deddington.org.uk).

So our research will continue even after publication of this book. It is our way of acknowledging the sacrifices that have been made by the men and women of this Parish and their families and friends.

About the authors

Michael Allbrook

Michael moved to Deddington in 2007 from Surrey where he had run his own recruitment business specialising in staff for Human Resources. His earlier career was in personnel management with several companies including EMI. He was appointed a Companion of the Chartered Institute of Personnel and Development in 1989. He married Sally in 1969 and their two daughters and their families live locally.

His grandfather, Arthur, served in WWI and volunteered to train in gas warfare, a silly decision some thought, but his knowledge was soon considered too great to risk his serving on the Front. Three uncles also served; Walter was so traumatised by his experiences that he returned a changed man. Ted was shot and died whilst on patrol in No Man's Land and Jack died from his wounds in 1917.

In WWII both his parents volunteered for, and were, Officers in the Royal Artillery and the Women's Royal Air Force. Two uncles also served and all survived. Uncle Edward, who was in Tanks in the Desert Rats, took part in the North African Campaign, the invasion and fighting in Italy and was posted home to join the Normandy invasions. At this point he was severely wounded near Falaise which resulted in his spending the next year in hospital.

Michael's birth coincided with D-Day and the arrival of the first flying bombs. For this reason his Mother and he moved from Essex almost immediately and then to London where one memory is walking to school and passing so many bombsites awash with rose bay willow herb and buddleia.

Rob Forsyth

Rob's grandfather served in the Royal Artillery in WWI, as did his uncle and father-in-law in WWII. His father was an RNVR officer in WWII, serving in Coastal Command and Air Sea Rescue. His nephew served in the Fleet Air Arm in the 1980s.

He grew up in Priors Marston, Warwickshire, and Tring, Hertfordshire. During his time in the navy (p.128) Rob and his wife, Maureen, lived in many places and when they moved to Deddington in 1977 with their children Nicola, Justin and Jonathan, their plan was to be here for a couple of years but, like lots of other people, have found many reasons for remaining in the Parish ever since.

He left the RN in 1981 to seek wider horizons than a periscope offered and worked for a number of high technology companies, the last of which was Westland Group plc as its Marketing Director.

On retirement from this second career (1999), he continued in the aerospace business as a consultant for a few years and was a founding director of The Oxford Channel, one of the first local TV stations in the country.

He is now fully retired but still fully occupied with parish history, golf, tennis and four grandchildren.